Great New Nonfiction Reads

Great New Nonfiction Reads

Sharron L. McElmeel

1995
LIBRARIES UNLIMITED, INC.
Englewood, Colorado

Copyright © 1995 Sharron L. McElmeel
All Rights Reserved
Printed in the United States of America

No part of this publication may be reproduced, stored in a retrieval system, or transmitted, in any form or by any means, electronic, mechanical, photocopying, recording, or otherwise, without the prior written permission of the publisher.

LIBRARIES UNLIMITED, INC.
P.O. Box 6633
Englewood, CO 80155-6633
1-800-237-6124

Photographs of book jackets found on the title page appear courtesy of: Lerner Publications/Carolrhoda Books for *Better Mousetraps: Product Improvements That Led to Success* by Nathan Aaseng, copyright 1990; Scholastic for *The Magic School Bus on the Ocean Floor* by Joanna Cole, copyright 1992; and Clarion Books for *Gray Wolf, Red Wolf* by Dorothy Hinshaw Patent, copyright 1990.

Louisa M. Griffin, *Production Editor*
Constance Hardesty, *Copy Editor*
Eileen Bartlett, *Proofreader*
Pamela J. Getchell, *Design and Layout*

Library of Congress Cataloging-in-Publication Data

McElmeel, Sharron L.
　Great new nonfiction reads / Sharron L. McElmeel ; drawings by Deborah L. McElmeel.
　　xvi, 225 p. 17x25 cm.
　　Includes bibliographical references and indexes.
　　ISBN 1-56308-228-4
　　1. Children--Books and reading.　2. Oral reading.　I. Title.
Z1037.M287 1994
[PN1009.A1]
028.1'62--dc20   94-20258
                                                                CIP

For E. J.
Michael
Deborah
Thomas
Matthew
Steven
Suzanne

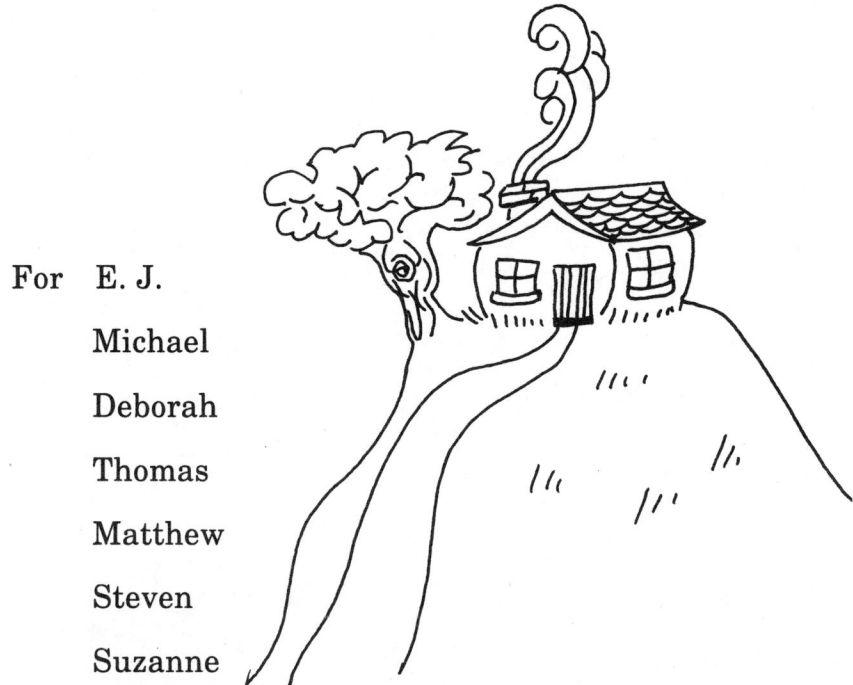

but especially for Michael and Deborah, who started the others on a quest for adventure and information and a sense of wanting to know more.

Contents

Acknowledgments xi

Introduction xiii

1 The World of Information Literature 1
   Choosing Books Worth Reading 3
      Garnering Interest: Points to Consider 4
      So Many Books, So Little Time 7
   Reading and Using Information Books with Young Readers ... 8
      Choosing the Book and Planning the Session 8
      Reading Aloud 8
      Encouraging Research 9
      Reading for Information 12
      Benefits of Reading Aloud 14
   Responding to Information Literature 15
      Selecting Response Activities 15
   Notes 17

2 Seeking Information 19
   The Bookshelf 20
      Adoption 20
      African Americans 21
      Airships 22
      Amish 24
      Animal Shelters 25
      Animal Words 26
      Animal World, Mysteries 27
      Animals, African 28
      Animals, Differences Among 30
      Animals, Endangered 31
      Animals, Extinct 32
      Apes 33
      Artists 34
      Asian Americans 37
      Authorship 39
      Automobile Racing 40
      Ballooning 41
      Bats 42

2 Seeking Information *(Continued)*
The Bookshelf *(Continued)*

Bears	43
Birds	44
Birds, Feathers	45
Blindness	46
Business	47
Butterflies	48
Canada	49
Careers	51
Cats	53
Chickens	54
Civil Rights	55
Constitutional Convention	56
Dinosaurs	57
Dinosaurs, Sites	57
Dolphins	59
Eagles	59
Easter	60
Ellis Island	61
Farming, Dairy	63
Farming, Trees	64
Firefighters	65
Fishing	66
Flight	67
Flight, Aviators	67
Flight, History	68
Fossils	70
Frogs	71
Galápagos Islands	72
Geography	73
Gettysburg Address	74
Hanukkah	75
Helping Others	76
Homelessness	77
Hopscotch	78
Horses	79
Houses	80
Ice Cream	81
Immigrants	82
Insects	83
Inventions, Accidental	85
Inventions and Inventors	86
Karate	87
Kites	88
Kwanzaa	89

Contents / ix

Letter Writing	90
Lighthouses	91
Machines	92
Meteors	94
Mexican Americans	94
Mexican Americans, Achievers	96
Money	97
Museums	98
Music, Origin of Hymns	99
Native Americans	101
Native Americans, History	102
Native Americans, Navajos	103
Native Americans, Pueblo	104
New York City	107
Ocean	108
Pandas	109
Pirates	110
Poets	112
Pollution	113
Ponds	114
Postal Service	114
Pussy Willow	115
Rain Forest	117
Recycling	118
Saint Lawrence Seaway	119
Scarecrows	120
Seasons	121
Sharks	122
Shipwrecks	123
Skeletons	124
Soccer	125
Solar System	127
Spiders	128
Tainos	129
Thanksgiving	130
Trains	132
Turtles	133
United States, History	134
Veterinarians	135
Warthogs	136
Washington, D.C.	137
Whales, Endangered	139
Whales, History	140
Windows	142
Wolves	143

x / CONTENTS

2 Seeking Information *(Continued)*
The Bookshelf *(Continued)*
 Worms 144
 Wounds and Injuries 145
Focus Books Arranged by Author 146
Focus Books Arranged by Title 150

3 Biographies 155
The Biography Bookshelf 156
 Abolitionist: Truth, Sojourner (1797-1883) 156
 Animal Researcher: Goodall, Jane (1934-) 158
 Artist: Cassatt, Mary (1844-1926) 160
 Artist: Goya, Francisco (1746-1828) 162
 Artist: Ringgold, Faith (1930-) 163
 Author: Hopkins, Lee Bennett (1938-) 165
 Author: Lindgren, Astrid (1907-) 166
 Author: Rylant, Cynthia (1954-) 167
 Author and Environmentalist: Carson, Rachel
  (1907-1964) 168
 Bullfighter: El Chino (Bong Way Wong) 169
 Civil Rights Activist: Parks, Rosa (1913-) 171
 Dancer: Ailey, Alvin (1931-1989) 172
 Entrepreneur: Strauss, Levi (1829-1902) 173
 King: Keita, Sundiata (d. 1255) 175
 King: Louis XIV of France (1638-1715) 177
 Naturalist: Muir, John (1838-1914) 178
 Physician: Picotte, Susan LaFlesche (1865-1915) 180
 Politician and Social Activist: Jackson, Jesse (1941-) ... 182
 President of the United States: Madison, James
  (1751-1836) 183
 President of the United States: Washington, George
  (1732-1799) 185
 Printer: Gutenberg, Johann (1397?-1468) 187
 Social Activist: Keller, Helen (1880-1968) 188
Focus Books Arranged by Biographee 190
Focus Books Arranged by Author 191
Focus Books Arranged by Title 192

Author/Title/Illustrator Index 195

Subject Index 211

About the Author 225

Acknowledgments

My family, as usual, has contributed to this book by generously giving of their time to help and assist in ways that allow me time for all the things I enjoy doing, including writing and teaching, and visiting with friends and family. To them a special thank you, especially to Deborah for drawing the illustrations that appear on the cover of this book and on the dedication page. Thank you to a special friend, Nancy Jennings of O. G. Waffle Bookhouse in Marion, Iowa, who suggested titles, brought out new books, shared copies of many books to be read and evaluated, and talked about good books. For their continued support of all my writing projects, I owe my appreciation to a very special group—Fold-Pak Consultants. The gathering of information and research was made easier through the cooperation of several publishers: My thanks especially to: Cyndy Kantrud, Lerner Publications/Carolrhoda Books; Louise Bates, Putnam & Grosset Group; Andrew H. Smith, Bantam Doubleday Dell; Jeffrey Kaye, Penguin USA; Darin S. Keesler, Harry N. Abrams; John Mason, Scholastic; Alison Wood, Clarion Books; Janice Boland, Richard C. Owen Publishers; Ken Geist, Farrar, Straus & Giroux; and Lisa A. McFadden, Macmillan Children's Book Group.

A very special thank you to David V. Loertscher, Libraries Unlimited, who has been involved in all 12 of my books. He is always looking for new ideas and is always the advocate for the author (and the reader). And for seeing that the market is found—a thank you to Debby Mattil.

Introduction

I wanted to title this book *The Latest and Greatest—Information Literature*, but marketing know-how won out. The title would have been too similar to my book *The Latest and Greatest Read-Alouds* (Libraries Unlimited, 1994). In reality this book does present the latest and greatest with the focus on information literature. Many of the very best read-aloud titles were included in *The Latest and Greatest Read-Alouds*, but we need to keep in mind that young readers are also very interested in books of information. This title presents books that are not only informational, but are well suited for sharing in large or small group read-alouds or, in some cases, are books that beg to be shared with a friend and discussed with energy and enthusiasm.

Recently, in a conversation about what type of book one young library patron wished to find, the seven-year-old patron declared, "I am going to be a paleontologist when I grow up. I am already studying about bones." This enthusiastic second-grader read Steven Kellogg's *Prehistoric Pinkerton!* (Dial, 1987) with interest, and he devoured *Digging Up Dinosaurs* by Aliki (Crowell, 1988).

A group of third-graders were introduced to the animals of Australia through Mem Fox's *Possum Magic* (Harcourt, 1983) and then later discovered Caroline Arnold's books *Kangaroo* (Morrow, 1987), *Koala* (Morrow, 1987), and such other titles as *Amazing Animals of Australia* by S. L. Barry (National Geographic, 1984), *The Australian Echidna* by Eleanor Stodart (Houghton, 1991), and *Wombats* by Barbara Triggs (Houghton, 1991). Teachers nurtured the young readers' delight in these books by encouraging their enthusiasm for new information and persuading them to make connections between the fiction that was read aloud and books that yielded additional information about topics of interest. Children have a natural curiosity about the world around them; the more that curiosity is stimulated, the more information is sought.

THE SCOPE AND PURPOSE OF THIS BOOK

The nonfiction titles featured in this book are excellent for reading aloud or sharing with young readers—but all types of nonfiction books are not included. Books included in this reference source fit both the definition of being within the nonfiction category and also

xiv / INTRODUCTION

titles that could be classified as "information books." For each focus book (main entry) complete bibliographic information and a target audience (for the reading aloud or sharing) is given. The target audience is intended to be the level/age that I would recommend as the primary audience for this title, although most books recommended here could be used with students above the target audience level with success. In some cases, the reading of specific titles might be successfully used with a group in a grade or age lower than the target audience. Following each main entry are connecting suggestions—suggestions for further reading.

The presentation of information in books has changed during the past few years. Instead of dry, boring texts that assume that those who want the information will read the text regardless, the new generation of information books attempts to attract readers, to interest them in the topic from the beginning, and to give them accurate, interesting information. The purpose of *Great New Nonfiction Reads* is to help parents and educators locate information books created by contemporary authors and illustrators. More than 600 books are listed, most with very recent copyrights and all available at the end of 1993. *Great New Nonfiction Reads* attempts to build on the reader's general knowledge of information books, expands that knowledge by identifying recent titles, and suggests topics and additional books to read.

The focus is on selecting books that can be easily shared with individuals or with a group of readers, and then make connections to other books for further reading. Efforts were made to suggest books on topics related to other readings, family activities, or curriculum topics. More than 120 titles are featured, and more than 500 books are suggested for further reading. The topics featured range from adoption to wounds (cuts and scrapes). The books and topics selected are my personal choices of books that I enjoy reading or sharing with young readers. I expect that many users of this book will not agree with all of my choices—and that is as it should be. Use the suggestions that appeal to you, but along the way be open to other titles that might interest you and your students. This book is intended to stimulate interest in information literature and to bring some excellent titles to your attention and, through you, to the children around you.

TIPS FOR SHARING INFORMATION BOOKS

Sharing information books requires somewhat different techniques than sharing books of fiction. Some information books may be read aloud in their entirety, while others are best shared by reading selections. In some cases, discussing the photographs and diagrams is the best way to introduce readers to a title. Transparencies of appropriate charts and diagrams will help make them visually accessible to a large group. Appropriate methods of sharing a book depend on the age of the audience. This book gives the target audience for each recommended title. The target audiences are not cast in concrete: Books for younger readers may serve as a thematic introduction for intermediate readers, while short segments, chapters, or pictures of a book for intermediate readers might be shared with readers in the primary grades.

Many titles could have been featured in this book. I chose those that immediately caught my interest and—equally important—left me wanting to know more, to read more. (Many of the books, especially the biographies, I found myself not wanting to close until I had finished.) In addition, I tried to include books that will help readers build their background for other reading. Indeed, a major goal of this book is to suggest books that will build background in subject areas that young readers will encounter. The multitude of excellent titles about some topics (and the popularity of some topics) encouraged the inclusion of more than one set of suggested titles about those topics. The comprehensive indexes list topics related to each recommended book, as well as topics related to the books recommended for further reading.

As with fiction, oral reading and responses to information literature will help children develop an appreciation for well-written literature and extend their thinking skills. Books that are filled with information fulfill children's curiosity and sense of wonder.

It is within the power of every parent, teacher, library media specialist, and public librarian to give children a rich experience with literature. While fiction can help children develop a sense of story, information books can help children build a sense of inquiry or involvement in the world. We must teach children to read, but more important, we must encourage them to want to read and learn. The very best way to do that is to give children *time to read and the inspiration to enjoy and learn*. Sharing books with children—reading aloud, showing pictures, stimulating their interest with bits of information from a book—will provide that inspiration and will help them aspire to know more.

The suggestions in this book should not be the deciding factor in your choice of books to share with young readers. The single most important criteria for selecting a book to share is whether or not *you*, the person presenting the book, enjoys it. In addition, you must consider your audience. The enjoyment you convey as you read aloud or share the book will be passed to your listeners. This book should give you a start in locating information books that you will enjoy introducing to children, books that they will enjoy, that will extend their reading interest, and that will motivate them to pursue more information.

USING THIS BOOK

Chapter 2 is arranged by topic, with suggested titles listed alphabetically. The list could be browsed. Chapter 3, which is shorter, focuses on biographies. The comprehensive indexes list all titles, authors, illustrators, and subjects related to the suggested titles and other topics discussed in this book. The indexes will help the reader locate titles to use as collaborative readings for thematic and curriculum units or titles that focus on topics being discussed within the classroom or in the family. The suggestions in this book, when teamed with the suggestions for fiction titles in *The Latest and Greatest Read-Alouds*, will help parents and educators bring a balanced array of literature to children.

Read, share, enjoy!

ONE

The World of Information Literature

With fiction for weft and information books for warp, a reader can weave a cloth filled with beautiful patterns and shimmering threads that brings glimmer to the reader's eyes and sparks the imagination. Weaving information books into a youngster's world of reading will enhance the child's ability to see beyond the imaginative into a world filled with real mysteries, adventures, and excitement.

Popular themes often occur in curriculum guides or units. For example, bears are a common theme in the early grades. In later grades other common themes are natural disasters, environmental concerns, and the American Revolution. For each theme, both fiction and nonfiction can be used.

For example, during a focus on bears, several books can give information about real bears as well as some not-so-real bears. Folktales, fairy tales, songs, and poetry like those contained in Mary Pope Osborne's collection *Bears, Bears, Bears: A Treasury of Stories, Songs, and Poems About Bears* (Silver, 1990) can and should be combined with photo-documentaries like *The Bear Family* by Dieter Betz (Tambourine, 1992); photo-filled information titles including *Amazing Bears* by Theresa Greenaway (Knopf, 1992); and books about endangered bears, such as *Where Are My Bears?* by Ron Hirschi (Bantam, 1992). Helen Kay's *The First Teddy Bear* (Stemmer House, 1985) tells of the origin of the teddy bear—how a toy maker was inspired by an incident involving President Theodore Roosevelt and a bear—and its popularity in the United States. Other information books can lead to mapping the location of endangered bears. In addition to Hirschi's *Where Are My Bears?* and similar information titles, Helen Gilks's *Bears* (Ticknor, 1993) can lead to other inquiry projects.

Many of the bear books cited above can be shared at home after the child or family visits a zoo with a bear exhibit. When a news item features a story about an increase in the bear population in Yellowstone National Park, books dealing with the locations and habitats of those and other bears might be interesting to share. When a child receives a new teddy bear, it might be accompanied by a copy of Kay's *The First Teddy Bear*.

Opportunities must be sought to weave information into the child's experience. Connections can be made regardless of whether the setting is home or school. For example, in conjunction with a school tasting party that features cranberry relish or a Thanksgiving dinner that includes cranberry sauce, William Jaspersohn's *Cranberries* (Houghton, 1991) gives much interesting information about how cranberries are grown, harvested, and made ready for the consumer. During a focus on growing things, the photographs and text in Elizabeth King's *The Pumpkin Patch* (Dutton, 1990) will help children understand the preparatio5n and work it takes to plow, plant, cultivate, and harvest pumpkins. The same book is appropriate to read at home in conjunction with the making of the first pumpkin pie of the season.

In addition to the hundreds of titles listed in this resource book, the subject access in the catalogs of school library media centers and public libraries yield many titles that can be used to build an information base on an infinite number of topics. Thematic units at school can be enriched with information books, and the same books can be read at home to answer the questions of young readers and to give them rich opportunities to observe and question their world.

We must be careful not to regard the reader of nonfiction as something less than a "real" reader. Often we laud those who read fiction as readers who really enjoy and savor books, while we look askance at those who are more attracted to nonfiction.

A number of years ago, a fifth-grade student's reading habits were the subject of a regularly scheduled parent–teacher conference. The teacher commented that this child, the third in the family that she had taught, was certainly not the reader his older brother and sister had been. The father said, "I think you have that wrong. He reads a lot. He just doesn't read what you and his mother (an elementary school educator) would choose for him to read." And, indeed, the child did read a lot. He read the sports page every day, devoured every issue of *Sports Illustrated,* studied books describing the best techniques for weight lifting, and read accounts of sports figures. He read the back of every sports card he could acquire.

In the years that followed he read directions to learn how to play Nintendo and construct a birdhouse, and he found out everything he could about his black Labrador puppy. Was he a reader? You bet he was! Did he read Laura Ingalls Wilder's Little House series, which everyone else in the family had read by the third grade? No, he found the series boring. He never did acquire a taste for reading fiction, but he continued to read for information. Given a choice he would always pick up an article or a book filled with information that interested him. Ten years later, when he was about to become a father, he kept track of the baby's prenatal development by reading books on the subject from the public library. He learned to weld by taking classes, reading the textbook, and reading collaborative material that explained the finer points of making various types of welds. Today, he continues to read the sports page on a daily basis as well as every issue of *Sports Illustrated,* and he has added *Golf Digest* to his regular reads. He reads the how-to articles in many periodicals and still prefers to read aloud information books to his young child.

Is this man a lifelong reader? Yes, without a doubt. Did any of his teachers consider him a reader? No, his parents only remember teachers lamenting his resistance to reading what they had chosen for him to read (almost always books of fiction). But times are changing, and today parents and educators view information books as valuable.

With this commitment to recognizing information books as literature, young readers who prefer to read for information can be recognized as readers. This is not to say that interest in other types of books should not be nurtured and encouraged. Those who read mostly fiction should be introduced to the world of information titles, and those who read mostly nonfiction should be introduced to the world of fiction. Still, we must recognize that different people have affinities for different types of books. After all, many adults prefer nonfiction, such as biographies. Count me among those who do. My all-time favorite reads are history, biography, and how-to books. We owe children the benefit of a balanced reading diet and the opportunity to choose their reading fare.

To encourage a balanced reading diet, we must have a firm commitment to include nonfiction in the repertoire of books we offer to young readers. Your attitude as the teacher, parent, or grandparent will play a large role in encouraging young readers to integrate information books with other types of books, such as fiction, poetry, or folklore.

CHOOSING BOOKS WORTH READING

Believable plot, realistic characters whom the reader cares about, accurate setting, consistent details, worthwhile theme, and natural language are points to consider when evaluating the merits of a work of fiction. Some of the same points are relevant to evaluating information books. Information books must be about a topic that readers care about, the information must be accurate, the details must be consistent, the information must be worthwhile, and the text must be written in natural language. Many books have some weak and some strong points, but it is the overall rating that one must be concerned with. In "If That Do No Good, That Won't Do No Harm: The Uses and Dangers of Mediocrity in Children's Reading,"[1] Sheila Egoff concludes that approximately 2.5 percent of children's books are excellent, 62.5 percent are mediocre, and 35 percent are extremely poor. If children are to be inspired, challenged, and motivated to read, the books we offer young readers must not be poor; they must rise above mediocrity. We need to continue to strive to find that 2.5 percent that are the excellent offerings.

Garnering Interest: Points to Consider

Information books that are about topics that readers care about, have information that is both accurate and worthwhile, contain consistent details, and are written in natural language will be most appealing to young readers. To determine an information book's potential appeal to young readers, consider the following points.

First Impressions: The Cover and Hook

The cover must be attractive. (Yes, one can judge a book by its cover, and children often do.) The information and illustrations on the first few pages must draw the reader into the interior pages. If the reader can be lured into the book, the first hurdle has been overcome. Carolyn Caywood, writing in the *School Library Journal* Teens & Libraries column,[2] states that readers assume that a book's cover describes its contents. Although Caywood speaks specifically of fiction for young adults, her comments offer food for thought. We should reassess the covers of all books that we encourage young readers to read. The book covers must be a first draw. Caywood says that color photographs sell books better than paintings. I believe that is also true of both the covers and illustrations of information books. Photographs enhance a book's overall credibility. Once the cover has drawn the reader in, the evaluation of the book's content can be made. While fiction must first of all tell a good story, a book of information must first promise to tell the reader something of interest. The book must immediately grab the reader's interest. Often the illustrations draw the reader in, but sometimes it is the opening line. For example, the opening sentence of *Predator!*, "Whenever you see a wild animal of any kind—from a fox trotting through the woods to a fly zipping around your bedroom—the chances are it's looking for something to eat"[3] made me want to know more. Reading the book I learned about food cycles, the efforts of some animals to protect themselves from predators, and how some predators actually help maintain the balance of animals and help humans control pests. Especially interesting was the chapter about camouflage; the information about mimicry and other protective coloration made me wonder at the complexity of nature. And all because I thought I'd quickly find out if flies bit me for my blood.

Evaluating the Contents

It should be obvious that, above all else, information books must be accurate. Books can give misleading information if they have serious omissions or if they are not up-to-date. If you are not an expert in the topic discussed, it is difficult to assess a book's accuracy, but there are some clues.

Credibility of the Author. Check the credibility of the author. Does the author have the appropriate background and experience for writing about the topic? What are the author's credentials? Information on the jacket flap may give information about the author's credentials and background. Sometimes the foreword discusses the author's research and experience.

Authors are cautioned to write about what they know, and often that is interpreted to mean that they should write about what they have experienced firsthand. If that were true, few books would be written about historical events or people because contemporary writers would not have the requisite experience. A broader interpretation recognizes thorough research as valid background for writing about a topic or experience. A bibliography of sources contributes to the credibility of information books.

Copyright Date. Another important indicator of quality is the copyright date. Information needs to be up-to-date. Obviously, a book titled *The Newest Automobiles* is misleading if the copyright date is 1973. Some people used to think that the copyright date mattered little for books dealing with historical topics. But we have come to know that new discoveries in history generate new thoughts about historical events. For instance, recently emphasized information regarding the Tainos, the natives who greeted Columbus in the Caribbean, has changed our thoughts about the honor (or dishonor) that should be accorded him. Ten years ago little was published about the atrocities suffered by the Tainos. New information has changed the perspective of that historical event. When new discoveries about historical events are made, those discoveries affect how facts are viewed and in some cases may change our interpretation of the events.

Balanced Presentation. Books that purport to examine an issue or situation must give a balanced presentation, giving accurate information on all sides of a topic. Many times an historical event is told from the point of view of the majority culture, and the facts are viewed from that perspective. For example, Native Americans killed buffalo for survival. They killed only those buffalo they needed for food and clothing. Yet many writers have described the hunting as slaughter. The term *slaughter* projects a more negative image than the term *hunted,* a term that reflects the need for the buffalo's meat and hide. Another example: Regardless of the motives of the white settlers or the Native Americans involved, an attack by Native Americans on settlers was most often referred to as a massacre, while attacks by pioneers on Native Americans were referred to as battles or attacks to protect their homesteads. The connotation is that Native Americans were thoughtless and indiscriminate but white settlers had to protect their property from intruders. That is unacceptable. Information books should be free of stereotypes; they should present balanced and unbiased accounts of events and situations.

Sometimes the point of view is clearly stated, and the value of the book is its presentation of that particular view. That is true of titles like Paul Goble and Dorothy Goble's *Brave Eagle's Account of the Fetterman Fight: 21 December 1866* (Pantheon, 1972; University of Nebraska, 1988). *Brave Eagle* clearly is intended to give a Native American's view of a battle that is recounted in many other books from the point of view of white soldiers involved in the attack.

Accuracy of Graphics. Another important consideration is the accuracy and clarity of the illustrations, charts, and graphs in the book. The visual representations should be as accurate as the text and should clarify concepts or information presented in the book. Well-illustrated books are very important in encouraging further exploration or experimentation. Illustrations also can involve the reader in gathering and interpreting information.

Anthropomorphism and Teleological Explanations. Avoid information books that treat animals in an anthropomorphistic manner. Giving animals human traits, or personifying them, is a common and legitimate literary device in books of poetry and fiction. However, when an animal is given human attributes in books of information, the device is called anthropomorphism. Because young children are thought to acquire new information most readily when it is connected to their experience, many writers of information books resort to anthropomorphism in an effort to make a connection for young readers. Anthropomorphism is unacceptable.

A related technique is teleological explanations for natural events. Leaves "basking in the sun" or the flow of the river "carving out a new river bed" are examples of teleological explanations. *Basking* and *carving* are human activities that do not accurately account for the scientific or natural purpose of the event.

Organization. A final point to consider when evaluating the contents of information books is their organization. Is it logical? Does the book include reference aids, such as a table of contents, index, glossary, bibliography, and a list of additional readings? Other reading aids, such as bold type or chapter headings, can do much to help the reader locate specific information.

In summary, the best information books meet standards in regard to accuracy and authenticity, have content that appeals to the intended audience, are told from a perspective that is clear to the reader, present information in a style that draws the interest of readers, include illustrations that extend and clarify the text, and are organized to help the reader obtain information.

So Many Books, So Little Time

None of us will have time to share all the good books we wish to share with young readers. There are simply too many books. After the valuative criteria have been applied, we must choose which books we will share with young readers. For choosing books to share with children there seems to be as many sets of criteria as there are books. Donna E. Norton discusses the evaluation of books for children in *Through the Eyes of a Child: An Introduction to Children's Literature* (Macmillan, 3d ed., 1990) as does Charlotte S. Huck et al. in *Children's Literature in the Elementary School* (Harcourt, 5th ed., 1993).

I prefer a very simple guide: If the book interests me I read it to children. I use this criterion whether the book is fiction, poetry, folklore, information, or other. I never read a book that doesn't interest me. There are simply too many books to waste my time or the children's time with something that doesn't bring a tear or a smile or inspire me to want to know more—which most good books do. My definition of a good book to read, regardless of the age of the child to whom I am reading, is whether or not the book evokes an emotional response. Those are the books I prefer to read to myself and those are the books I read and share with children. Readers of this book, *Great New Nonfiction Reads*, will not necessarily agree with all of the selections I have included in the following chapters. That is the way the world is. The lists of general information books and biographies are among the very best of those published in the past few years. The books included are merely suggestions—my suggestions. We are all different and we will all have different responses to specific titles. I happen to like the books included on this list; I like them a lot. Some readers will make different choices and some listeners will ask to have different titles to read over and over again. The most important criteria is that the read-aloud or sharing session is a positive experience for both the reader and listeners.

There is no magic list of books that all children must hear before they pass out of childhood. The most important thing is that children are exposed to books, reading, and the world of information. Sharing literature and a love of reading and learning is one of the most valuable gifts that any adult can pass on to children. And it's never too early or too late to share that gift.

READING AND USING INFORMATION BOOKS WITH YOUNG READERS

Sharing information books effectively does not happen by accident. The appropriate book must be selected; the seating arrangement must encourage your audience to become active listeners and provide for joint viewing of graphics and illustrations; the reader's voice must convey enthusiasm; and opportunities for collaborative reading or response activities must be provided.

Choosing the Book and Planning the Session

When choosing a book to read or share with children, keep in mind their collective background of experience and depth of knowledge. A child does not need to know every word that is read aloud; one of the goals of reading aloud is to stretch the listener's vocabulary. However, the words must be used in a meaningful and logical context.

If a book is to be read in one sitting, consider the length of the book you choose. If the read-aloud will extend over two or more sessions, ascertain stopping points in the book. When a read-aloud or sharing session extends to two or more sessions, it is especially important that the previous reading session be summarized before subsequent readings begin. A simple question, "Can anyone tell me what we have learned (or read about) so far?" will get the discussion started. After the discussion, read the next segment.

Reading Aloud

When you read aloud a book of information, consider the size of the group to whom you are reading. The presentation style must fit your personality, but it also must fit the group or child to whom you are reading. If you are a parent reading at home to your child or children, sharing a large, comfortable chair or sofa is the best choice. Simply stated: Get cozy and close. If you can do so comfortably, put your arms around your children and read aloud in a clear, energetic voice. Voice your own curiosity about the information; your enthusiasm for reading for more information should be evident. Encourage your children to voice their questions and feedback. Information books generate discussion and interaction. Not only the text proper but the captions and content of pictures and illustrations will stimulate discussion.

Be aware of the reaction of your listeners. Their level of interest will tell you how much of the material to read aloud and how much to summarize. Eye contact with the audience and energetic reading will do much to hold your listeners' interest.

When sharing a heavily illustrated book, gather your listeners as close to you as possible. If you are reading to just one or two children, sit beside one another and hold the book together. If the group is larger, try to get all the children close enough to see the illustrations. Transparencies or enlargements of some of the illustrations may help in sharing sessions with larger groups. I always make sure the book is available to students to browse and enjoy independently after the reading.

If children are allowed to daydream, draw pictures at their desks, or do work sheets, their half-hearted listening will reinforce the idea that listening and reading are not important. In fact, just the opposite is true. If at all possible bring the listeners to a reading carpet or a similar intimate space where they will not be preoccupied with other activities and can give their full attention to the book. If this is not possible, move the desks to the edge of the room and arrange the chairs in a big circle in the center of the room. Taking the time to rearrange the furniture may seem disruptive, but with a little practice the arrangement will come quickly and pay dividends. The effort will serve to highlight the importance of the activity.

Encouraging Research

Learning in the information age demands that educators ensure that students use information effectively. As partners in the educational process, parents and others who have the best interests of children in mind, participate by stimulating children's interest in the world. At school or at home children can be encouraged to use information in meaningful contexts. Curriculum contexts include creating and interpreting graphs in math class, discussing current issues in social studies, completing science labs or projects, or writing essays and reports on selected topics. At home the use of information manifests itself in such activities as selecting a television show to view, purchasing a product, deciding on a career, or preparing a party menu.

Motivating children to read has traditionally involved reading fiction aloud, giving booktalks, sharing information about the author, and holding special reading promotions. Motivating children to research and to read information books involves similar activities. Using information books to stimulate a child's interest in a topic is highly successful. Reading aloud from an information book or sharing some of the facts and pictures from the book whets the appetite of listeners and encourages them to seek more information. Given the opportunity they will locate other sources of materials and read more about the topic.

As we explore the realm of information books we begin to realize how much information there is in the world. The idea is not to attempt to teach children everything there is to learn but to inspire them to be interested in learning and excited about learning new information. If you are successful in that endeavor, then the children you inspire will continue to learn throughout their lifetimes.

Collaborative Reading: Making Connections

Much can be done to stimulate reading in information books. Motivation to read can come from a visit to a museum, farm, or other place of interest; an event; or questions that arise in discussions, presentations, or other readings.

- A visit to a nature center to observe a demonstration on making maple syrup could interest a reader in Kathryn Lasky's *Sugaring Time* (Macmillan, 1986) or Diane Burns's *Sugaring Season: Making Maple Syrup* (Carolrhoda, 1990).
- A litter of puppies born in a household might motivate a reading of Joanna Cole's *My Puppy Is Born* (Morrow, 1991) or Heiderose Fischer-Nagel's *A Puppy Is Born* (Putnam, 1985).
- Reading the Little House series by Laura Ingalls Wilder could interest youngsters in *The Little House Cookbook: Frontier Foods from Laura Ingalls Wilder's Classic Stories* by Barbara M. Walker (HarperCollins, 1979) or *The Laura Ingalls Wilder Songbook* edited by Eugenia Garson (HarperCollins, n.d.). Readers might become interested in writing to some of the historical sites of the Wilder homes to gather more information.
- Watching a wasp build a nest could lead to a reading of Bert Kitchen's *And So They Build* (Candlewick, 1993) or Bianca Lavies's *Wasps at Home* (Dutton, 1991).

Just as activities can lead to the reading of information books, so can the reading of fiction lead to the reading of nonfiction. Arnold Lobel's Frog and Toad series has regularly motivated the search for information about frogs and toads. Children who want to know about the real-life characteristics of Lobel's characters eagerly read *Frogs, Toads, Lizards, and Salamanders* by Nancy Winslow Parker and Joan Richards Wright (Greenwillow, 1990); *Amazing Frogs and Toads* by Barry Clarke (Knopf, 1990); and *Frogs* by Gail Gibbons (Holiday, 1993). They visit ponds and creeks in search of tadpoles they can watch develop, and they watch frogs and toads jump across moist grass in yards dampened by rain. They become excited about learning.

Almost any fiction book can be connected to an information book. As fiction is read and enjoyed, information books can be suggested as collaborative reading material.

- Reading about the life of Gary Paulsen (the author of *Hatchet* [Bradbury, 1987] and other novels for middle-grade readers) in his *Woodsong* (Bradbury, 1990) might interest some students in the Iditarod, a prestigious, 1,049-mile dogsled race from Anchorage to Nome, Alaska. Sources on this topic include periodical articles, such as those about Libby Riddles in *National Wildlife* (February-March 1986, pp. 40-45) or *Sports Illustrated* (February 17, 1986, pp. 90-102); books about contestants, such as *Susan Butcher and the Iditarod Trail* by Ellen M. Dolan (Walker, 1993); or general books about training of sled dogs, such as *Racing Sled Dogs* by Michael Cooper (Clarion, 1988).

- Enjoy the series of cranberry books by Wende Devlin and Harry Devlin (*Cranberry Birthday* [Four Winds, 1988], *Cranberry Mystery* [Four Winds, 1984], *Cranberry Thanksgiving* [Parents, 1971], and several other titles) and then introduce William Jaspersohn's *Cranberries* (Houghton, 1991).

- Read *Spiders in the Fruit Cellar* by Barbara M. Joosse (Knopf, 1983) and then introduce Alexandra Parsons's *Amazing Spiders* (Knopf, 1990) and Maria M. Mudd's 14-page pop-up book, *The Spider* (Stewart, 1992).

- After reading *The Tiny Seed* by Eric Carle (Picture Book, 1987), share Erika Markmann's *Grow It! An Indoor/Outdoor Gardening Guide for Kids* (Random, 1991).

- Laugh at the letters in *The Jolly Postman or Other People's Letters* by Janet Ahlberg and Allan Ahlberg (Little, Brown, 1986) and then introduce the basics of writing letters with Loreen Leedy's *Messages in the Mailbox: How to Write a Letter* (Holiday, 1991) and Gloria Skurzynski's *Here Comes the Mail* (Bradbury, 1992). Skurzynski's book uses up-to-date illustrations to show how to properly address an envelope.

These connections and others suggested in this book can make the difference in helping young readers learn to understand and follow written instructions, put readings in context, summarize main ideas, locate specific facts and details, distinguish fact from fiction, interpret charts and graphs, use operating manuals, and understand technical and abstract materials. Integrating information books into the curriculum and into a child's home reading experience will provide opportunities to give children experiences in writing clearly and legibly. Children may also learn to take notes and develop outlines; organize information; compose letters, reports, and memoranda; proofread and edit material; locate sources of information; cite reference sources correctly; draft a project proposal; respond appropriately to oral directions; present oral information and directions; observe verbal and nonverbal cues; and participate in discussions.

Fiction and nonfiction literature provide children with models of good writing and present opportunities for building writing skills through innovations on the text and extensions of the concepts within the text. Well-structured books of information also model the product of research and logical organization.

Reading for Information

Early readers learn how to read narrative forms of literature; reading for information requires different approaches. When the reader seeks specific information, the process of reading becomes part of the information problem that needs solving. Readers must first identify the information they need to have in order to accomplish the task that they have identified. To do this, the reader must have formulated the goal or objective for obtaining the information. If the reader wishes to build her/his background of knowledge about a particular subject then the reading technique is very similar to the reading of a narrative. This is especially true if the information book is written in a narrative form. However, if the goal for reading the book extends beyond a quest for general background information other techniques for reading and researching will need to be used. Young readers will need to access strategies for how and when to use indexes, the table of contents, chapter headings, bold headings, picture captions, and other conventions used to organize information in nonfiction books. In addition the reader will need to be aware of the purposes and scope of various reference materials (printed or electronic) such as dictionaries, encyclopedias, indexes, periodicals, and other reference sources, as well as human resources. Seeking information for a specific purpose often involves sources of information other than books. The reader interested in specific information about a topic or in a specific type of information will often need to brainstorm a list of possible sources; investigate the sources and the organization of the source; read the texts and the accompanying information to locate the information needed; and pursue the information in other sources until each bit of information needed or wanted is located.

We cannot seek information that we do not know exists. Information books expand a reader's awareness into places and times not experienced. They give information about topics that will help readers make decisions, to investigate other opportunities for learning, and to build a general schematic background.

Reading and Using Information Books with Young Readers / 13

Thinking About the Reading Selection

Young readers can be taught to reflect on the informational reading they have done with the following questions:

- What is the book about?
- What is the name of the author?
- What makes the author qualified to write the book?
- When was the book published?
- Did the book have illustrations and graphics?
- Did the illustrations and graphics give information not offered in the text itself?
- What bit of information did you most enjoy learning?
- Do you need or want more information about the topic?
- What did you find out that you didn't know before?
- Are there other books about this topic that you might read?
- What information would you like to share with a friend?

As readers become more accomplished in reading for information and more comfortable with information gathering, they may begin to assess their reading material more thoroughly. They might consider

Content

- What is the book about?
- Was the information clearly presented?
- Did the title give accurate clues about the scope of the book?
- Do I need more information than this book provides?

Credibility

- Is the author qualified to write about this topic? (Check the author's background and sources used in writing the book by checking the book jacket, title page, introduction, foreword, and other books by the author.)
- Is the information up-to-date? (Check the copyright date and the currency of the information presented.)
- Does the author indicate whether the information in the book is fact or opinion? Key phrases like "I think," "Scientists believe," or "In the opinion of some," will give clues.

Style

- Was the information presented in a clear and direct manner?
- Was the information organized?
- Is the information told in a factual manner, or is the information fictionalized?
- Does the book make you want to know more?

Illustrations

- Do the illustrations give additional information?
- If graphs, charts, or other graphics are used, are they easy to read and do they give useful information?
- Are the labels and captions accompanying the illustrations or graphs clear and concise?

Organization

- Does the book include a table of contents or index? If so, did they help you quickly locate the information you needed?
- Did the headings and subheadings help you peruse the book to find out what type of information it contained?

Benefits of Reading Aloud

Several studies affirm the value of reading aloud to young children and the positive relationship of that activity to learning to read early. In a significant study reported by Dolores Durkin in 1966,[4] a common factor in the homes of children who learned to read early was respect for books. All of Durkin's early readers had been read to as toddlers and some had been read to as early as infancy. In a study in Scotland,[5] Margaret Clark noted a similar pattern. She found that, while the families she studied were not economically equal, they did share a pattern of frequent use of the public library and respect for the value of books and reading. One of the most dramatic situations supporting the value of reading was reported by Dorothy Butler. Doctors had diagnosed a multiple-handicapped girl, Cushla, as severely retarded but she was read to from the age of four months. Cushla eventually learned to read well beyond her chronological age, much to the astonishment of her doctors. Cushla's impressive story is told in *Cushla and Her Books* by Dorothy Butler (Horn Book, 1980).

Not only does reading aloud profoundly affect the early development of a child's reading attitudes and abilities, but reading aloud seems to have a long-term effect on the reading behavior of children. In her doctoral dissertation (Ohio State University, 1974), Judith Sostarich cites a comparative study of sixth-grade students. Sostarich identified active and nonactive readers. Although students in each group could read equally well, the active readers chose to read often while the nonactive readers seldom read on their own. Sostarich investigated the students' backgrounds and discovered a definite pattern: The active readers had been frequently read to as toddlers, some as infants. In some of the frequent readers' families, books were still read aloud.

RESPONDING TO INFORMATION LITERATURE

Children respond to reading in varied ways. Many share their feelings and thoughts about what they have read by sharing the information they have learned. This need to share may motivate them to write an entry in their reading journal, give an informal booktalk to a friend, or participate in a more formal classroom activity. In all cases the response must be enjoyable and chosen by the reader. Choice makes the sharing meaningful. Responses chosen by others (that is, dictated) leave little room for real involvement from the reader. For example, it is doubtful that every child in a classroom would choose at any one time to create a mobile. Although dictating responses is counterproductive, encouraging some responses is valuable. Reading by its nature is a solitary activity. Responses allow and provide a vehicle for interaction between readers, whether or not they are reading the same title. Using the information in a book to provide the basis for some type of response activity encourages the reader to reflect on what the book was about. Response activities also give other children an opportunity to learn about the book from the reader. The responses provide an opportunity for other readers to participate in a discussion and to promote further involvement with the book and its information.

Selecting Response Activities

Response activities must always be purposeful, and the reader must understand the purpose. All activities should be enjoyable and should extend literature through diverse forms of response. Activities may incorporate the expressive arts, such as art, music, drama, or writing, or they may incorporate cooking or games. The product of the activity is no more important than the interaction and involvement of those engaging in the activity. While choice of response is an important aspect of responding to literature, children must be given some guidelines and models. Connections must be modeled, and various activities considered. Reading another book should always be one response alternative.

Response activities at home differ little from response alternatives that might be appropriate at school. However, some activities may be easier to accomplish in one setting than in the other. For example, drama activities may be easier to accomplish in a school setting because there are other students to participate. However, in families with more than one child, the same opportunity may be present. Cooking activities often take less preplanning if done in the home, but cooking is possible in the classroom. The novelty of cooking in the classroom contributes to the enjoyment of this response opportunity.

Twenty-Five Responses for Information Books

1. Compile lists or charts of information you learned from the book.

2. Create a fact sheet about the topic discussed in the book.

3. Create a game that incorporates some of the information in the book. Base your game on a popular board game or a television game show.

4. Create a three-dimensional model of an illustration in the book.

5. Create a book jacket for the book.

6. Create a pop-up version of the book.

7. Create a travel brochure.

8. Dramatize a scene from the book.

9. If the book includes a musical score (as in *Amazing Grace: The Story Behind the Song* by Jim Haskins), learn to sing the song and record it.

10. Learn about the author and defend her or his credentials.

11. Locate a recipe that is related to information in the book.

12. Locate several books on the same subject. Read the books and compare information.

13. Locate other books or articles that deal with the same topic, setting, or event. Read and compare the information. Create a Venn diagram to show the information that is common to both books and the information that is unique to each book.

14. Make a chart depicting interesting information from the book.

15. Make a list of questions you still have about the topic, event, or setting.
16. Make a mural that shows some of the information from the book.
17. Make a poster advertising the book.
18. Make a time line of the events in the book.
19. Make an information web depicting the areas of information that could be incorporated into further investigation.
20. Make an audiotape of you reading the book for your classmates to listen to.
21. Record on audiotape an interview with the book's author (played by a fellow reader) regarding the research that she or he did to write the book.
22. Record on audiotape an interview with the book's illustrator (played by a fellow reader) regarding the background information she or he had to research to create authentic illustrations.
23. Videotape a documentary that tells some of the information from the book.
24. Write a book report.
25. Write a book review.

Reading information books will help young readers to answer questions and to build a solid schematic background. Responding to information books will give readers an opportunity to clarify, share, and evaluate the information they have learned. After readers are introduced to the world of information, they will begin to make their own connections and identify their own focus books. A valued response to the reading of one book is when the book encourages or motivates the reading of another.

NOTES

[1] Sheila Egoff, "If That Don't Do No Good, That Won't Do No Harm: The Uses and Dangers of Mediocrity in Children's Reading," *Issues in Children's Book Selection: A School Library Journal/Library Journal Anthology.* Bowker, 1973, pp. 3-10.

[2] Carolyn Caywood. "Judge a Book by Its Cover." *School Library Journal* (Vol. 39; No. 8; August 1993), p. 58.

[3] Bruce Brooks, *Predator!* Farrar, 1991, p. 3.

[4] Dolores Durkin, *Children Who Read Early*. New York: Columbia Teachers College Press, 1966.

[5] Margaret Clark, *Young Fluent Readers*. London: Heinemann Educational Books, 1976.

TWO

Seeking Information

For many children learning to read brings a new sense of independence to explore the world of knowledge. Young children show their curiosity with their constant question "Why?" As they develop the ability to obtain information from reading, they come to realize that it is no longer always necessary to ask someone "Why?" The answers to many of their questions can be found in books.

The introduction of information books to young people should begin early. Reading ability among children of the same age varies widely, and so does their interest in the world of information. It is hoped they will develop an enjoyment of independent reading by sharing book experiences with their classmates, parents, siblings, and others. In many cases the child's interest level may be above her or his reading level. Daily read-aloud sessions or sharing of information books will help satisfy the child's thirst for stimulating information literature, enhance memory, and build on prior knowledge. Sharing information books helps listeners build an understanding of the importance of research and organization, chronological ordering and historical perspective, the use of inference to make predictions, and other author techniques.

Careful selection of books can do much to help children gain a sense of the immense amount of information in the world and to understand the viewpoints and attitudes of other cultures and groups of people. When selecting titles to read an attempt should be made to present a balanced picture of the world, an unbiased view of people and their cultures, and a sense of the world as a place filled with information. When selecting books to share the child's background experience and depth of knowledge must be taken into consideration. Take the time to find out what they are interested in learning. Read books with them and observe their reactions, their interests, and their responses. Read about the familiar and the unfamiliar. Read about animals, plants, and places to go. Read about writers, scientists, artists, and common people who contributed to our society. Read about events in history, inventions, predictions for the future, things to do, and things to make. Find books that interest you, and share them with the same enthusiasm that you share a good novel or picture book. Find books that lead the young people with whom you share them to investigate to find more information, to develop varied interests, and to expand their view of the world.

THE BOOKSHELF

Adoption

Banish, Roslyn, with Jennifer Jordan-Wong. **A Forever Family.** Illustrated by Roslyn Banish and Jennifer Jordan-Wong. HarperCollins, 1992. 44 pp. ISBN 0-06-021673-5. (362.7 Ban).
Target Audience: Grades 4-6; Ages 9-11

Jennifer Jordan-Wong is the eight-year-old adopted daughter of Susan B. Jordan and Ron Wong. She was seven years old when they adopted her in a ceremony that many friends attended. But before that she had lived in foster homes and had talked to social workers who help children whose parents are unable to take care of them. Now that she lives with her adoptive mom and dad, she has a room of her own and many cousins and aunts and uncles. Her grandparents love her, and they look at pictures together. Her grandfather taught her to write her name in Chinese. She does many things with her forever family. But she does have many questions, questions that are not answered in the book but that will stimulate discussion and thinking about the different situations that children find themselves in.

Connections: Families of Choice

Adoption is a legal term for the act of creating a legal relationship of parent and child when it does not naturally exist. Adoption was practiced by the early Romans, and their adoption laws influenced the civil laws of many countries today.

Keiko Kasza has written a deceptively simple picture book that could be used to introduce the topic of adoption and foster care. The book, *A Mother for Choco* (Putnam, 1992), tells of a chick's search for a mother.

There are many types of families of choice today. Cynthia Rylant's fictional picture books *When I Was Young in the Mountains* (Dutton, 1982) and *The Relatives Came* (Bradbury, 1985) are set in the Appalachian Mountains and based on the time she was living with her grandparents. Later, after her mother finished nursing school, Cynthia lived with her mother in Beaver, West Virginia. Poems that focus on the days spent in Beaver are collected in *Waiting to Waltz: A Childhood* (Bradbury, 1984). The poems tell of her years as a 14-year-old "single kid," a kid alone while her mother worked.

Other authors have written novels that focus on different types of family arrangements. They include: *The Pinballs* by Betsy Byars

(Harper, 1977; Scholastic, 1979), about foster children; *Mama One, Mama Two* by Patricia MacLachlan (Harper, 1982), about a girl with an ill mother and a foster mother; *Edgar Allan* by John Neufeld (NAL, 1969), about a white family that adopts an African-American child; *The Great Gilly Hopkins* by Katherine Paterson (Crowell, 1978), in which a foster preteen adjusts to her changing family structure; *Just Like a Real Family* by Kristi Holl (Atheneum, 1983), about a child with a single parent and surrogate grandparent; and *The War with Grandpa* by Robert Kimmel Smith (Delacorte, 1984), in which a child's grandfather comes to live with the family.

Vera B. Williams's books often feature a family, headed by a mother, that includes a grandmother and children. Williams's titles include: *A Chair for My Mother* (Greenwillow, 1982); *Something Special for Me* (Greenwillow, 1983); *Music, Music for Everyone* (Greenwillow, 1984); and *Three Days on a River in a Red Canoe* (Greenwillow, 1981). Mavis Jukes writes about situations in which there are "broken families," although she prefers to call them "mending families." Patricia MacLachlan wrote a novel about a single father searching for a wife, *Sarah, Plain and Tall* (Harper, 1985) and other books that focus on aunts, grandparents, or foster care.

African Americans

Haskins, Jim. **One More River to Cross: The Stories of Twelve Black Americans.** Scholastic, 1992. 151 pp. ISBN 0-590-42896-9. (920 Has). (Photograph of the jacket is courtesy of the publisher and is reprinted with the permission of Scholastic.)

Target Audience: Grades 4-6; Ages 9-11

A collective biography of 12 African Americans who have made major contributions to life in America. Opportunities that were closed to African Americans because of the color of their skin were opened through the courage and persistence of the people profiled in this book. Dr. Charles Drew discovered a method for storing blood plasma, a technique that makes it possible to store blood for use in crises. Fannie Lou Hamer worked to gain equal rights for all Americans.

Eddie Robinson was a winning football coach. Madam C. J. Walker founded her own business and became a millionaire. Crispus Attucks, a hero of the American Revolution era, was killed during the Boston Massacre. Matthew Henson was codiscoverer of the North Pole. Marian Anderson, an opera singer, opened concert hall doors to African Americans. Ralph Bunche was a diplomat and the first African American to win the Nobel Peace Prize. Romare Bearden was "the most celebrated black American artist of the twentieth century." Shirley Chisholm was a political leader and congresswoman who, in 1972, sought the Democratic party's nomination for president of the United States. Malcolm X was a Black Muslim leader. And Ronald McNair was an astronaut aboard the ill-fated *Challenger*.

Connections: Notable African Americans

African Americans are Americans whose ancestors came from Africa. Some came by way of the Caribbean Islands, and some came directly to the United States. Most came as slaves brought by slave traders.

David A. Adler's *A Picture Book of Martin Luther King, Jr.* (Holiday, 1989), a well-written biography of the African American civil rights leader, is a good introduction to King's life and work. Eric Weiner wrote the story of antislavery spokesperson Frederick Douglass in *The Story of Frederick Douglass, Voice of Freedom* (Dell, 1992).

Other biographies focus on talented contemporary African Americans. Titles include: *Alvin Ailey, Jr.* by Kathilyn Solomon Probosz (Bantam, 1991); *Alvin Ailey* by Andrea Davis Pinkney (Hyperion, 1993); *Katherine Dunham: Black Dancer* by Carol Greene (Children's Press, 1992); *Leontyne Price: Opera Superstar* by Sylvia B. Williams (Children's Press, 1990); *Barbara Jordan: Congresswoman* by Linda Carlson Johnson (Blackbird Press, 1990); *Colin Powell* by Jonathan Everston (Bantam, 1991); and *The Real McCoy: The Life of an African-American Inventor* by Wendy Towle (Scholastic, 1993).

African-American inventors worked with Thomas Edison, invented the shoe last machine, and developed a method of sugar refining that is still used today. Some of these inventors are featured in *Outward Dreams: Black Inventors and Their Inventions* by Jim Haskins (Walker, 1991); and *Extraordinary Black Americans* by Susan Altman (Children's Press, 1988).

Airships

Munro, Roxie. **Blimps.** Illustrated by Roxie Munro. Dutton, 1989. n.p. ISBN 0-525-44441-6. (629.133 Mun).
Target Audience: Grades 2-5; Ages 7-10

Unlike hot-air balloons, a helium-filled blimp does not float willy-nilly through the sky, driven by wind and air currents. Blimps are driven by propellers and steered by rudders on their tail fins. After a blimp is filled with helium, it must be held down by lead-filled bags and bowlines. As each passenger boards the blimp, lead is removed in amounts that equal the weight of the passenger. After everyone is aboard, the bowlines are released, and the pilot and copilot maneuver the blimp as it rises. The passengers sit in the craft's cabin, called the gondola, which has broad windows and is simply furnished. The gondola hangs from the bottom of the blimp. A blimp usually flies 1,000-3,000 feet above the ground and does not go higher than two miles. The average speed, 28-30 miles per hour, is slower than most cars. Blimps are often used for advertising purposes and are used for sightseeing tours over several of the world's major cities, including San Francisco, London, Munich, and Sydney. Wherever a blimp lands the ground crew stands in formation as it signals the wind direction and provides a target for the blimp's landing. After the blimp is locked down, the lead bags are placed on the blimp. Blimps are rarely deflated once they are inflated.

Connections: Adventurous Flights

An airship is a lighter-than-air aircraft that moves on its own power and can be steered in any direction. Airships were once called dirigibles. Airships that resemble huge cigars are sometimes called zeppelins after the designer Count Ferdinand von Zeppelin of Germany. Small airships, or blimps, played a vital role in World War II by protecting ships against submarine attacks. Blimps located submarines and attacked them with depth charges. After the war the United States Navy used blimps to patrol the coasts of the United States. Flights made in airships were often dangerous and usually adventurous.

Other adventurous flights were taken by pilots of early planes. These pilots include Charles Lindbergh, Amelia Earhart, Jacqueline Cochran, and Ruth Law. Books about their exploits include *Coming Out Right: The Story of Jacqueline Cochran, the First Woman Aviator to Break the Sound Barrier* by Elizabeth Simpson Smith (Walker, 1991); *Flight: The Journey of Charles Lindbergh* by Robert Burleigh (Philomel, 1991); *Clear the Cow Pasture, I'm Coming in for a Landing! A Story of Amelia Earhart* by Robert Quackenbush (Simon, 1990); and *Ruth Law Thrills a Nation,* written and illustrated by Don Brown (Ticknor, 1993).

Information about flying in hot air balloons can be found in Neil Johnson's highly illustrated *Fire & Silk: Flying in a Hot Air Balloon* (Little, Brown, 1991).

Amish

Ammon, Richard. **Growing Up Amish.** Illustrated with photographs, maps, and drawings. Atheneum, 1989. 102 pp. ISBN 0-689-31387-X. (973 Amm).
Target Audience: Grades 4-6; Ages 9-11

Anna and her family are Amish. They live on a farm without electricity or tractors. The clothes they wear are of a simple style, dark blue or black without zippers or buttons. *Growing Up Amish* is an account of Anna and her daily life in an Amish community in Pennsylvania. The children attend the local Amish school, raise farm animals, and do their farm chores. Anna and everyone in her family work hard but they also play. They go on picnics; take a trip together to buy a horse; go to school parties; and enjoy participating in sporting events, including hockey, volleyball, baseball, sledding, and fishing. Indoor activities include reading, indoor games, singing, and eating meals together. The book includes traditional recipes for food, poems, songs, and games.

Connections: Amish Stories

Amish families are described in *An Amish Family* by Phyllis Reynolds Naylor (Lamplight, 1974) and *Amish People: Plain Living in a Complex World* by Carolyn Meyer (Atheneum, 1976). Photographs of the Amish and their lifestyle are scarce because the Amish prefer not to be photographed. Thus, Patricia Polacco's beautifully illustrated picture book *Just Plain Fancy* (Bantam, 1990), which shows many painted images of the Amish way of life, is a valuable addition to the body of work.

The Amish were named for Jacob Ammann, leader of a group of people who broke away from the Swiss Mennonites in the 1690s. The Amish came to the United States in 1728 and today live in 23 of the 50 states. The largest communities exist in Ohio, Pennsylvania, Indiana, Iowa, and Illinois. There is also a large community in Ontario, Canada. Many Amish and Mennonite communities are close to one another. Such is the case in Kalona, Iowa, where the Mennonite Historical Society of Iowa, located in the Mennonite Museum in the Kalona Historical Village, provides much information about various sects in the Mennonite and Amish communities. A community museum, the Wall Museum, is operated by another community group, the Kalona Historical Society. For more information about the Kalona community write: Kalona Historical Society, P.O. Box 292, Kalona, IA 52247. Amish or Mennonite communities in your state or in a nearby state may have similar historical organizations or museums you could contact for information.

Animal Shelters

Kitchen, Bert. **And So They Build.** Illustrated by Bert Kitchen. Candlewick, 1993. n.p. ISBN 1-56402-217-X. (591.56 Kit).
Target Audience: Grades 2-5; Ages 7-10

The many ways that animals build shelters are shown in pictures and discussed in the text. The satin bowerbird, living in the rain forest of eastern Australia, builds a bower of bright objects to attract a mate. The male mallee fowl digs three-foot-deep pits and piles them high with vegetation. After the pit warms to 90 degrees Fahrenheit, he digs a hole for his mate to lay her eggs. Termites build their shelter in the shape of a column with an umbrella-shaped roof. Harvest mice weave a nest around stalks in fields, and swallows build nests on sheltered ledges or beams using semicircular layers of mudballs, grass, and straw. Paper wasps build unique, paperlike combs of hexagonal cells. The shelters of the tailorbird from Asia, the bowl-and-doily spiders, the gladiator tree frog, a three-spined stickleback, caddis-fly larva, and beavers are also included. This is a fine introduction to unusual and interesting shelters created by animals.

Connections: Shelters for Animals

Some animals spend all of their lives moving about and never build a shelter. Other animals build shelters only when they need protection for their young. And still others, such as the chipmunk, build lifetime shelters and seldom venture far from them. Some animals do not actually build shelters but live within a defined territory and discourage other animals from invading that territory.

And So They Build introduces some of the more exotic shelters that animals build. A somewhat longer book, *Animal Homes and Societies* by Billy Goodman (Little, Brown, 1992), focuses on the many types of animal social behavior, including loners, such as the tiger, and the more sociable, such as the Portuguese man-of-war.

Other books include information about individual animals, such as *Raccoons* by K. M. Kostyal (National Geographic, 1987). In Kostyal's book the young raccoon is shown peeking from a hole in a tree, which the raccoon uses as a den. In a section at the end of the book called "More About Raccoons," the author tells about other places that raccoons often choose for dens. The final section of this book could serve as a model for readers to use in creating information pages about other animals.

How Animals Care for Their Babies by Roger B. Hirschland (National Geographic, 1987) mentions the nests built by squirrels and several kinds of birds. In *Africa's Animal Giants* by Jane R. McCauley

(National Geographic, 1987), many large animals are shown in their natural habitats.

Animal Words

MacCarthy, Patricia. **Herds of Words.** Illustrated by Patricia MacCarthy. Dial, 1990. n.p. ISBN 0-8037-0892-0. (428.1 Mac).
Target Audience: Grades K-3; Ages 5-8

Patricia MacCarthy has created beautiful silk batiks that represent groups of animals and other things. The text recites the collective nouns for various animals and objects shown: peacocks, hippos, hares, eagles, swine, ships, sailors, walruses, aircraft, horsemen, geese, crocodiles, flamingos, eggs, goldfinches, swans, treasure, stars, witches, owls, teal, partridges, larks, snipe, badgers, oxen, otters, flies, salmon, horses, constables, squirrels, ferrets, trees, hounds, leopards, and antelope.

Connections: Nouns About Animals

MacCarthy's book features groups of animals and objects to introduce young readers to the collective nouns for those groups. An earlier title by MacCarthy, *Animals Galore!* uses similar illustrations in bright, flowing colors to introduce many other collective nouns for animals. Animals represented in *Animals Galore!* include lions, elephants, penguins, eels, wolves, dolphins, toads, ants, water buffalo, crows, cats, gnats, parrots, monkeys, geese, sheep, piglets, and whales.

Brian Wildsmith and Ruth Heller have created books that deal with collective nouns. *Brian Wildsmith's Wild Animals* (Watts, 1967) speaks of flocks and herds of wild animals as well as other groups, for example, a "shrewdness of apes," an "array of hedgehogs," and a "troop of kangaroos." *Brian Wildsmith's Birds* (Watts, 1967) uses oil paintings to illustrate flocks of birds as well as a "congregation of plover," a "nye of pheasants," and a "wedge of swans." Ruth Heller illustrates her collective nouns in *A Cache of Jewels and Other Collective Nouns* (Grosset, 1987). The rhyming text and illustrations introduce a "drift of swans," a "clutch of eggs," and a variety of other collective nouns.

Collective nouns create interesting word play opportunities. Books by Marvin Terban capitalize on young people's interest in words. Among Terban's titles are *Guppies in Tuxedos: Funny Eponyms* (Clarion, 1988); *The Dove Dove: Funny Homograph Riddles* (Clarion, 1988); *Funny You Should Ask: How to Make Up Jokes and Riddles with Wordplay* (Clarion, 1992); *Hey, Hay! A Wagonful of Funny Homonym Riddles* (Clarion, 1991); *Mad As a Wet Hen! And Other Funny*

Idioms (Clarion, 1987); *Punching the Clock: Funny Action Idioms* (Clarion, 1990); *Superdupers: Really Funny Words!* (Clarion, 1989); *Too Hot to Hoot: Funny Palindrome Riddles* (Clarion, 1985); and *Your Foot's on My Feet! And Other Tricky Nouns* (Clarion, 1986).

Animal World, Mysteries

Taylor, David. **Animal Magicians: Mystery and Magic of the Animal World.** Illustrated by various artists. Extraordinary Animals series. Lerner, 1989 (Boxtree, 1988). 48 pp. ISBN 0-8225-2175-X. (591 Tay). (Photograph of the jacket is courtesy of the publisher and is reprinted with the permission of Lerner Publications/Carolrhoda Books.)
Target Audience: Grades 4-6; Ages 9-11

There are many mysteries in the animal world, and this book examines 10 of them. The development of pearls within the body of an oyster is discussed in the first chapter. Another chapter focuses on the giant panda, one of the world's oldest and most endangered animals. Other mysteries of the animal kingdom discussed in this book involve electric eels; electric rays; luminous animals, such as dragonfishes and diademed squid; bats; moths and other insects, including the praying mantis; chameleons; hummingbirds; and scorpions. Each chapter gives basic information about the animal and about the mystery that surrounds its existence. A glossary and index are included.

Connections: Skeletons and Other Information About Animals

One of the most interesting books about animals is *Inside the Whale and Other Animals* by Steve Parker, illustrated by Ted Dewan (Doubleday, 1992). Dewan's illustrations show cross-sections of many animals. Twenty-two animals are featured, including the blue whale, giant tortoise, honeybee, scorpion, mountain gorilla, and the great white shark. An interesting look at the skeletons of several animals is given in *The Glow-in-the-Dark Book of Animal Skeletons* by Regina Kahney, illustrated by Christopher Santoro (Random, 1992).

The complex nature of habitats is explored in *Windows on Wildlife* by Ginny Johnston and Judy Cutchins (Morrow, 1990). The relative intelligence of animals is the topic of *How Smart Are Animals?*

by Dorothy Hinshaw Patent (Harcourt, 1990). Other books deal with strange facts about animals. One especially attractive book that examines reptiles and strange facts about them is *Frogs, Toads, Lizards, and Salamanders* (Greenwillow, 1990) and *Bugs* (Greenwillow, 1987), both by Nancy Winslow Parker and Joan Richards Wright. Interesting and unusual facts about animals are incorporated into two particularly interesting titles: *An Elephant Never Forgets Its Snorkel: How Animals Survive Without Tools and Gadgets* by Lisa Gollin Evans (Crown, 1992) and *Bees Dance and Whales Sing: The Mysteries of Animal Communication* by Margery Facklam (Little, Brown/Sierra, 1992).

One of the chapters in Taylor's book piques interest in natural camouflage by discussing the changing colors of a chameleon. Camouflage is the topic of *Animal Camouflage: A Closer Look* by author-illustrator Joyce Powzyk (Bradbury, 1990). Powzyk presents examples of six types of camouflage.

General information and many facts about animals are included in *Zoo Clues: Making the Most of Your Visit to the Zoo* by Sheldon L. Gerstenfeld (Viking, 1991); *And Then There Was One: The Mysteries of Extinction* by Margery Facklam (Little, Brown/Sierra, 1990); and *Why Is a Frog Not a Toad? Discovering the Differences Between Animal Look-Alikes* by Q. L. Pearce (Lowell House, 1992).

Animals, African

Bare, Colleen Stanley. **Who Comes to the Water Hole?** Illustrated with photographs by Colleen Stanley Bare. Cobblehill, 1991. n.p. ISBN 0-525-65073-3. (599 Bar).
Target Audience: Grades K-3; Ages 5-8

Ever wonder what a warthog looks like? And does a wildebeest really exist? These and other animals are shown at a watering hole in Southern Africa. During the eight-month dry season, there is one refuge: a watering hole. Here animals come seeking a drink. The animals come in ones, twos, threes, and more. They drink and drink and satisfy their thirst. The endangered white rhinoceros and the tick bird that often is with the rhino are among the first visitors. Other animal visitors include wild pigs (warthogs), baboons, zebras, several types of antelope, wildebeests, hippopotami, crocodiles, yellow-billed storks, woolly-necked storks, ostriches, monkeys, mongooses, meerkats, giraffes, elephants, lions, leopards, cheetahs, and hyenas.

Connections: Animals of the Savannah and Rain Forest (Regions of Africa)

More information about some of the animals that live in the African savannah can be located in titles focusing on specific animals or families of animals. Information about crocodiles can be found in Dorothy M. Souza's *Roaring Reptiles* (Carolrhoda, 1992), which describes the physical characteristics, habitat, and life cycle of crocodilians: alligators, crocodiles, caimans, and gavials. Another title that describes the crocodile and its life cycle is *Crocodiles* by Alison Tibbitts and Alan Roocroft (Capstone Press, 1992). The baboon is featured in Lynn M. Stone's *Baboons* (Rourke, 1990) and the zebra is featured in Caroline Arnold's *Zebra* (Morrow, 1987) and in Linda C. Wood's *Zebras* (Wildlife Education, 1993). Arnold focuses on a zebra by investigating the zebra in a zoo setting and Wood describes the zebra and its natural habitat. Antelope are the focus of Mary Hoffman's *Antelope* (Raintree, 1987). Caroline Arnold has featured another savannah animal in *Hippo* (Morrow, 1989). Photographs by Richard Hewett show the hippos in the San Francisco Zoo and in the wild. One of the most interesting titles about hippos is *Jane Goodall's Animal World: Hippos* by Miriam Schlein (Bryon Preiss/Atheneum, 1989). The physical characteristics, behavior, and life cycle of the ostrich is described in Emilie U. Lepthien's *Ostriches* (Children's Press, 1993). The rare Rothschild giraffe is featured in Betty Leslie-Melville's *Daisy Rothschild* (Doubleday, 1987). *Giraffes: The Sentinels of the Savannas* by Helen Roney Sattler (Lothrop, 1990) describes the habits and natural habitat of the giraffe, as well as the giraffes' relationship to humans. The life of the lion in the savannah is the focus of *The Lion and the Savannah* by Dave Taylor (Crabtree, 1989). The fastest mammal on earth, the cheetah, is the subject of *Cheetahs* by Linda C. Wood and Cynthia L. Jenson (Wildlife Education, 1993).

Another area of Africa that has different types of animals is the tropical rain forest. *At Home in the Rain Forest* by Diane Willow (Charlesbridge, 1991) features a variety of rain forest plants and animals. The text is brief and must be supplemented with information from more in-depth titles.

Eight animals are depicted in double-page spreads featuring photographs and two or three line drawings in *Jungle Animals* by Angela Royston (Aladdin, 1991). More than 50 tropical birds are introduced in a short survey from the Eyewitness Junior series, *Amazing Tropical Birds* by Gerald Legg (Knopf, 1991).

Creating a chart of animals that live in the savannah region of Africa and animals that live in the rain forest may help young readers formulate theories about common characteristics of animals living in each region, the food the animals eat, etc.

Animals, Differences Among

Pearce, Q. L. **Why Is a Frog Not a Toad? Discovering the Differences Between Animal Look-Alikes.** Illustrated by Ron Mazellan. Lowell House, 1992. n.p. ISBN 1-56565-025-5. (591 Pea).
Target Audience: Grades K-3; Ages 5-8

This book shows and describes subtle differences between similar animals. Honeybees and yellow jackets (wasps) are similar in size but different in the structure of their homes and their stingers. Each has a distinctive shape, and each honeybee dies after it stings a victim. The wasp's stinger can be used over and over again. An alligator and a crocodile can be distinguished by the shape of the snout and the visibility or invisibility of the teeth when the mouth is shut. Coyotes and wolves are seldom seen together. The wolf is considerably larger, growing to at least 6 feet long and 2-3 feet high at the shoulder. The coyote is seldom longer than 4 feet and 1-2 feet tall at the shoulder. An adult male coyote weighs up to 60 pounds making it considerably smaller than a male wolf, which can weigh as much as 165 pounds. The beaks of the goose and duck give away their identities. In addition, the duck has a shorter neck and a flatter and more streamlined body than a goose. Upon carefully studying the spots on a jaguar and a leopard, those animals can be identified. A leopard's spots are dark rosette shapes, while those of the jaguar are clusters of four or five large spots around a central ring. The short, stocky body of a toad can be easily differentiated from the longer-legged frog. In addition, the toad's skin is rough, bumpy, and often dry, while the frog's skin is smoother and often brightly colored. Other pairs of animals for which identification clues are given include antelope and deer, turtles and tortoises, rabbits and hares, apes and monkeys, and butterflies and moths.

Connections: Animal Pairs

Each of the pairs in Pearce's book lends itself to related readings. For example, the comparison of the wolf and coyote could be used in conjunction with *Wolves* by R. D. Lawrence (Little, Brown/Sierra, 1990); *Amazing Wolves, Dogs & Foxes* by Mary Ling (Knopf, 1991); *Gray Wolf, Red Wolf* by Dorothy Hinshaw Patent (Clarion, 1990); and *Wild, Wild Wolves* by Joyce Milton (Random, 1992).

Compare frogs and toads by reading *Frogs* by Gail Gibbons (Holiday, 1993), which focuses on the life cycle of the frog from egg, to embryo, tadpole, and tiny frogs. The final double-page spread illustrates the differences between frogs and toads.

Christopher Maynard's *Amazing Animal Facts* (Knopf, 1993) answers more than 500 questions about animals. Among the questions are: What is a butterfly? What are frogs? Are toads frogs? and Do crocodiles cry?

Information about other animals in Pearce's title can be found in *Look Out for Turtles* by Melvin Berger (HarperCollins, 1992); *Apes* by Tess Lemmon (Ticknor, 1993); *Wasps at Home* by Bianca Lavies (Dutton, 1991); *Monarch Butterfly* by Gail Gibbons (Holiday, 1989); and *Where Butterflies Grow* by Joanne Ryder (Lodestar, 1989).

Information about crocodiles and alligators is included in *Never Kiss an Alligator!* by Colleen Stanley Bare (Cobblehill, 1989).

Animals, Endangered

Paladino, Catherine. **Our Vanishing Farm Animals: Saving America's Rare Breeds.** Illustrated with photographs. Little, Brown, 1991. 32 pp. ISBN 0-316-68891-6. (636 Pal).

Target Audience: Grades K-3; Ages 5-8

Most of us know about endangered animals that live in the wild, such as the elephant, leopard, and rhinoceros, but most of us do not think about the cows, horses, pigs, or other farm animals that might be endangered. Many of these animals are just like the Rothschild giraffe or the black rhino—specific breeds are vulnerable to extinction. When settlers came to America, they brought with them hardy animals that served a variety of purposes. Cows were beasts of burden, milk producers, and a source of meat. Gradually cows began to be developed specifically for dairy purposes or for meat production. There were dairy cows and beef cattle. As those animals became more profitable for the owners, the other more versatile breeds were less sought after, and they began to die out. In the introduction to her book, Paladino explains why it is important that each breed of animal be preserved—our future, she says, may rely on them. The endangered animals discussed in this book include: the Dutch Belted cow, Gloucester Old Spots pig, Guinea hog, Navajo-Churro sheep, American Mammoth jackstock, Ancona and Black Australorp chicken, and American Bashkir Curly horse. The final pages of the book list many other breeds of cattle, goats, asses, pigs, and sheep that the American Minor Breeds Conservancy considers to be endangered.

Connections: More Endangered Animals

Compare the plight of the animals mentioned in Paladino's book to the endangered status of the Rothschild giraffe or the black rhino. Read about some of the wild endangered animals in *Daisy Rothschild: The Giraffe That Lives with Me* by Betty Leslie-Melville (Doubleday, 1987); *Saving the Peregrine Falcons* by Caroline Arnold (Carolrhoda,

32 / Seeking Information

1985); *Endangered Animals* by Victor H. Waldrop (National Wildlife, 1989); and *As Dead As a Dodo* by Peter Mayle (Godine, 1982).

John Burningham has written a wonderful introductory picture book to endangered animals that are found in the wild, *Hey! Get Off Our Train* (Crown, 1990). Use the information about endangered farm animals to write and illustrate an innovative version of Burningham's text to reflect the plight of the farm animals introduced in Paladino's book.

To find out more about other endangered farm animals, write to the American Minor Breeds Conservancy, P.O. Box 477, Pittsboro, NC 27312.

Animals, Extinct

Pallotta, Jerry. **The Extinct Alphabet Book.** Illustrated by Ralph Masiello. Charlesbridge, 1993. n.p. ISBN 0-88106-471-8. (591.52 Pal).

Target Audience: Grades K-3; Ages 5-8

Each of the 26 letters of the alphabet represents a creature that is endangered or no longer exists. The list includes such unusual creatures as the akioloa (a bird), coelurosauravus (a gliding reptile), quagga (an animal related to the zebra), and the white dodo (a bird). One of the animals listed as extinct is the coelacanth, a fish once thought to be extinct because it was discovered as a fossil. Since then the coelacanth has been found in small numbers. The book's main contribution to knowledge about extinct animals is its alphabetical list of animals that are extinct. This book can be used as a quick, introductory read-aloud before proceeding to a focus on one or more of the many animals.

Connections: Extinct or Endangered Animals

Endangered animals are those that are in danger of becoming extinct (nonexistent). Animals that are dying out but still exist in nature, such as the giant panda, are said to be endangered. An excellent source of information about many of those animals is the *Macmillan Children's Guide to Endangered Animals* by Roger Few (Macmillan, 1993). Maps in each section show the location of the habitat of each animal. An informational paragraph names the country where the animal is presently found and gives other statistical information. More than 20 sources for more information about protection and conservation activities on behalf of animals throughout the world are given.

Apes

Lemmon, Tess. **Apes.** Illustrated by John Butler. Ticknor, 1993. 32 pp. ISBN 0-395-66901-4. (599.88 Lem).
Target Audience: Grades K-3; Ages 5-8

Facts about apes are the focus of this book. However, additional sections focus specifically on orangutans, chimpanzees, gibbons, and gorillas. The author also discusses threats to apes and efforts to protect them. All apes are forest dwellers. According to the world map that shows the distribution of apes in the world, chimpanzees and gorillas inhabit the eastern, western, and central regions of Africa; gibbons reside on the Asian continent in countries such as Thailand and Malaysia; and orangutans live in Borneo and Sumatra and two islands in Southeast Asia. Family groups, eating habits, play, and other activities are discussed for each type of ape. Destruction of ape habitats is seriously endangering their existence. Baby chimpanzees are often captured for pets, but clothing them (as many people do) makes their hair fall out, and most of them die within a few months. In Taipei, Taiwan, it is fashionable to keep an orangutan as a pet. In fact, Lemmon says, there are more orangutans living in the city than in the jungle, their natural habitat. People all over the world, including the United States, keep orangutans as pets. Baby gibbons are often sold as pets, and many die of starvation or neglect. Because apes are so much like humans, scientists use them to test drugs and for other types of experiments. Hunters used to kill mountain gorillas and sell their hands and heads as souvenirs. They are now among the most endangered animals in the world. Armed guards now patrol the forests and attempt to protect the apes, but there is still danger. Some are caught in traps intended for antelope, and the smaller lowland gorillas are still captured for sale to zoos.

Connections: Protecting Endangered Animals

Over the years the chimpanzee has become an endangered animal. Jane Goodall has spent many years observing the behavior of chimpanzees. Information about Goodall's work is presented in *Jane Goodall: Friend of the Chimps* by Eileen Lucas (Millbrook, 1992). Goodall's work focuses on the information she gained from many years of field study. For example, Goodall was the first to document that animals—chimpanzees specifically—make and use tools to obtain food. Before her study it was thought that only humans made tools.

Other books about endangered animals include *Daisy Rothschild: The Giraffe That Lives with Me* by Betty Leslie-Melville (Doubleday, 1987); *Saving the Peregrine Falcons* by Caroline Arnold (Carolrhoda, 1985); and *As Dead As a Dodo* by Peter Mayle (Godine, 1982). Mayle's title presents 16 vanished species in words and paintings. Several titles by Ron Hirschi focus on the endangering of bears and other animals. The books in Hirschi's One Earth series show how the animals look, and the simple text discusses the animals' disappearance and suggests activities to protect the species. Titles include: *Where Are My Bears?* (Bantam, 1992); *Where Are My Prairie Dogs and Black-Footed Ferrets?* (Bantam, 1992); *Where Are My Puffins, Whales and Seals?* (Bantam, 1992); and *Where Are My Swans, Whooping Cranes, and Singing Loons?* (Bantam, 1992).

Sometimes endangered animals are kept in zoos. *Windows on Wildlife* by Ginny Johnston and Judy Cutchins (Morrow, 1990) focuses on six natural habitat exhibits in the United States. Photographs and text take readers behind the scenes to learn about the life of a lowland gorilla in the Ford African Rain Forest at Zoo Atlanta in Atlanta, Georgia; rockhopper penguins at Sea World's Penguin Encounter in Orlando, Florida; birds, insects, and gharials in the Jungle World building at the Bronx Zoo in New York City; hippopotami at the Hippoquarium at the Toledo Zoo (Ohio); birds in the R. J. Reynolds Forest Aviary in the North Carolina Zoological Park in Asheboro, North Carolina; and giant kelp in the Monterey Bay Aquarium in Monterey, California. A final chapter in *Windows on Wildlife* focuses on the pros and cons of life in the wild versus life in captivity. This chapter would be useful to begin a brainstorming session in which students list additional pros and cons of keeping animals in captivity.

Artists

Cummings, Pat, comp. and ed. **Talking with Artists: Conversations with Victoria Chess, Pat Cummings, Leo Dillon and Diane Dillon, Richard Egielski, Lois Ehlert, Lisa Campbell Ernst, Tom Feelings, Steven Kellogg, Jerry Pinkney, Amy Schwartz, Lane Smith, Chris Van Allsburg, and David Wiesner.** Illustrations consist of a variety of childhood photographs, new photographs taken by a variety of photographers, artwork from the artist's childhood, and some illustrations taken from current work. Bradbury, 1992. 96 pp. ISBN 0-02-724245-5. (741.6 Cum).

Target Audience: Grades 4-6; Ages 9-11

Cummings gives basic biographical information about each artist and records their responses to eight questions: Where do you get your ideas from? What is a normal day like for you? Where do you work? Do you have any children? Any pets? What do you enjoy drawing the most? Do you ever put people you know in your pictures? What do you use to make your pictures? and How did you get to do your first book?

⁂ Connections: The Artists' Books

Each of the artists interviewed by Cummings has illustrated several books for young readers. Selected titles by each illustrator are listed below. Each list would help young readers connect the illustrators' biographical information with their work.

Victoria Chess: *The Complete Story of the Three Blind Mice* by John W. Ivimey (Joy Street, 1990); *A Hippopotamusn't and Other Animal Verses* by J. Patrick Lewis (Dial, 1990); *Tommy at the Grocery Store* by Bill Grossman (HarperCollins, 1989); *Slither McCreep and His Brother, Joe* by Tony Johnston (Harcourt, 1992); and *Ghosts! Ghostly Tales from Folklore* by Alvin Schwartz (HarperCollins, 1991).

Pat Cummings: *Petey Moroni's Camp Runamok Diary* by Pat Cummings (Bradbury, 1992); *Clean Your Room, Harvey Moon* by Pat Cummings (Bradbury, 1991); *C.L.O.U.D.S.* by Pat Cummings (Lothrop, 1986); *Go Fish* by Mary Stolz (HarperCollins, 1991); *Good News* by Eloise Greenfield (Coward, 1977); *I Need a Lunch Box* by Jeannette Caines (HarperCollins, 1988); *Willie's Not the Hugging Kind* by Joyce Durham Barrett (HarperCollins, 1989); and *Two and Too Much* by Mildred Pitts Walter (Bradbury, 1990).

Leo Dillon and Diane Dillon: *The Tale of Mandarin Ducks* retold by Katherine Paterson (Lodestar, 1990); *Aida* retold by Leontyne Price (Gulliver, 1990); *Moses's Ark: Stories from the Bible* by Alice Bach and J. Cheryl Exum (Delacorte, 1989); (illustrated by Leo Dillon and Diane Dillon with Lee Dillon) *Pish, Posh, Said Hieronymus Bosch* by Nancy Willard (Harcourt, 1991); *The Race of the Golden Apples* by Claire Martin (Dial, 1991); *Miriam's Well: Stories About Women in the Bible* by Alice Bach and J. Cheryl Exum (Delacorte, 1991); *Northern Lullaby* by Nancy White Carlstrom (Philomel, 1992); *Ashanti to Zulu: African Traditions* by Margaret Musgrove (Dial, 1976); and *Why Mosquitoes Buzz in People's Ears* by Verna Aardema (Dial, 1975).

Richard Egielski: *Oh, Brother* by Arthur Yorinks (Farrar, 1989); *Ugh* by Arthur Yorinks (Farrar, 1990); *Sid and Sol* by Arthur Yorinks (Farrar, 1990); *Hey, Al!* by Arthur Yorinks (Farrar, 1986); *Christmas in July* by Arthur Yorinks (HarperCollins/di Capua, 1991); *The Tub People* by Pam Conrad (HarperCollins, 1989); and *The Lost Soldier* by Pam Conrad (HarperCollins/Geringer, 1992).

Lois Ehlert: *Color Farm* by Lois Ehlert (HarperCollins, 1990); *Feathers for Lunch* by Lois Ehlert (Harcourt, 1990); *Fish Eyes: A Book You Can Count On* by Lois Ehlert (Harcourt, 1990); *Red Leaf, Yellow Leaf* by Lois Ehlert (Harcourt, 1991); *Circus* by Lois Ehlert (HarperCollins,

1992); *Chicka Chicka Boom Boom* by Bill Martin, Jr., and John Archambault (Simon, 1989); *Moon Rope: A Peruvian Folktale; i Un lazo a la luna: Una leyenda peruana* by Lois Ehlert and translated by Amy Prince (Harcourt, 1992); and *THUMP, THUMP, Rat-a-Tat-Tat* by Gene Baer (HarperCollins/Zolotow, 1989).

Lisa Campbell Ernst: *Sam Johnson and the Blue Ribbon Quilt* by Lisa Campbell Ernst (Lothrop, 1983); *Ginger Jumps* by Lisa Campbell Ernst (Bradbury, 1990); *Miss Penny and Mr. Grubbs* by Lisa Campbell Ernst (Bradbury, 1991); *Zinnia and Dot* by Lisa Campbell Ernst (Viking, 1992); *Walter's Tail* by Lisa Campbell Ernst (Bradbury, 1992); and *Gumshoe Goose, Private Eye* by Mary DeBall Kwitz (Dial, 1991).

Tom Feelings: *Jambo Means Hello: Swahili Alphabet Book* by Muriel Feelings (Dial, 1974); *Moja Means One: Swahili Counting Book* by Muriel Feelings (Dial, 1972); *Daydreamers* by Eloise Greenfield and Tom Feelings (Dial, 1981); and *Now Sheba Sings the Song* by Maya Angelou (Dial, 1987).

Steven Kellogg: *The Island of the Skog* by Steven Kellogg (Dial, 1973); *Pinkerton, Behave!* by Steven Kellogg (Dial, 1979); *Is Your Mama a Llama?* by Deborah Guarino (Scholastic, 1989); and *Jimmy's Boa and the Big Splash Birthday Bash* by Trina Hakes Noble (Dial, 1989).

Jerry Pinkney: *The Misadventures of Brer Rabbit, Brer Fox, Brer Wolf, the Doodang, and Other Creatures* retold by Julius Lester (Dial, 1990); *The Talking Eggs: A Folktale from the American South* by Robert D. San Souci (Dial, 1989); *Drysolong* by Virginia Hamilton (Harcourt, 1992); and *In for Winter, Out for Spring* by Arnold Adoff (Harcourt, 1991).

Amy Schwartz: *Camper of the Week* by Amy Schwartz (Orchard/Jackson, 1991); *Mother Goose's Little Misfortunes* by Amy Schwartz and Leonard Marcus (Bradbury, 1990); *Blow Me a Kiss, Miss Lilly* by Nancy White Carlstrom (HarperCollins, 1990); *Fancy Aunt Jess* by Amy Hess (Morrow, 1990); *The Lady Who Put Salt in Her Coffee* by Lucretia Hale (Harcourt, 1989); and *Magic Carpet* by Pat Brisson (Bradbury, 1991).

Lane Smith: *Glasses (Who Needs 'Em?)* by Lane Smith (Viking, 1991); *The Big Pets* by Lane Smith (Viking, 1991); *The True Story of the Three Little Pigs by A. Wolf* by Jon Scieszka (Knopf, 1989); *The Good, the Bad, and the Goofy* by Jon Scieszka (Viking, 1992); and *The*

Stinky Cheese Man and Other Fairly Stupid Tales by Jon Scieszka (Viking, 1992).

Chris Van Allsburg: *Just a Dream* by Chris Van Allsburg (Houghton, 1990); *The Z Was Zapped* by Chris Van Allsburg (Houghton, 1987); *The Polar Express* by Chris Van Allsburg (Houghton, 1985); and *Swan Lake* by Mark Helprin (Houghton/Ariel, 1989).

David Wiesner: *Free Fall* by David Wiesner (Clarion, 1988); *Hurricane* by David Wiesner (Clarion, 1990); *Tuesday* by David Wiesner (Clarion, 1991); *June 29, 1999* by David Wiesner (Clarion, 1992); *The Sorcerer's Apprentice* by Marianna Mayer (Bantam, 1989); *Kite Flier* by Dennis Haseley (Four Winds, 1986); and *Tongues of Jade* by Laurence Yep (HarperCollins, 1991).

Reading some of each artist's books and enjoying their artwork will help make the interviews meaningful. While reading each of the interviews, determine whether there are common elements in the artists' early lives that led them to the world of art and children's books. Was the goal of becoming an artist something each of them had as a very young child, or did the goal come later in life? How did each of the artists come to create art for children's books, by luck or design?

Asian Americans

Morey, Janet Nomura, and Wendy Dunn. **Famous Asian Americans.** Illustrated with photographs. Cobblehill, 1992. 170 pp. ISBN 0-525-65080-6. (920 Mor).
Target Audience: Grades 4-6; Ages 9-11
A collective biography of 14 Asian Americans who have achieved prominence. The first is José Aruego, children's book author and illustrator. Aruego, a native of the Philippines, was a classmate and good friend of Benigno Aquino. Aquino was assassinated in 1983 and his widow, Corazon Aquino, became president of the Philippines in 1986. Before Aruego attended art school he earned a law degree, but he abandoned his career when he came to New York. Other notables that are profiled in this book include people of Chinese, Korean, Japanese, Vietnamese, and Cambodian heritage. Their accomplishments include a wide range of activity. Included are profiles of Connie Chung, news journalist; An Wang, founder and owner of Wang Laboratories; and sports figures, politicians, and many other notables.

Twelve other notables are profiled in this book. Michael Chang, the son of Chinese immigrants, became, at the age of 17, the youngest male and the first American man in 34 years to win the French Tennis Open. Connie Chung is of Chinese heritage, is a nationally-known television broadcaster. Myung-Whun Chung, born in South Korea, has achieved acclaim as an orchestra conductor, particularly for his work with the Opera de la Bastille in Paris, France. Wendy Lee Gramm, an economist of Korean heritage, serves the U.S. Government as the chair of the Commodity Futures Trading Commission. Daniel K. Inouye is a U.S. Senator of Japanese heritage. Maxine Hong Kingston is an author and educator who blends together her Chinese heritage with the culture of her American homeland. June Kuramoto came to the United States from Japan, at the age of five, and has become an accomplished musician. She plays the traditional koto in a group that combines the music of western instruments with her koto and Japanese percussion instruments. Haing Ngor became a medical doctor in his native Cambodia and then suffered the horrors of war as the Khmer Rouge took over the country. And although he emphasizes his work to help other refugees and especially children left orphaned in many Asian countries, he is perhaps best known for his role in the movie, *The Killing Fields*, for which he won an Oscar as best supporting actor. Another actor is a refugee from Vietnam— Dustin Nguyen has played Harry Ioki in television's "21 Jump Street," acted in "Magnum P.I.," and was a cast member for seven months on "General Hospital" and now, in addition to his work as an actor, works hard to keep children from drugs and gangs. As an American astronaut, Ellison S. Onizuka became the first Asian American in space and a hero to the Japanese Americans across the United States. He died in the explosion of the *Challenger* in 1986. I. M. Pei, an American born in China, is a noted architect who has designed a museum for the Rock and Roll Hall of Fame in Cleveland, Ohio, an enlarged and modernized historic museum associated with The Louvre in Paris, and a towering 72-story bank in Hong Kong among hundreds of other innovative architectural projects. Samuel C. C. Ting was born in Michigan but was raised in China where he and his family suffered many hardships. After returning to the United States to study he has become one of the most celebrated physicists in the world and earned the 1976 Nobel Prize in Physics. An Wang, a Chinese native, is the founder and owner of Wang Laboratories, a computer company that has grown from one employee and $600 in funding to a company with annual sales of $2.4 billion and about 20,000 employees.

༄༅ Connections: China and Other Asian Countries

Asian Americans are Americans whose ancestors came from countries in Asia or the Pacific Islands. Sometimes this group of people is referred to as Asian Americans/Pacific Islanders, but most sources group all peoples from the continent of Asia or from islands in the Pacific Ocean as one group. However, it is important to remember that, just as other racial, ethnic, or geographic groups contain subgroups that may differ vastly from one another, so Asian Americans differ from one another depending on their heritage or country of origin.

Page xviii of Morey's book features a map of Asia. Use the map to locate the countries of origin of the people featured in the biographical chapters. To help readers learn about these regions, the following resources are suggested: *The Land and People of China* by John S. Major (Lippincott, 1989); *Inside China* by Ian James (Watts, 1989); *Land of Yesterday, Land of Tomorrow: Discovering Chinese Central Asia* by Brent Ashabranner (Cobblehill, 1992); *Japan* by Ian James (Watts, 1989); *Cambodia* by Claudia Canesso (Chelsea, 1989); *The Land and People of Cambodia* by David P. Chandler (Lippincott, 1991); and *The Land and People of Korea* by S. E. Solberg (Lippincott, 1991). Additional titles can be found by looking up specific countries in the catalog of a school or public library.

Authorship

Bauer, Marion Dane. **What's Your Story? A Young Person's Guide to Writing Fiction.** Clarion, 1992. 134 pp. ISBN 0-395-57781-0. (808.3 Bau). (Photograph of the jacket is courtesy of the publisher and is reprinted with the permission of Clarion Books.)
Target Audience: Grades 4-6; Ages 9-11

Every young person who writes or dreams of being a writer will enjoy these tips on how to write fiction. Bauer talks about characters, plot, point of view, dialogue, endings, and revision. Fourteen chapters explore where good story ideas come from and how to develop ideas into stories that readers will enjoy. Practical suggestions are given for creating believable plots and creating enough story tension to hold readers' interest. Bauer says the success of a writer owes 90 percent to the practice of the craft and 10 percent to inspiration. Her book is intended to help one develop the craft, but the writer must still seek the inspiration that will bring the story energy and passion. Each chapter can be shared or read aloud and will give young writers suggestions for strengthening their own writing.

Connections: Writing Tips

Bauer has succeeded in giving writing tips that will have a practical impact on the habits of young writers. Another book that may give helpful tips or ideas is *Where Do You Get Your Ideas?* by Sandy Asher, illustrated by Susan Hellard (Walker, 1987). Asher includes all of her own "secrets" for generating ideas and includes suggestions from many other favorite authors whom she interviewed. Jamie Gilson, Lila Perl, William Sleator, Patricia Reilly Giff, Marjorie Weinman Sharmat, Dean Hughes, C. S. Adler, Ellen Conford, Kristi Holl, Robert Kimmel Smith, and Robert Burch are among those who tell the stories behind their stories. More books for intermediate-age writers (ages 8-12) are *How to Read and Write Poetry* by Ann Cosman (Watts, 1979); *Write Your Own Story* by Vivian Dubrovin (Watts, 1984); and *In Your Own Words, A Beginner's Guide to Writing* by Sylvia Cassedy (Doubleday, 1979). Younger writers may wish to read *How a Book Is Made* by Aliki (Crowell, 1986) and *Writing for Kids* by Carol Lea Benjamin (Crowell, 1985).

Automobile Racing

Sullivan, George. **Racing Indy Cars.** Illustrated with photographs. Cobblehill, 1992. 63 pp. ISBN 0-525-65082-2. (796.7 Sul).
Target Audience: Grades 4-6; Ages 9-11

This book is a must for those interested in automobile racing. On the straightaway some Indy cars can race at 235 miles per hour, but they were not always that fast. Changes in design, materials used to make the automobiles, and development of more efficient engines, have made Indy cars some of the fastest in the world. The cars are not only among the fastest but are also among the safest race cars in the world. The development of special safety clothes has helped to improve the drivers' safety. Information about the race team, statistical information about a typical car, costs involved in putting a race car in a race, elements that change the dynamics of a race, racing strategy, and many photographs help to bring the reader into the world of racing. A glossary of racing words and terms helps readers speak the language of the racing world, and an index helps readers refer to specific information to read again.

Connections: Racing the Cars

One of the greats in car-racing circles, Michael Andretti, is the subject of his own account of racing cars at the famed Indianapolis Motor Race, *Michael Andretti at Indianapolis* by Michael Andretti, Robert Carver, and Douglas Carver (Simon, 1992). This first-person account will appeal to youngsters who are captivated by the inside story of the race. Andretti describes the inner workings of the race and the people behind the scenes.

Ballooning

Johnson, Neil. **Fire & Silk: Flying in a Hot-Air Balloon.** Illustrated with photographs and drawings. Little, Brown, 1991. n.p. ISBN 0-316-46959-9. (797.5 Joh).
Target Audience: Grades K-3; Ages 5-8

Photographs and drawings take readers from the first flight carrying passengers to the annual hot air balloon festival in Albuquerque, New Mexico. The first flight with passengers took place in September 1783, when a hot air balloon carried a sheep, a duck, and a rooster. By November of that year Joseph Montgolfier and his brother, Étienne Montgolfier, decided that the hot air balloon was safe for human passengers. They hung a basket under their giant blue and gold balloon and launched it with a scientist and a soldier. What started as a novelty now fills festival skies with multicolored and novel-shaped balloons. Hot air ballooning delights both those who fly in the oldest way known and those who simply enjoy the sight of the gigantic shapes of brilliant silky cloth in the sky.

Connections: Other Balloon Enthusiasts

Gary Paulsen is a well-known author of fiction titles for young adults. He has written popular titles, such as *Hatchet* (Bradbury, 1987); *The Voyage of the Frog* (Orchard, 1989); *The Cookcamp* (Orchard, 1991); and *Canyons* (Delacorte, 1990). During the early part of his writing career, Paulsen lived in the Southwest and was a balloon enthusiast. Out of that experience came *Launching, Floating High, and Landing If Your Pilot Light Doesn't Go Out* (Raintree, 1979). Since Paulsen has become a popular author and speaker, Delacorte republished that humorous account of hot air ballooning as *Full of Hot Air: Launching, Floating High, and Landing* with illustrations by Mary Ann Heltshe (Delacorte, 1993).

Since the first flights for pleasure, several organizations have used hot air balloons for important research. Information about some of those research projects is given in *Research Balloons: Exploring Hidden Worlds* by Carole S. Briggs (Lerner, 1988).

A simple book that uses the functions involved in hot air ballooning to demonstrate concepts such as up and down or push and pull is *A Rainbow Balloon: A Book of Concepts* written and illustrated with photographs by Ann Lenssen (Cobblehill, 1992).

Bats

Milton, Joyce. **Bats: Creatures of the Night.** Illustrated by Judith Moffatt. Grosset, 1993. 48 pp. ISBN 0-448-40193-2. (599.4 Mil).
Target Audience: Grades K-3; Ages 5-8

This volume, written for the primary-aged reader, tells almost everything anyone wants to know about bats. Bats are not blind. There are more than 1,000 kinds of bats, some as large as a Canada goose and others much smaller. And yes, vampire bats do drink the blood of animals but not of humans. In that respect bats are no different from most animals, as most animals do feed on other living things eating insects and sometimes fish, fruit, and the juices of flowers, as well as preying on other animals. Other interesting facts about bats are revealed as the author discusses the lives of approximately 100 brown bats that live in an old barn.

Connections: Watching for Bats

Many people think that bats are creepy creatures to be feared and despised. But the beauty of bats is the subtle message of the picture book *Bat Time* by Ruth Horowitz (Four Winds, 1991). *Bat Time* depicts a calm, quiet summer evening during which Leila and her father watch for bats.

More factual information about bats and their habits is included in a title in the Eyewitness Junior series, *Amazing Bats* by Frank Greenaway (Knopf, 1991) and in *A First Look at Bats* by Millicent E. Selsam and Joyce Hunt (Walker, 1991). A somewhat longer book aimed at the intermediate audience, *Bats* by Sharon Sigmond Shebar and Susan E. Shebar (Watts, 1990), attempts to dispel myths about bats and presents interesting and fascinating facts about the mammals.

Bats are also featured in *A Promise to the Sun: An African Story* by Tololwa M. Mollel (Little, Brown, 1992). That book is a Pourquoi story that explains why bats fly at night. Many colorful birds are part of the story, but the star of the book is the plain little bat.

Some readers may wish to follow the directions in *Bats, Butterflies, and Bugs: A Book of Action Toys* by S. Adams Sullivan (Little, Brown, 1990) to make a three-dimensional bat. The bat could be used in retelling *A Promise to the Sun* or other stories.

Bears

Gilks, Helen. **Bears.** Illustrated by Andrew Bale. Ticknor, 1993. 32 pp. ISBN 0-395-66899-9. (599.74 Gil).
Target Audience: Grades K-3; Ages 5-8

A survey of eight types of bears presents the animals' physical characteristics, habits, and behavior. An introductory section provides general information about all types of bears. The polar bear is described as an excellent swimmer and as living in one of the coldest places on earth. They are the largest carnivores that live on land, and they are very dangerous. The brown bear lives on more continents than any other bear. The size and color of the brown bear vary greatly; this class of bear includes the North American bear commonly referred to as the grizzly. The most common bear in North America is the American black bear. Strangely enough black bears are not always black; sometimes they are brown or cream colored. The sun bear is the smallest of all bears. It lives in jungles in Asia. Sun bears do not hibernate because their habitat is warm all year and food is seldom scarce. They get their name from a yellow crescent on their chest. The sloth bear was originally thought to be a type of sloth because it can hang upside-down from branches. It lives in forests in India, Sri Lanka, and Nepal. Other bears included in the book are the Asiatic black bear, the bespectacled bear, and the giant panda. No bear is common today and two, the bespectacled bear and the giant panda, are very rare. A two-page map of the world clearly shows the distribution of bears throughout the world.

Connections: Bear Facts

A very basic book that gives many facts about bears is *Amazing Bears* by Theresa Greenaway (Knopf, 1992). Accounts of episodes involving bears include Helen Kay's account of Theodore Roosevelt's encounter with a young bear, an incident that resulted in the development of the first teddy bear. Kay's book, *The First Teddy Bear* (Stemmer

House, 1985) is an interesting read-aloud for both primary and intermediate students. Dieter Betz's *The Bear Family* (Tambourine, 1992) is a photo-documentary of the Alaskan grizzly that introduces an 11-year-old female and her two cubs. A title translated from French, *Bears* by Gallimard Jeunesse and Laura Bour (Scholastic, 1992) gives a simple introduction to bears, what they eat, how they care for their young, and how they play. The book also warns against feeding bears in the wild and provides other cautions.

Birds

Bash, Barbara. **Urban Roosts: Where Birds Nest in the City.**
Illustrated with photographs. Little, Brown/Sierra, 1990. n.p. ISBN 0-316-08306-2. (598.2 Bas).
Target Audience: Grades K-3; Ages 5-8

When cities and new developments take over land once inhabited by birds, the birds are left without places to build nests, roost, and raise their young. Many have adapted to the new surroundings. The rock dove (pigeon) preferred rocky cliffs; now it substitutes the nooks and crannies of tall buildings made of stone, brick, and glass for those rocky cliffs. Bash details many other places where birds find refuge—tiled roofs, a work glove hanging on a line, an old shoe on a porch. Owls find similar places to have their young, although their activity generally takes place at night, when the adults hunt for rats and mice to bring back to the young. Even the killdeer finds a spot to lay the eggs where they will be camouflaged. Other birds discussed in the book include swallows, crows, starlings, peregrine falcons, and snowy owls.

Connections: Birds at Home in Your Neighborhood

Jim Arnosky has created *Crinkleroot's Guide to Knowing the Birds* (Bradbury, 1992), which has Woodsman Crinkleroot showing children how to identify birds and how to attract them to their backyards. Those who wish to know more about the birds mentioned in *Urban Roosts* and about other birds that may be in their backyards will want to read this title as well as *Birds* by Jill Bailey and David Burnie (Dorling, 1992); *Barn Owls* by Wolfgang Epple (Carolrhoda, 1992) or the much simpler *Owl* by Mary Ling (Dorling, 1992); *House Sparrows Everywhere* by Caroline Arnold (Carolrhoda, 1992); *Pigeons* by Miriam Schlein (Crowell, 1989); and *About Birds: A Guide for Children* by Cathryn Sill (Peachtree, 1991). *Our Yard Is Full of Birds* by Anne Rockwell (Macmillan, 1992) is a very simple introduction to the many types of birds one might find in a city (or country) backyard.

Birds, Feathers

Patent, Dorothy Hinshaw. **Feathers.** Illustrated with photographs by William Muñoz. Cobblehill, 1992. 64 pp. ISBN 0-525-65081-4. (598.2 Pat).
Target Audience: Grades 4-6; Ages 9-11

This book contains more than most readers will ever need to know about birds and their feathers, but it is an interesting book about a topic that will intrigue many readers. More than 40 percent of the world's vertebrate species are birds. Feathers are important to birds whether or not the bird flies. The ostrich's feathers insulate and protect the bird's body, but the feathers weigh less than one-tenth what a similar amount of fur would weigh. This lightweight covering allows the ostrich to run like the wind, despite the fact that it only has two legs. The book discusses six kinds of feathers: contour feathers, semiplume feathers, down feathers, afterfeathers, filoplumes, and bristles. A few birds have powder-down feathers. Topics include how feathers grow, keeping feathers clean, growing new feathers, and how wings and feathers contribute to flight. The reasons some birds are brightly plumed while others are dull and camouflaged is discussed.

Connections: The World of Birds, Amphibians, Fish, Reptiles

Feathers examines just one aspect of a bird's existence. An Eyewitness Book, *Bird* by David Burnie (Knopf, 1988), examines birds' ability to fly or move swiftly, the structure of feathers, courtship, camouflage, feet and tracks, beaks, nest building, and many other topics about birds. Similar studies of other types of animals are presented in other Eyewitness Books: *Amphibian* by Dr. Barry Clark (Knopf, 1993), *Fish* by Steve Parker (Knopf, 1990), and *Reptile* by Colin McCarthy (Knopf, 1991). (There is an Eyewitness series and an Eyewitness Junior series, both from Knopf.)

Blindness

Alexander, Sally Hobart. **Mom Can't See Me.** Illustrated with photographs by George Ancona. Macmillan, 1990. n.p. ISBN 0-02-700401-5. (617.7 Ale).
Target Audience: Grades 4-6; Ages 9-11

The author tells the story of her blindness through the words of her nine-year-old daughter, Leslie. At the age of 26, blood vessels in the author's eyes began to break, causing her to become completely blind. The author, through her daughter's words, describes how she identified Leslie among the babies in the nursery by her big feet. Now the mother listens for noises that let her know what Leslie and her brother are doing, and she even detects that Leslie has sneaked some cookies by smelling the chocolate chips on Leslie's breath. Black-and-white photographs show Leslie and her family in everyday activities: riding bikes, reading aloud, telling stories, baking, and camping out. A few tricks that Leslie uses to fool her mother are included. Older readers will recognize the irony of including the tricks in a book that is actually written by Leslie's mother.

Connections: Coping with Blindness

In 1992, a second book by Sally Hobart Alexander was published. That title, *Mom's Best Friend,* illustrated with photographs by George Ancona (Macmillan, 1992), focuses on Leslie's mom and her efforts to obtain and work with a new guide dog after her first dog, Marit, died. Leslie's mom has to go to the guide dog school for a month or more so that the dog can get used to her, and even after they come home, the dog has to get used to the new surroundings and to bond with Leslie's mom. Leslie and her brother Joel aren't allowed to play with the dog until the acclimation period is over. Alexander's second book gives even more insight into the life of a blind person.

To read books to her children, Alexander uses the braille system, in which letters of the alphabet are represented by six dots in a cell. The braille alphabet was developed by Louis Braille, a blind Frenchman who was 15 years old when he developed the system. Braille's story is told in Dennis Brindell Fradin's *Remarkable Children: Twenty Who Made History* (Little, Brown, 1987).

Other authors have told stories of how fictional characters deal with blindness. Gloria Whelan's *Hannah* (Knopf, 1991), takes place in 1897 just as the braille method of reading and writing is reaching America. Nine-year-old Hannah doesn't know anything about reading and writing. Until Miss Robbins, the new teacher, comes to live with Hannah's family, Hannah isn't even allowed to go to school. A preteen boy faces a similar challenge in the contemporary story *Carver* by Ruth Yaffe Radin (Macmillan, 1990). When he moves back to his mother's hometown, he learns that he will have to attend a regular school. Several other novels use the challenge of blindness as a theme. Patricia MacLachlan tells the story of a boy who attempts to "see" like his blind grandfather in *Through Grandpa's Eyes* (Harper, 1980).

Jean Little, writing for more mature readers, is legally blind. She writes about a teenager with poor vision in *From Anna* (Harper, 1972). Anna's high school years are the subject of another book, *Listen for the Singing* (Dutton, 1977; HarperCollins, 1991). The stories about Anna are set in Canada in the late 1930s and are based on many incidents from Little's own life. Susan Gaitskell has written a fictionalized account of Jean Little's life for primary readers. That book, *A Story of Jean* (Oxford, 1989), tells about the teasing Jean endured because she was almost blind and her efforts to overcome her unhappiness by turning to stories and books. Little's memoir, which describes the challenges of her failing vision, is *Little by Little: A Writer's Education* (Viking, 1988) and its sequel, *Stars Come Out Within* (Viking, 1991).

Thomas Bergman has written a series of books about children who live with a variety of challenges. One of the books, *Seeing in Special Ways: Children Living with Blindness* (Gareth Stevens, 1989), features several children who converse with Bergman. The dialogues between Bergman and each of the children are accompanied by photographs of the child who is talking. Thomas, a nine-year-old who wishes that someday he will be able to drive a car, says, "But I don't suppose I ever will." Andrew was born blind because his mother had German measles while she was pregnant; Katie, another nine-year-old, weighed only one pound when she was born, and too much oxygen damaged her eyes. George A., an eight-year-old, wishes that he could feel the images on television. In addition to these children, several other children tell their individual stories of how they get along with their blindness.

Business

Aaseng, Nathan. **Close Calls: From the Brink of Ruin to Business Success.** Illustrated with photographs. Inside Business series. Lerner, 1990. 80 pp. ISBN 0-8225-0682-3. (650.14 Aas). (Photograph of the jacket is courtesy of the publisher and is reprinted with the permission of Lerner Publications/Carolrhoda Books.)
Target Audience: Grades 4-6; Ages 9-11

This book chronicles the stories behind the beginning, failure, and eventual success of several companies, including DuPont, Folger's,

Heinz, Woolworth's, Dow Chemical, 3M, Ohio Art, Hallmark, and Chrysler. Sandpaper that wouldn't sand and a fire that destroyed all of one company's inventory are just two of the disasters chronicled. These disasters brought the companies involved to the brink of ruin. Other stories focus on entrepreneurs: Frank W. Woolworth was not a particularly successful salesperson: before founding his company, he was fired from one job, had his salary reduced at another, and had difficulty staying with one employer. He found his niche with window displays; one of them, a display of five-cent items, was the beginning of a successful chain of five-and-dime stores. Similar tales of success surround each of the nine companies or products profiled in Aaseng's book.

Connections: From Rags to Riches

There are many stories of business success and people who succeeded in adverse situations. *Madame C. J. Walker: Self-Made Millionaire* by Patricia McKissack and Fredrick McKissack (Enslow, 1992) is the true story of an African American woman who exhibited remarkable persistence and belief in herself, founded her own company, and became a millionaire. Other titles that tell stories of people who triumphed over adverse situations are *From Rags to Riches: People Who Started Businesses from Scratch* by Nathan Aaseng (Lerner, 1990); *Midstream Changes: People Who Started Over and Made It Work* by Nathan Aaseng (Lerner, 1990); *Great Women in the Struggle: An Introduction for Young Readers* by Toyomi Igus, Veronica Freeman Ellis, and Diane Patrick (Just Us, 1992); and *One More River to Cross: The Stories of Twelve Black Americans* by Jim Haskins (Scholastic, 1992). Each story in these collections is a source of inspiration and courage. Sharing the stories with students should help some readers establish goals for themselves.

Butterflies

Lasky, Kathryn. **Monarchs.** Illustrated with photographs by Christopher G. Knight. Harcourt/Gulliver Green, 1993. 64 pp. ISBN 0-15-255296-0. (595.78 Las).
Target Audience: Grades K-3; Ages 5-8

The tale of these monarch butterflies begins in a cubbyhole on an island off the coast of Maine. As many as 400 eggs are laid among the leaves in the cubbyhole. Lasky explains the development from egg to caterpillar to chrysalis to butterfly. The book also gives an account of a woman in Penobscot Bay, Maine, who is an expert on butterflies. She keeps many chrysalides surrounded by milkweed and watches them develop into butterflies. The woman, Clara Waterman, releases the butterflies into her yard. She works with children who come to learn about the butterflies. Sometimes she takes the children to the cubbyhole to collect caterpillars and chrysalides.

From Clara's garden the monarchs migrate south. Lasky tells us that all of the late-summer monarchs who live east of the Rocky Mountains migrate to Mexico for the winter. As they fly south the butterflies land during the late afternoon. They look for nectar-filled flowers, especially purple and yellow ones. They cannot fly if the temperature falls below 55 degrees Fahrenheit. By November the monarchs stream into Mexico, where the climate is warm, water is plentiful, and nectar-filled flowers grow. The largest colony is at El Rosario, Mexico. The citizens of El Rosario promote the butterflies as a tourist attraction. Another winter refuge for monarchs is Pacific Grove, California, where citizens celebrate their annual arrival with a parade. Near the end of February the monarchs begin to become more active, and by late April or May the first generation of spring butterflies have begun their flight north and have reached the southern states. By June the butterflies will have arrived in the mid-latitude states of Virginia, Missouri, Iowa, and Delaware. By July the butterflies will have moved farther north, as far as Canada, where the cycle begins once again.

Connections: Migrating Butterflies

Dr. Fred Urquhart's 1976 landmark discovery of the winter habitat of monarch butterflies is the subject of Bianca Lavies's *Monarch Butterflies: Mysterious Travelers* (Dutton, 1992). The migration habits of the monarch are also the subject of *The Great Butterfly Hunt: The Mystery of the Migrating Monarchs* by Ethan Herberman (Simon, 1990). The monarch is the subject of *Monarch Butterfly* by Gail Gibbons (Holiday, 1989), while the majesty of all butterflies is presented in *Where Butterflies Grow* by Joanne Ryder (Lodestar, 1989).

John Still's *Amazing Butterflies and Moths* (Knopf, 1991) brings together a fascinating, photo-filled overview of butterflies and moths. A simple explanation of the life cycle of a butterfly is presented in *Butterfly* by Moira Butterfield (Simon, 1992) and in *Butterfly* by Mary Ling (Dorling, 1992).

Canada

Harrison, Ted. **O Canada.** Illustrated by Ted Harrison. Ticknor, 1992 (Kids Can Press, 1993). n.p. ISBN 0-395-66075-0. (971 Har).
Target Audience: Grades K-3; Ages 5-8

Ted Harrison, a native of England who emigrated to Canada, has painted his vision of each province of Canada to introduce Americans to the "beautiful land to the north." The book opens with a two-page spread of a political map of Canada. Each province's borders are clearly shown, large cities and their locations are identified. Newfoundland and Labrador are depicted with an illustration of the sea. Newfoundland, the easternmost province, is an island. Labrador is on the mainland, edged by the Labrador Sea. The illustration depicting Nova Scotia shows a picturesque fishing village. Nova Scotia is almost entirely surrounded by water. Prince Edward Island is shown with rolling farmlands, white farm houses, and many lighthouses to warn fishermen and sailors about the dangerous coral reefs and sandbars. The varied countryside of New Brunswick is represented by farmland beside the sea. Not pictured are the temperate forests that make up 85 percent of New Brunswick. Beautiful cities with old stone houses represent the French-speaking province of Quebec. The most populous Canadian province, Ontario, is illustrated with a baseball team (Toronto is the home of the Toronto Blue Jays), hot air balloons, and the rolling countryside that surrounds Toronto. An endless field of sunflowers and a farm set against a sky in shades of blue represent Manitoba. The great wheat-producing province of Saskatchewan is shown as prairie, with a member of the Royal Canadian Mounted Police, or Mounties, riding across the prairie. Saskatchewan's landscape moves into an illustration depicting Alberta, whose rolling foothills lead to the peaks of the Rocky Mountains. The coastal waters of British Colombia's Pacific shoreline are illustrated for that province. The cold, desolate north country, the Yukon Territory, is depicted with mountains reflecting in the snowy land dotted by homes with smoking chimneys. Finally, the illustration depicting the vast province of the Northwest Territories shows a caribou and a wolf trail across the barren ground, a land marked with an "inukshuk," or figure of stone blocks. Inukshuk are trail markers built by the Inuit, a native people. The final two pages of the book have the music and words (in English and in French) for "O Canada," Canada's national anthem.

Connections: Our Northern Neighbor

Harrison's book offers a clear and comprehensible overview of each province of Canada. Several titles have examined the history and geography of specific regions of Canada in more detail. Some excellent titles include those in Suzanne LeVert's Let's Discover Canada series, published by Chelsea, which include *Northwest Territories* (1992), *Yukon* (1992), and 10 other titles focusing on each Canadian province. The prairie of Canada is effectively described in an alphabet book, *A Prairie Alphabet* by Jo Bannatyne-Cugnet (Tundra, 1992). Lushly painted, detailed illustrations are included for each letter of the alphabet.

Each page contributes to a view of the Canadian prairie. Accounts of the Canadian gold rush are told in *Klondike Fever: The Famous Gold Rush of 1898* by Michael Cooper (Clarion, 1989) and *Gold! The Klondike Adventure* by Delia Ray (Lodestar, 1989). The St. Lawrence Seaway, which serves both Canada and the United States, is the subject of Gail Gibbons's *The Great St. Lawrence Seaway* (Morrow, 1992).

Careers

Johnson, Neil. **All in a Day's Work: Twelve Americans Talk About Their Jobs.** Illustrated with photographs by Neil Johnson. Little, Brown, 1989. 90 pp. ISBN 0-316-46957-2. (331.7 Joh).
Target Audience: Grades 4-6; Ages 9-11
  Through personal interviews and photographs of each of the subjects, the author has captured a view of 12 individuals who are enthusiastic about the way they earn their livings, who have a perspective of their jobs, and who can articulate the reasons they continue in their careers. They include a musician with a symphony, a detective, cotton farmer, television journalist, judge, computer programmer, restaurateur, social worker, air force pilot, nurse, assembly-line worker, and teacher.

Connections: Investigating Other Job Opportunities

Each of the careers highlighted in the Johnson title could lead to more investigation into the specific vocational field. For example: Two of the careers included in the Johnson title are related to law enforcement (judge and detective). A book that might provide more information on careers in that field include: *Careers in Law Enforcement and Security* by Paul Cohen and Shari Cohen (Rosen, 1990) and a book, by Joan Hewett, focusing specifically on the role of a public defender. That book, *Public Defender: Lawyer for the People* (Lodestar, 1991) includes information about the role of a public defender—a defense lawyer appointed by the court to defend suspects who cannot afford to hire a lawyer. In order to present the information Joan Hewett and photographer Richard Hewett follow Janice Fukai, a public defender in Los Angeles County, California, as she inspects a crime scene to gather clues to help in a client's defense, questions propspective jurors, and selects members of the jury. In the courtroom they observe her questioning of witnesses—carefully calculated to help her client's case. The Hewett title offers a quick look into the life of one person doing her job. Any discussion of law enforcement may logically lead to a discussion among young readers of their personal

52 / Seeking Information

rights. Information about that aspect is included in *Up Against the Law: Your Legal Rights As a Minor* by Ross R. Olney and Patricia J. Olney (Lodestar, 1985).

The Cohen book cited above is one title in a series of titles for young adults that has been created by the Rosen Publishing Group; a series focusing on careers in various segments of our society. In addition to the law enforcement title other titles are: *Careers in Computer Sales* by Lawrence Epstein (Rosen, 1990); *Careers in Fashion Retailing* by Pat Koester (Rosen, 1990); and *Careers in Banking and Finance* by Patricia Haddock (Rosen, 1990).

Intermediate readers will enjoy reading *A Week in the Life of an Airline Pilot* by William Jaspersohn (Little, Brown, 1991), which details the work of Captain Ralph Larson as he and his crew fly from New York to New Delhi, India. *The Astronaut Training Book* by Kim Long (Lodestar, 1990) is a guide for those who are interested in pursuing an aerospace career.

Other careers are the focus in books that take a look at the many jobs behind the scenes in the making of equipment for ball games, *Bat, Ball, Glove* by William Jaspersohn (Little, Brown, 1989) and in the making of a motorcycle, *Motorcycle: The Making of a Harley-Davidson* by William Jaspersohn (Little, Brown, 1984). Jaspersohn shows people who design the motorcycle and those who manufacture, test run, and sell it.

Titles that are particularly suited to sharing with younger readers are *Trucker* by Hope Herman Wurmfeld (Macmillan, 1990), *A Carpenter* by Douglas Florian (Greenwillow, 1991), *A Potter* by Douglas Florian (Greenwillow, 1991), and *An Auto Mechanic* by Douglas Florian (Greenwillow, 1991).

Community helpers are the focus of *To the Rescue* by Hope Irvin Marston (Cobblehill, 1991) and *Fire Fighters*, a pop-up book created by Peter Seymour and illustrated by Norm Ingersoll (Lodestar, 1990). *Fire Fighters* shows the type of equipment and some of the work that firefighters do. Seymour and Ingersoll have also created *Pilots* (Lodestar, 1992), which looks at what it is like to fly a jetliner and what it takes to become a pilot.

While specific careers in various industries are covered in the books cited above, Millbrook Publishing has created a series of career books that focus on the type of person who enters the career. The Millbrook series includes: *Careers for People Who Like People* by Russell Shorto (Millbrook, 1992); *Careers for People Who Like to Perform* by Russell Shorto (Millbrook, 1992); and *Careers for Animal Lovers* by Russell Shorto (Millbrook, 1992). More career information for those who like animals can be found in the "Connections" section accompanying Gail Gibbons's book *Say Woof! The Day of a Country Veterinarian* (Macmillan, 1992). See page 135.

Another source of information about careers are the parents, aunts and uncles, and grandparents of those who are interested in learning more about careers. Invite them to talk about their careers.

Cats

Ryden, Hope. **Your Cat's Wild Cousins.** Illustrated with photographs by Hope Ryden. Lodestar, 1991. 48 pp. ISBN 0-525-67354-7. (599.74 Ryd).

Target Audience: Grades K-3; Ages 5-8

The African wildcat is the ancestor of the house cat, but it is nearing extinction. In this country the African wildcat can be found only in the San Diego Zoo. The lion, the king of beasts, is so powerful that it can knock over and kill a buffalo. It is the lioness that does most of the hunting, but after the kill has been made, the larger and stronger male forces the lioness to stand aside to wait for the leftovers. This is the origin of the expression "getting the lion's share." Other cats featured in Ryden's book include the caracal, a cat who "uses its short tail like some kind of cartoon character"; the cheetah, the fastest cat in the world; the black-footed cat, the smallest cat in the world; the serval, a long-legged cat that lies down like a dog; the leopard, a cat that can adapt to a variety of habitats and is the only large cat to make regular use of trees; the tiger, the largest member of the cat family; the marbled cat, which is slightly larger than the domestic cat but has a long, thick tail that leads those who see it to think that it is attached to a much larger cat; Pallas's cat, whose face resembles that of a monkey; the snow leopard, an expert jumper that can leap as far as 49 feet; the fishing cat, a cat from southeastern Asia that does not mind getting wet; the ocelot, often sought for its beautiful coat of rust, brown, and black on a white or cream background; the jaguarundi, a cat that more closely resembles a marten or a mink and whose chirping sounds like a bird; the jaguar, the biggest and strongest New World cat; the bobcat, which lives only in North America; the Canada lynx, a skilled hunter that preys on snowshoe hares; and the puma, a New World animal that resembles a lion.

Connections: All Kinds of Cats

Seven varieties of big cats are featured in *Big Cats* by Seymour Simon (HarperCollins, 1991). Basic animal facts interspersed with bits of trivia are included in *Cat* by Juliet Clutton-Brock (Knopf, 1991). Like the other volumes in the Eyewitness series, *Cat* is illustrated with clear photographs that clarify the information in the text. Somewhat shorter than Clutton-Brock's title are Ron Hirschi's *What*

Is a Cat? (Walker, 1991) and *Where Do Cats Live?* (Walker, 1991), which present interesting essays and crisp, color photographs.

Chickens

Hariton, Anca. **Egg Story.** Dutton, 1992. n.p. ISBN 0-525-44816-6. (598 Har).
Target Audience: Grades K-3; Ages 5-8

Bright watercolors illustrate this account of an egg from the time it is laid through its incubation under the hen's body to the chick's birth after 21 days. The rooster wakes the farm animals to stretch and yawn or flap their wings. The gray hen cackles in the hen house because she has just laid an egg. A description of the inside of the egg is given, along with the information that the chick will hatch in 21 days. Illustrations show how the chick develops within the egg. The book tells how the hen keeps the chick from sticking to the inside of the eggshell and how the chick breaks out of the shell to become one of the farm animals.

Connections: Animals That Hatch from Eggs

Chickens are not the only animals that hatch from eggs. Patricia Lauber presents information about a variety of eggs, including ostrich, python, and monarch butterfly eggs, in *What's Hatching Out of That Egg?* (Crown, 1979, 1991). Black-and-white photographs highlight the information.

On one double-page spread in *Reptiles* by Colin McCarthy (Knopf, 1991), photographs showing the eggs of snakes, lizards, crocodilians (caimans and alligators), turtles, and tortoises accompany information about the eggs. On a following page in the same book, several photographs depict reptiles hatching. A similar photographic treatment is given to eggs of water birds and waders, eggs of land birds, and extraordinary eggs in *Birds* by David Burnie (Knopf, 1988). Another section in Burnie's book depicts seven stages of a pheasant chick hatching.

Compare the size of an egg with the animal that hatched from it. Determine whether there is a pattern to the ratio of the size of the egg to the size of animal hatched. Pictures or descriptions of eggs of various size can be found in books like Burnie's *Birds* and in books about the animals that hatch from eggs.

Civil Rights

Rochelle, Belinda. **Witnesses to Freedom: Young People Who Fought for Civil Rights.** Illustrated with photographs. Lodestar, 1993. 98 pp. ISBN 0-525-67377-6. (323.1 Roc).
Target Audience: Grades 4-6; Ages 9-11

Rochelle pays tribute to the individuals, particularly young people, who contributed to the civil rights movement. The first young person whose story is told is Barbara Johns, who attended R. R. Moton High School for black students in Farmville, Virginia. Johns instigated a boycott at the high school to force officials to make improvements to the school. The town's white school was far superior to R. R. Moton High School in terms of supplies, textbooks, furniture, and other necessities. The boycott was only partially successful. The National Association for the Advancement of Colored People filed suit to force improvements at the school and to force the integration of all schools in Farmville. Five years after the struggle began, city officials closed all of the schools in Prince Edward County, Virginia, a move intended to prevent integration. Barbara Johns's efforts began protests all over America. Other stories in *Witnesses to Freedom* tell about the children involved in the desegregation efforts that became part of the Supreme Court case *Brown* v. *Board of Education of Topeka, Kansas*; the children involved in the Little Rock Nine efforts to integrate Little Rock, Arkansas schools; the Montgomery, Alabama bus boycott, lunch counter sit-ins, freedom rides, the Children's Crusade, the March for Jobs and Freedom in Washington, D.C.; and efforts to obtain voting rights.

Connections: Striving for Civil Rights

The stories told by Belinda Rochelle are stories of young people who participated in efforts to make the place a better place for all people. Several books for young readers chronicle the stories of many others who participated in these efforts. David A. Adler tells the story of Martin Luther King, Jr. in his account of King's civil rights efforts, *Martin Luther King, Jr.: Free at Last* (Holiday, 1986) and in *A Picture Book of Martin Luther King, Jr.* (Holiday, 1989). Other books about King's life include *Meet Martin Luther King, Jr.* by James T. De Kay (Random, 1989) and *The Life and Death of Martin Luther King, Jr.* by James Haskins (Lothrop, 1977). Rosa Parks, who was one of the first to refuse to leave her seat on a Montgomery bus and thus brought about the beginning of the Montgomery bus boycott, is the subject of several books, including *A Picture Book of Rosa Parks* by David Adler (Holiday, 1993) and *Rosa Parks: My Story* by Rosa Parks and James Haskins (Dial, 1992). A survey of the struggle for civil rights for African

Americans is included in *Blacks in America, 1754-1979* by Florence Jackson (Watts, 1980) and *The Civil Rights Movement in America from 1865 to the Present* by Patricia McKissack and Fredrick McKissack (Children's Press, 1991).

Constitutional Convention

Maestro, Betsy, and Giulio Maestro. **A More Perfect Union: The Story of Our Constitution.** Illustrated by Giulio Maestro. Lothrop, 1987. 48 pp. ISBN 0-688-06839-1. (342.73 Mae).
Target Audience: Grades 4-6; Ages 9-11

In May 1787, representatives of the 13 American colonies met in Philadelphia to figure out what to do about some of the problems they were having working together as one nation. Instead of creating solutions to the problems of each of the colonies, the convention began to talk about forming a new government. This book chronicles the roles of George Washington and colony representatives, the need for the Bill of Rights, and the struggle to ratify the Constitution.

Connections: A Perspective on the Constitution

Jean Fritz tells the story of the writing of the Constitution in *Shh! We're Writing the Constitution,* illustrated by Tomie dePaola (Putnam, 1987). Fritz's straightforward writing style and her inclusion of interesting details add another dimension to the story. Fritz's biographies of five people who played a part in the forming of the nation include: *And Then What Happened, Paul Revere?* (Coward, 1973), *What's the Big Idea, Ben Franklin?* (Coward, 1976), *Where Was Patrick Henry on the 29th of May* (Coward, 1975), *Why Don't You Get a Horse, Sam Adams?* (Coward, 1974), and *Will You Sign Here, John Hancock?* (Coward, 1976). A longer, and more detailed account of a man involved in the writing of the Constitution is Fritz's *The Great Little Madison* (Putnam, 1989), which tells the story of James Madison and his friendship with Thomas Jefferson and their efforts to establish a viable national government for the new nation to be known as the United States of America.

Dinosaurs

Aliki. **Dinosaur Bones.** Illustrated by Aliki. Let's-Read-and-Find-Out Science Book series. Crowell, 1988. 32 pp. ISBN 0-690-04549-2. (567.9 Ali).
Target Audience: Grades K-3; Ages 5-8

In 1676, a giant fossil bone was described as a human thigh bone. Later Dr. Robert Plot discovered that it was a dinosaur bone. Dinosaurs became extinct more than 65 million years ago. From the discovery of bones and other fossils, paleontologists are able to learn about life during the time when dinosaurs roamed the earth. Scientists are still finding fossils and are still learning about prehistoric animals. An explanation of the work of the early paleontologists and a description of the prehistoric eras when dinosaurs developed and evolved are included. The author suggests that there are many things that we do not know about dinosaurs. As new information is uncovered by scientists, the author says that she "check[s] in at the museum and read[s] my new books for the latest news."

Connections: More About Dinosaurs

Other excellent information titles include *New Questions and Answers About Dinosaurs* by Seymour Simon (Morrow, 1990); *Macmillan Children's Guide to Dinosaurs and Other Prehistoric Animals* by Philip Whitfield (Macmillan, 1992); *The Dinosaur Questions and Answer Book* by Sylvia Funston (Little, Brown, 1992); and *Where to Find Dinosaurs Today* by Daniel Cohen and Susan Cohen (Cobblehill, 1992).

Bernard Most has written many humorous and fun books using dinosaurs. His *Four and Twenty Dinosaurs* (Harcourt, 1990) parodies favorite nursery rhymes, and his *The Littlest Dinosaur* dispels the myth that all dinosaurs were huge. Most discusses the research necessary to create an accurate fiction book in a videotape, *Get to Know Bernard Most* (Harcourt, 1993). Readers may wish to offer Most their ideas for other dinosaur books. Send him a letter at 3 Ridgecrest, Scarsdale, NY 10583.

Dinosaurs, Sites

Cohen, Daniel, and Susan Cohen. **Where to Find Dinosaurs Today.** Illustrated with photographs. Cobblehill, 1992. 210 pp. ISBN 0-525-65098-9. (567.9 Coh).
Target Audience: Grades 4-6; Ages 9-11

Those who love dinosaurs will delight in this title, which tells the location of hundreds of dinosaurs throughout the United States and Canada. I used the index to locate Iowa, and sure enough there was an entry that confirmed the book's authenticity in my mind: "University of Iowa, Museum of Natural History." I know the museum's fine exhibits firsthand, but few other people know about it. The Cohens not only managed to find this little-known exhibit, they also managed to find 148 other locations that dinosaur lovers will enjoy visiting. The places range from museums with scientific displays like the one at the University of Iowa to fun displays like the twice-life-size, steel-and-concrete model of *Brontosaurus* with a gift shop in its stomach near the Wheel Inn Restaurant on Interstate 10 at Cabazon, California, or the Dino-Store in Birmingham, Alabama, which sells more than 120 different dinosaur T-shirts. In addition to giving basic information about specific dinosaur sites, the Cohens impart much incidental information about dinosaurs in the course of discussing the sites. For example, they explain that, although the name *Brontosaurus* has been replaced by the scientific term *Apatosaurus,* many tourist sites and museums are reluctant to change the name in their displays. Reading about the entries is an interesting experience, and it seems that a dino-trip would be just as much fun.

Connections: Dinosaur Fun

Dinosaurs are the topic of several titles that will encourage interest in Aliki's *Dinosaur Bones* (Crowell, 1988) and *Digging Up Dinosaurs* (Crowell, 1981; rev. 1988) will interest readers in paleontology. Another title, *Dinosaur Dig* by Kathryn Lasky (Morrow, 1990), recounts the Knight family's summer trip to the western United States, where they helped a paleontologist uncover dinosaur fossils. On the trip were Kathryn Lasky Knight, her husband and the book's photographer Christopher Knight, and their two children.

One of the first entries in *Where to Find Dinosaurs Today* features the expert in the field of dinosaurabilia, Dean Hannotte. Hannotte collects hundreds of items connected with dinosaurs. His apartment is filled floor to ceiling with dinosaur memorabilia. His apartment is not a museum, but if people call ahead, he may invite them to see his collection. The authors suggest that if you write to him, he will write back. Dean Hannotte's address is 151 First Avenue, New York, NY 10002. Decide what questions you wish to ask him, then write a class letter. Be sure to enclose a self-addressed, stamped envelope for his reply.

Dolphins

Behrens, June. **Dolphins.** Illustrated with photographs. Children's Press, 1989. 48 pp. ISBN 0-516-00517-0. (599.5 Beh).
Target Audience: Grades 4-6; Ages 9-11
Ancient Greeks told stories about dolphins that saved lives and guided ships to safety. Dolphins are members of the cetacean group of mammals; they are relatives of whales and porpoises. The dolphin's fluke—a flat, horizontal tail—and its flippers help the dolphin swim. Indeed, the dolphin is one of the fastest swimmers in the sea. Scientists have studied and tracked the movement of dolphins for decades. Because of their intelligence and their ability to respond to commands and perform tricks, many dolphins are used as performers in marine parks. Information about various types of dolphins is included in the text and photographs. Some information is included about the killer whale, or orca, which is the largest member of the dolphin family.

Connections: Observing Dolphins

Dolphins are charming and entertaining in marine exhibits and in the sea, and they are interesting animals to observe. Many who have observed the animals have written about them in *Dolphins* by Sharon Bokoske and Margaret Davidson (Random, 1993); *Dolphins and Porpoises* by Dorothy Hinshaw Patent (Holiday, 1987); and *The Dolphins and Me* by Don Reed and illustrated by Pamela Carroll and Walter Carroll (Little, Brown, 1989).

Those who enjoy reading about dolphins might also be interested in whales and sharks. Books include *Whales and Other Creatures of the Sea* by Joyce Milton (Random, 1993); *Sharks and Other Creatures of the Deep* by Philip Steele (Dorling, 1991); *Seals, Sea Lions and Walruses* by Dorothy Hinshaw Patent (Holiday, 1990); and *Where Are My Puffins, Whales, and Seals?* by Ron Hirschi (Bantam, 1992).

Eagles

Lang, Aubrey. **Eagles.** Illustrated with photographs by Wayne Lynch. Little, Brown/Sierra, 1990. 64 pp. ISBN 0-316-51387-3. (598.9 Lan).
Target Audience: Grades 4-6; Ages 9-11
Since ancient times the eagle has been revered as a symbol of strength and courage. Native Americans believed in the power of the eagle, and its feathers were part of some tribes' ceremonial clothing. Eagles have been the emblem of many nations and are often immortalized in carvings on buildings, monuments, and flags. The bald eagle is the

national bird of the United States. The 59 species of eagles can be divided into four major groups that inhabit both of the American continents, Europe, Asia, and Africa. The eagle is a predator who helps to control the population of many smaller animals. Descriptions of the characteristics of the eagle (its keen eyesight spawned the phrase *eagle-eyed*) give readers interesting information about the interdependence of the eagle and nature. Charts depict how eagles use air currents to soar through the air, migration routes, and how pesticides move through the food chain. A final chapter portrays the plight of the eagle, whose future is threatened by human progress. The eagle's habitat has been destroyed and rivers have been polluted with chemicals that kill the fish eagles eat. Many of the species are protected species and considered endangered.

Connections: Endangered Animals

Many other endangered animals are featured in *Macmillan Children's Guide to Endangered Animals* by Roger Few (Macmillan, 1993). This atlas focuses on endangered animals from various continents and islands. Maps in each section show the location of the usual habitat of each of featured animal. Few's book will stimulate additional reading and investigation about other endangered animals. *Junkyard Bandicoots and Other Tales of the World's Endangered Species* by Joyce Rogers Wolkomir and Richard Wolkomir (Wiley, 1992) is an interesting collection of short vignettes about familiar and not-so-familiar endangered animals. The book gives information about conservation efforts and discusses a few species that are extinct. Other books cited in connection with Jerry Pallotta's *The Extinct Alphabet Book* (see page 32) present information about other endangered animals.

Fact sheets about endangered animals are available from the World Wildlife Fund. In addition, the organization's catalog lists newsletters, atlases, books, and other educational materials. The catalog and fact sheets can be obtained from: World Wildlife Fund, U.S., 1250 24th Street N.W., Washington, DC 20037.

Easter

Gibbons, Gail. **Easter.** Illustrated by Gail Gibbons. Holiday, 1989. n.p. ISBN 0-8234-0737-3. (394.2 Gib).
Target Audience: Grades K-3; Ages 5-8

While not promoting the Christian holiday in a didactic manner, Gibbons does not back away from presenting the origins of the holiday in Christian tradition. After the origin is presented, Gibbons presents symbols of Easter, explains the origin of the word *Easter,* describes traditions, such as Easter egg hunts, egg-rolling contests, the giving of Easter baskets, Easter dinners, and Easter parades. Gibbons's watercolor illustrations complement the text in this balanced view of the holiday.

Connections: Traditions of Easter and Passover

Gibbons's *Easter* serves as a general introduction to the holiday whose secular traditions are featured in many titles for young readers. Those wishing to know more about the traditions and symbols of Easter will want to read *Lilies, Rabbits, and Painted Eggs: The Story of the Easter Symbols* by Edna Barth, illustrated by Ursula Arndt (Clarion, 1970). The story behind the religious celebration is told in *The Easter Story,* written and illustrated by Brian Wildsmith (Knopf, 1993), and in *Easter: The King James Version,* illustrated by Jan Pienkowsi (Knopf, 1989).

Many people do not celebrate Easter but focus on Passover and the coming of spring. *Passover As I Remember It* by Toby Knobel Fluek and Lillian Fluek Finkler (Knopf, 1994) tells of life in a Polish village in the 1930s. A young girl tells of helping her family prepare for the Passover seder over a period of months. Deep-hued watercolors by Toby Knobel Fluek help readers visualize the Jewish traditions associated with Passover.

A universal Easter tradition is beautifully decorated eggs. Decorated eggs are featured in many picture books, including the 1951 Caldecott award-winning *The Egg Tree* by Katherine Milhous (Scribner's, 1950) and *The Great Big Especially Beautiful Easter Egg* by James Stevenson (Greenwillow, 1983). The Ukrainian art of painting eggs, *pisanky,* is an element in *Rechenka's Eggs* by Patricia Polacco (Philomel, 1988); *Nina's Treasures* by Stefan Czernecki and Timothy Rhodes (Sterling, 1990); and *Chicken Sunday* by Patricia Polacco (Philomel, 1992).

Ellis Island

Jacobs, William Jay. **Ellis Island: New Hope in a New Land.** Illustrated with photographs. Scribner's, 1990. 34 pp. ISBN 0-684-19171-7. (304.8 Jac).
Target Audience: Grades 4-6; Ages 9-11

Ellis Island became the first stopping point for hundreds of immigrants to the United States. The immigrants arrived by the hundreds on ships that were cramped and foul smelling. Upon their arrival the immigrants were inspected by guards and doctors at Ellis Island. On March 27, 1907, the day described in Jacobs's book, more than 16,050 immigrants arrived on the island. Most could not speak English and had to be questioned through an interpreter. If any defects (deafness, heart problems, mental illness, lameness, or trachoma, an eye disease) were detected, the immigrant's coat was marked with chalk and he or she was separated from the other immigrants. The examination time was stressful for many families, because if a person was barred from entry, the family had to decide whether that person would return home alone or whether the rest of the family would go, too. The decision was especially difficult if the person barred was a young child. Those who passed the health examination had to answer personal questions about their occupation, finances, and who was meeting them. Passage through Ellis Island took about four hours, and about two of every one hundred people were sent back home. Those who were admitted to the United States were finally able to meet their relatives or friends. During the processing many of the immigrants were given new names: for example, Sapirov was changed to Shapiro, Smalovsky became Smith, and Jacobovitz became Jacobs.

Millions of people were processed through Ellis Island before 1954, when Ellis Island was shut down. The buildings were left in disrepair until 1976, when the United States celebrated its bicentennial. At that time Congress allocated funds to restore the buildings on Ellis Island, and a museum was developed. With the contributions of thousands of people the restoration fund created a memorial to the thousands of immigrants whose names were inscribed on the Immigrant Wall of Honor.

Connections: Experiences at Ellis Island

Joan Lowery Nixon has written a fictionalized story of Russian Jews who landed at Ellis Island. *Land of Hope* (Bantam, 1992), set in the early 1900s, describes the Levinsky family's experiences at Ellis Island. Grandfather's limp and age cause him to be refused admittance to the United States, and he must return across the ocean. Rebekah, his 15-year-old granddaughter, finds the news devastating but is determined to achieve her goal of a better life in America. Another Ellis Island title by Nixon, *Land of Promise* (Bantam, 1993), tells the story of 16-year-old Rose Carney who travels to Chicago where she meets her father, who had immigrated earlier from their Irish farm. Rose gets a job and with her father saves money to send for Rose's mother and younger sisters.

A title by Ellen Levine, *If Your Name Was Changed at Ellis Island,* illustrated by Wayne Parmenter (Scholastic, 1993), answers many questions about immigrants and their experiences at Ellis Island. "Why did people come to America?" and "Did every immigrant come voluntarily?" are among the questions that are answered. Ellis Island is also the subject of *Sam Ellis's Island* by Beatrice Siegel (Four Winds, 1985). A picture book by Maxinne Rhea Leighton, *An Ellis Island Christmas* (Viking, 1992) relates the experiences of the fictional Kyrsia, her mother, and her brothers, who leave Poland to travel to the United States to join the children's father. The family arrives on Christmas Eve. The softly rendered, sepia illustrations by Dennis Nolan help to show the young girl's hopes and fears as the family is processed through Ellis Island.

Farming, Dairy

McFarland, Cynthia. **Cows in the Parlor: A Visit to a Dairy Farm.** Illustrated with photographs. Atheneum, 1990. n.p. ISBN 0-689-31584-8. (637 McF). (Photograph of the jacket is courtesy of the publisher and is reprinted with the permission of Macmillan Children's Book Group.)
Target Audience: Grades K-3; Ages 5-8

Clear Creek Farm is a dairy farm. Twice each day the cows need to be milked. In winter, spring, summer, and fall the job is the same. From what (and where) the cows eat to how they are milked in the dairy parlor is shown in photographs and discussed in the text. The birth of new calves helps the female cow to keep on producing milk, but the calf is given its own pen and after the first day is fed milk from a bottle. If the calf is female it will become a member of the milking herd. The routine is repeated day after day throughout the year.

Connections: Dairy Farming

The story of a morning milking on a wintery day is told in *Morning Milking* by Linda Lowe Morris (Picture Book, 1992). The scenes are detailed in watercolor images of warmth and gentleness. Gail Gibbons's *The Milk Makers* (Macmillan, 1985) and Aliki's *Milk from Cow to Carton* (HarperCollins, 1992) also deal with dairy farms and bringing milk from the farm to the consumer. Aliki's book was originally published in 1974 with the title *Green Grass and White Milk*.

Farming, Trees

Jordan, Sandra. **Christmas Tree Farm.** Illustrated with photographs. Orchard, 1993. n.p. ISBN 0-531-05499-3. (635.9 Jor).

Target Audience: Grades K-3; Ages 5-8

Photographs illustrate this account of what occurs on the Clarks's Christmas tree farm. The farm has been in the family for several generations. Each spring bags and cartons of seedlings arrive at the farm. The young trees are planted in the spaces left by the trees that were cut down during the previous season. From that time on the seedlings must be watered, weeded, and cared for. Grass around the seedlings and the larger trees must be cut, and the older trees must be pruned to a nice shape. Each autumn the trees tall enough to be cut during the forthcoming Christmas season are measured and tied with colored-coded tape. The color of the tape tells customers how tall the tree is. Some people want to plant their trees after Christmas, so gardeners come to the farm to dig up some of the trees, roots and all. A burlap bag covers the roots and dirt. In November the farm opens for business and customers, many of whom are old friends, come to buy trees. Then the process starts all over again.

Connections: Types of Farms

The positive and negative aspects of farming are discussed in *The American Family Farm* by Joan Anderson (Harcourt, 1989). Photographs by George Ancona depict life on a farm. There are many types of farms. One of the more interesting farming operations, a modern day maple sugar farm, is described in *Sugaring Season: Making Maple Sugar* by Diane Burns (Carolrhoda, 1990). Another interesting farming operation is the focus of *Cranberries* by William Jaspersohn (Houghton, 1991) (photograph of the jacket is courtesy of the publisher and is reprinted with the permission of Houghton Mifflin Children's Books) which details the steps that are taken to grow, harvest, and bring cranberries to market. Corn production is illustrated in *Corn Belt Harvest* by Raymond Bial (Houghton, 1991). *An Apple a Day: From Orchard to You* by Dorothy Hinshaw Patent (Cobblehill, 1990) summarizes how apples are grown, harvested, stored, and sent to market. The steps taken to grow pumpkins are detailed in *The Pumpkin Patch* by Elizabeth King (Dutton, 1990). King's photographs cover the plowing, planting, cultivating, and harvesting of the pumpkins.

In addition to farms that raise plants for food, many farming operations raise animals for food or for other products, such as wool. The events that take place on a hog farm are the subject of a photo-essay in *Joel: Growing Up a Farm Man* by Patricia Demuth (Dodd, 1982), and raising sheep for wool is the topic of *Spring Fleece: A Day of Sheepshearing* by Catherine Paladino (Little, Brown, 1990).

Eight farmers are profiled in *You Call That a Farm? Raising Otters, Leeches, Weeds, and Other Unusual Things* by Sam Epstein and Beryl Epstein (Farrar, 1991). Each of the farmers raise endangered animals, medicines, food, or consumer goods. Parrots for zoos, alligators for leather, catfish for food, and mysid shrimp for testing poisons are among the items produced by these unusual farmers.

Firefighters

Kuklin, Susan. **Fighting Fires.** Illustrated with photographs. Bradbury, 1993. n.p. ISBN 0-02-751238-X. (628.9 Kuk).
Target Audience: Grades K-3; Ages 5-8

This photo-essay portrays the work of firefighters. The text and photographs show the equipment used, including pumpers, rigs, and turnout coats. Various roles of firefighters are discussed, from the job of truckies and roof men to the pumper crew. Ample photographs show fire equipment, including riggers, pumpers, and other special equipment, as well as action photographs and award ceremonies honoring firefighters for bravery.

Connections: Firefighters and Firefighting

Fire safety and prevention is a common topic discussed with young people. Fire evacuation plans should be made for homes, and fire drills scheduled for schools. Kuklin's book shows the role of firefighters. Another book that may be useful is *Fire! Fire!* by Gail Gibbons (Crowell, 1984). Forest fires and the firefighting techniques necessary to control major natural disasters are discussed in *Forest Fires* by Christopher Lampton (Millbrook, 1991). *Forest Fires* is one book in the Disaster! series.

Fishing

Gibbons, Gail. **Surrounded by Sea: Life on a New England Fishing Island.** Illustrated by Gail Gibbons. Little, Brown, 1991. n.p. ISBN 0-316-30961-3. (974.1 Gib).
Target Audience: Grades K-3; Ages 5-8

The sea surrounds this island fishing village. Many of the island folk spend the winter on the mainland, but in the spring they return to the island to prepare for the new season. Spring has the lobstermen getting their traps and ships ready for the upcoming fishing season. The text introduces fishing as a career and focuses on the social life enjoyed by the people in the fishing village during one year.

Connections: Around the Year

Gibbons's book takes a look at life during one year on a fishing island. Donald Hall covered a similar time span in the life of a settler's family in 1832. Donald Hall's *Ox-Cart Man,* illustrated by Barbara Cooney (Viking, 1979), follows a family through the year. The family grew crops and made clothing, candles, brooms, and an ox cart. The ox-cart man took the goods to a nearby village to sell them and returned with food and some materials and seeds with which to begin the cycle once again.

Look at your own activities throughout a year. Can the activities that occur year after year be charted to give someone in another part of the country an idea of a year in your life?

Flight

Brown, Don. **Ruth Law Thrills a Nation.** Illustrated by Don Brown. Ticknor, 1993. n.p. ISBN 0-395-66404-7. (629.13 Bro).
Target Audience: Grades K-3; Ages 5-8

In 1916, Ruth Law attempted to fly from Chicago to New York City in one day. Unable to purchase a larger airplane, she had to make the flight in what she called her "baby machine." Because she added an extra gas tank to the plane, she had to remove the lights so that the plane would not weigh too much. The lack of lights meant that she had to arrive in New York City before nightfall. She flew for six hours before she had to land to refuel. She had flown, nonstop, for 590 miles. At 3:24 p.m. Ruth Law set out once again for New York City, but nightfall forced her to land two hours short of her goal. The next morning she continued to New York City, where she was greeted by an army general and a military band. Newspapers heralded her accomplishment, a banquet was held in her honor, and President Woodrow Wilson called her great. Ruth Law failed in her attempt to fly from Chicago to New York in one day, but she did set a U.S. nonstop, cross-country record of 590 miles. That record held for a full year, until it was broken by another female pilot, Katherine Simpson.

Connections: Flights That Made History

The spirit of flight is the focus of *Plane Song* by Diane Siebert (HarperCollins, 1993). It is a poetic tribute to planes and flying and to some of the original, courageous aviators. The best-known female aviator is probably Amelia Earhart, who is the subject of several biographies. Two of the most thorough and readable are *Clear the Cow Pasture, I'm Coming in for a Landing! A Story of Amelia Earhart* by Robert Quackenbush (Simon, 1990) and *Amelia Earhart: Flying for Adventure* by Mary Dodson Wade (Millbrook, 1992). The accomplishments of other female aviators are chronicled in *At the Controls: Women in Aviation* by Carole S. Briggs (Lerner, 1991).

Flight, Aviators

Burleigh, Robert. **Flight: The Journey of Charles Lindbergh.** Illustrated by Mike Wimmer. Philomel, 1991. n.p. ISBN 0-399-22272-3. (629.13 Bur). (Photograph of the jacket is courtesy of the publisher and is reprinted with the permission of Putnam & Grosset Group.)
Target Audience: Grades 4-6; Ages 9-11

68 / Seeking Information

On May 20, 1927, 25-year-old Charles Lindbergh set off in a small airplane, *The Spirit of St. Louis,* to fly solo across the Atlantic Ocean, from New York to Paris, France. The trip was more than 3,600 miles long and lasted more than 33 hours. During the flight Lindbergh struggled to stay awake and wrote frequent entries in his diary. When he finally saw land (England) his spirits revived. In Paris the cheering crowd almost crushed Lindbergh and his plane. Two French aviators helped him, and police guarded his plane. Newspapers heralded Charles Lindbergh with headlines proclaiming "American Hero Safe in Paris." Lindbergh had arrived, both in Paris and in the history books.

Connections: Adventurers in Flight

Charles Lindbergh is one of the best-known adventurers in the history of flight. Amelia Earhart was another adventurer who made many flights, but while she was on an around-the-world flight she apparently crashed and died. The story of her life and exploits are told in *Amelia Earhart: Flying for Adventure* by Mary Dodson Wade (Millbrook, 1992). Another pilot, Ruth Law, astounded the nation when in 1916 she attempted a solo flight from Chicago to New York. The account of her flight is the subject of *Ruth Law Thrills a Nation,* written and illustrated by Don Brown (Ticknor, 1993).

Flight, History

Moser, Barry. **Fly! A Brief History of Flight Illustrated.** Illustrated by Barry Moser. HarperCollins/Willa Perlman, 1993. n.p. ISBN 0-06-022893-8. (629.13 Mos).
Target Audience: Grades 4-6; Ages 9-11

Double-page spreads illustrate various events in the history of flight as described by the author. It begins with "The First Ascent" in 1783, arranged by Joseph Montgolfier and Étienne Montgolfier, who put a duck, a sheep, and a rooster in a basket and sent them aloft beneath a hot air balloon. Later the Montgolfier brothers sent a man, Jean François Pilâtre de Rozier, aloft in the same balloon. From that beginning Moser takes us through significant events in the history of flight: the flight by Sir George Cayley in 1849; the development of the first practical glider by Otto Lilienthal in 1891; the Wright brothers' contribution to the development of the airplane; the 1907 flight of the first helicopter; and other significant events in aviation history, right down to present efforts to put space stations in Earth's orbit. A tag line at the bottom of each double-page spread lists other significant events that took place around the time of the pictured event. For example, 1903 is the year that the Wright brothers made great strides in the development of the airplane. The tag line reads, "1896, first motion picture shows in New York City; 1898, Marie and Pierre Curie discover radium; 1901, Pablo Picasso's Blue Period begins; 1902, Beatrix Potter's *The Tale of Peter Rabbit* published." The final 16 pages of the book contain historical notes concerning each of the pictured events.

Connections: History of Flight

A first introduction to flight for the very young reader (and perhaps some older readers) is *Airplanes and Flying Machines* by Gallimard Jeunesse (Cartwheel, 1992). Jets, gliders, and hot air balloons are illustrated with bright colors and enhanced with transparent overlays. The overlays depict the machine in flight or provide an inside view of the flying machine. The text is minimal but the illustrations are so much fun that older students will find the book interesting. Fun bits of information about flight are in *Flight! Free As a Bird* by Siegfried Aust (Lerner, 1991) and *Amazing Flying Machines* by Robin Kerrod (Knopf, 1992). Explanations of pilot duties and the history of aviation are included in *Pilots and Aviation* by Carter M. Ayres (Lerner, 1990) and *Distance Flights* by Don Berliner (Lerner, 1990). In *Before the Wright Brothers* (Lerner, 1990), Don Berliner chronicles 15 inventors of flying machines in chronological order, from George Cayley to the Wright brothers. The book is illustrated with photographs and engravings and provides an understandable introduction to aeronautics.

Striking photographs taken by Wilbur Wright and Orville Wright chronicle the first days of the flying machine in *The Wright Brothers: How They Invented the Airplane* by Russell Freedman (Holiday, 1991) (photograph of the jacket is courtesy of the publisher and is reprinted with the permission of Holiday House, Inc.). A picture book, *Flight: The Journey of Charles Lindbergh* by Robert Burleigh (Philomel, 1991), details Charles Lindbergh's solo flight from New York to Paris. Chuck Yeager broke the sound barrier in 1947, and his story is told in *Breaking the Sound Barrier* by Nathan Aaseng (Messner, 1992). A pop-up book, *Pilots: A Pop-Up Book* by Peter Seymour (Lodestar, 1992), briefly presents the roles of various pilots who fly commercial jets, military jets, stunt planes, and helicopters. The book uses pop-ups with movable flaps and parts to stimulate interest in the planes.

Flight barriers that are being broken today have to do with space flight. Edward F. Dolin details the history of manned and unmanned American and Russian space flights in a photo-filled book, *Famous Firsts in Space* (Cobblehill, 1989). Another excellent reference on events in space exploration is *Opening the Space Frontier* by Ray Spanenburg and Diane Moser (Facts on File, 1989). Forecasts of the future of flight are enumerated in *Dream Planes* by Thomas G. Gunning (Dillon, 1992). The dreams are based on airplanes now in the planning stages.

Fossils

Aliki. **Fossils Tell of Long Ago.** Illustrated by Aliki. Let's-Read-and-Find-Out Book series. Crowell, 1972; rev. ed., 1990. 32 pp. ISBN 0-690-04844-0. (560 Ali).

Target Audience: Grades K-3; Ages 5-8

Aliki's interest in fossils developed early in the 1970s, when she wrote and illustrated the first edition of this book. It was during a trip to Greece with her family that her then-young son, Jason, found a fossil of a brachiopod. The result of that discovery and her research became a very basic introduction to fossils and how they are formed. Statements about the changes in the earth and climate are mentioned, but the focus is on the creatures that lived long ago. Aliki is known for incorporating bubble speech into her illustrations, and she uses the technique to give additional information to the reader. The final pages compare making a hand print in clay to the formation of a fossil.

Connections: Fossils and Changes

Aliki first published *Fossils Tell of Long Ago* in 1972. When she revised the book in 1990, she made subtle content changes in both text and illustrations. If both editions are available, compare and contrast them and discuss why Aliki made the changes. More information about fossils can be found in *Dinosaurs Down Under: And Other*

Fossils from Australia by Caroline Arnold (Clarion, 1990) and a book in the Eyewitness series, *Fossil* by Paul D. Taylor (Knopf, 1990). Both the Arnold and Taylor titles feature superb photographs showing actual fossils and people at work putting together museum exhibits.

Many cities have natural history museums. Locate and visit a natural history museum in your area, and take notes regarding the types of exhibits. *Making Your Own Nature Museum* by Ruth B. MacFarlane (Watts, 1989) will give you detailed advice on collecting, preparing, preserving, and displaying natural history items. The information covers plants, insects, bones, minerals, and fossils. MacFarlane includes information regarding safety and legality.

Frogs

Bailey, Jill. **Frogs in Three Dimensions.** Illustrated by Jérôme Bruandet. Viking, 1992. n.p. ISBN 0-670-84336-9. (597.8 Bai).
Target Audience: Grades K-3; Ages 5-8

As a means of motivating and encouraging students to investigate amphibians, specifically the frog, this book will serve well. The brief text covers habitat, feeding, movement, reproduction, and defense in the simplest of terms. Bruandet's paper engineering is the key to engaging the reader. Each page has a series of pop-ups or pull-outs that illustrate a particular concept. For example, on one page, a frog leaps for an insect and then swallows it. Other pop-outs illustrate the evolution of the frog from a single cell, to multiple cell, to tadpole, and finally to frog. In addition to the information given, older students will be intrigued with the paper engineering.

Connections: Frogs and Toads

Joanna Cole gives details about a frog's body in *A Frog's Body*, illustrated by Jerome Wexler (Morrow, 1980). Other books that give interesting facts about frogs include *Amazing Frogs and Toads* by Barry Clarke, illustrated by Jerry Young (Knopf, 1991); *The Complete Frog: A Guide for the Very Young Naturalist* by Elizabeth A. Lacey, illustrated by Christopher Santoro (Lothrop, 1989); and *Frogs & Toads* by Helen Riley (Thompson Learning, 1993).

Read about how to make pop-up books in Joan Irvine's *How to Make Pop-Ups* (Morrow, 1988) and *How to Make Super Pop-Ups* (Morrow, 1992). Irvine gives step-by-step instructions with clear diagrams for making many different types of pop-ups and special-effects books. To research the subject matter for your pop-up books, read reference works, such as the especially useful Eyewitness series and Eyewitness Junior series published by Knopf.

Galápagos Islands

McGovern, Ann. **Swimming with Sea Lions and Other Adventures in the Galápagos Islands.** Photographs by Ann McGovern. Scholastic, 1992. 48 pp. ISBN 0-590-45282-7. (508.866 McG).
Target Audience: Grades 4-6; Ages 9-11

Accompanying Mike McDowell of Quark Expeditions, Ann McGovern visited the Galápagos Islands and photographed the adventure. The Galápagos Islands are located hundreds of miles west of Ecuador, South America. The archipelago includes 15 large islands and more than 36 smaller ones. Ann McGovern and a dozen other passengers (including the ship's crew) spent two weeks on the boat *Mistral* exploring the Galápagos Islands. The islands are the home of giant tortoises; the islands get their name from the Spanish word for tortoise, *galápagos*. The book is written as the diary of a young boy who accompanies his grandmother on a trip to the islands. Entries touch on the endangered status of the Galápagos tortoises, the climate and plants, and the penguins that live on the islands. (Galápagos penguins are the only penguins in the world that live on the equator.) Entries also talk about the island's sandy beaches, the lava rocks that make walking barefoot difficult, the salt lagoons where flamingos live, and the fur seals. Other animals on the islands include red-footed boobies, blue-footed boobies, masked boobies, frigate birds, marine iguanas, pelicans, albatrosses, lava lizards, and swallow-tailed gulls.

Connections: Strange and Interesting Animals

Tortoises big enough to ride, birds with bright red or blue feet or with black masks and orange eyes, and sea lions that go swimming with humans inhabit the Galápagos Islands. Some of these strange and interesting animals are included in Jerry Pallotta's series of alphabet books. Pallotta's *The Bird Alphabet Book,* illustrated by Edgar Stewart (Charlesbridge, 1986) features the blue-footed booby for the letter *B*. The blue-footed booby is among the birds of Galápagos Islands featured in *The Bird Atlas* by Barbara Taylor, illustrated by Richard Orr (Dorling, 1993). Other birds of the islands in the atlas include the Galápagos penguin, flightless cormorant, Galápagos dove, waved albatross, cactus finch, tree finch, woodpecker finch, and the ground finch.

In *Swimming with Sea Lions,* McGovern presents information through journal entries. The idea of writing postcards or journal entries while on a trip or vacation is used in *Postcards from Pluto: A*

Tour of the Solar System by Loreen Leedy (Holiday, 1993) and in *Stringbean's Trip to the Shining Sea* by Vera B. Williams and Jennifer Williams (Greenwillow, 1988). Use these books in conjunction with *Swimming with Sea Lions* to stimulate interest in keeping a journal while on holiday trips. Sending postcards to a person who will save them to create a cumulative account of the trip makes the writing more palatable than journal entries that often have no real audience. If a student leaves school to go on a family vacation, encourage the student to write postcards and send them to classmates.

Geography

Leedy, Loreen. **Blast Off to Earth! A Look at Geography.**
Illustrated by Loreen Leedy. Holiday, 1992. 32 pp. ISBN 0-8234-0973-2. (910 Lee).
Target Audience: Grades 4-6; Ages 9-11

Mr. Quark and his fellow space robots and aliens are flying to Earth to explore the planet to learn very basic information about the planet that "looks like a big blue marble." The aliens discover that 70 percent of Earth is covered with water and that Earth has its own moon. While most discussions of geography involve climate, land formations, animal life, and people, Leedy focuses on the poles, the equator, the seven continents, and the four large oceans.

Connections: Mapping the Earth

As the Crow Flies: A First Book of Maps by Gail Hartman (Bradbury, 1991), is an introduction to maps that presents a look at different geographical areas from the perspective of an eagle, rabbit, crow, horse, and gull. The end papers link all of the animals' territories. A first atlas, *Macmillan First Atlas* by Nicola Wright, Tony Potter, and Dee Turner (Macmillan, 1992), is well suited for young children. The atlas explains maps and includes several double-page maps of the continents and countries of the world. Maps and puzzles about geographical regions are included in a book for primary students, *Puzzle Maps U.S.A.* by Nancy L. Clouse (Holt, 1990). A similar book for older students is *Where in the World Are You? A Guide to Looking at the World* by Kay Cooper (Walker, 1990).

City or county planning and development departments have large-scale maps of the area. Many departments sell copies of these maps for a nominal fee. Most of these maps are wall size, and most come in several large sheets that will have to be pieced together. If these maps are available obtain a copy of the entire set for your community. Laminate them before hanging them, and then use a transparency marker to mark significant locations. Make a key or legend to identify the names of the locations that have been marked. Using the map as a base, develop a more detailed map of your neighborhood. Create a key to different types of buildings.

Gettysburg Address

Fritz, Jean. **Just a Few Words, Mr. Lincoln: The Story of the Gettysburg Address.** Illustrated by Charles Robinson. Grossett, 1993. 48 pp. ISBN 0-448-40171-1. (973.7 Fri).
Target Audience: Grades 4-6; Ages 9-11

This book gives an account of the development and delivery of Abraham Lincoln's memorable speech, which he read at the dedication of the cemetery at the Gettysburg battlefield. The cemetery was built during the Civil War to bury soldiers killed in the Battle of Gettysburg. The dedication date was set for November 19 at the request of the featured speaker, Edward Everett, the nation's grandest speaker, who needed time to prepare his speech. President Lincoln was invited to say only a few words. Lincoln had his speech prepared by November 15, and three days later he took a train to Gettysburg. He arose the next morning and rode a horse to the ceremony where thousands of people, many with children on their shoulders, assembled. The people had to wait for some time for Edward Everett to arrive. His speech was two hours long. By comparison, the President's speech was only 10 sentences, 271 words. Lincoln read his speech and sat down.

Connections: The Life of Lincoln

Abraham Lincoln served as the 16th president of the United States and presided over the government during the Civil War. He proclaimed freedom for slaves and sought to unify the country. The speech he gave at Gettysburg is often quoted and memorized. It has been remembered infinitely longer than the message Edward Everett delivered in his two-hour speech. Lincoln was assassinated by John Wilkes Booth before he completed his second term as president.

Authors have chosen to emphasize various aspects of Lincoln's life. In 1940 Edgar Parin d'Aulaire and Ingri Mortenson d'Aulaire were awarded the Caldecott award for their beautifully illustrated biography of Lincoln, *Abraham Lincoln* (Doubleday, 1939). Stone lithographs were used to create the illustrations for the original edition.

Later the d'Aulaires re-illustrated the title. They did not want to go to all the work, but the publisher needed the illustrations in a format that could be used with new printing technology. Those who have access to both the 1939 version and the 1957 version will notice subtle differences in most of the illustrations. But the most significant aspect of both versions of the book is that the d'Aulaires conclude the book with Lincoln sitting in a chair: They do not acknowledge his assassination. Other writers include the assassination in their accounts of Lincoln's life.

William Jay Jacobs dispels several myths about Lincoln and speaks of the great things he accomplished in *Lincoln* (Scribner's, 1991). The 42-page book is filled with direct quotes gleaned from solid research. In *A Memorial for Mr. Lincoln* (Putnam, 1992) Brent Ashabranner focuses on Lincoln's presidential years as he describes the search for an appropriate memorial and speaks about the work of the Lincoln Memorial's architect, Henry Bacon, and sculptor, Daniel Chester French. A collection of oft-repeated anecdotes from Lincoln lore is included in Ruth Belov Gross's *True Stories About Abraham Lincoln* (Lothrop, 1990). A picture book that summarizes the life of Lincoln from birth to death is David A. Adler's *A Picture Book of Abraham Lincoln* (Holiday, 1989). A particularly useful time line of Lincoln's life is appended at the end of Adler's book.

Hanukkah

Ehrlich, Amy. **The Story of Hanukkah.** Illustrated by Ori Sherman. Dial, 1989. n.p. ISBN 0-8037-0718-5. (296.4 Ehr).
Target Audience: Grades 4-6; Ages 9-11

When Antiochus decreed that the Jews should forsake their laws, he sent his army to drive the Jews from their temple, destroy the holy books, and defile the temple. The Jews fought back against seemingly insurmountable odds. After Mattathias died, his son, Judah the Maccabee, led his people against the soldiers. Judah and the Jews triumphed and marched into Jerusalem. They cleansed the temple, rebuilt the altar, and searched for pure oil to light the lamp in order to rededicate the temple to God. They found only one day's supply of oil. They used it to light the lamp and set about to make more pure oil. The one day's supply of oil kept the lamp burning for eight days and eight nights, and by that time more pure oil had been made. Each year the eight days are commemorated by the celebration of Hanukkah.

76 / Seeking Information

⚘ Connections: Hanukkah Stories

Other retellings of the origin of Hanukkah include Roni Schotter's *Hanukkah!* (Little, Brown, 1990), Miriam Chaikin's *Hanukkah* (Holiday, 1990), and Jenny Koralk's *Hanukkah: The Festival of Lights* (Lothrop, 1990). Those who wish to explore the origins of the holiday with the very young will be interested in the board book by Tomie dePaola, *My First Chanukah* (Putnam, 1989). DePaola introduces the candles, food, and games that celebrate "Judah the Maccabee and his brothers."

Those who wish to learn more about the symbols of Hanukkah or Jewish symbols in general may consult Miriam Chaikin's *Menorahs, Mezuzas, and Other Jewish Symbols* (Clarion, 1990). The text discusses a wide variety of Jewish symbols.

The traditions of the holiday are sometimes incorporated into fiction. Eric A. Kimmel tells such a story in his book *The Chanukkah Guest,* illustrated by Giora Carmi (Holiday, 1990). The guest turns out to be a hungry bear that is mistaken for a rabbi who is supposed to visit Bubba Brayna. She serves him the "best potato latkes in the village." Before the night is over and the bear leaves, both he and the villagers are happy. Another of Kimmel's stories is *Hershel and the Hanukkah Goblins,* illustrated by Trina Schart Hyman (Holiday, 1989). The story is a trickster tale told in the tradition of old Yiddish folk tales.

Sing the songs and play the games associated with Hanukkah. Family traditions are included in *A Family Hanukkah* by Bobbi Katz, illustrated by Caryl Herzfeld (Random, 1993). The book includes traditional Hanukkah songs such as *The Dreidel Song* and explains the use of the dreidel. A package containing a paperback edition of this book along with a plastic dreidel and a cassette tape are available from Random House.

Helping Others

Ashabranner, Brent. **People Who Make a Difference.** Illustrated with photographs by Paul Conklin. Cobblehill, 1989. 135 pp. ISBN 0-525-65009-1. (920.073 Ash).
Target Audience: Grades 4-6; Ages 9-11

This book contains stories of 14 people who are making a difference in their communities. These people have been inspired to use their talents and efforts to make life better for groups of people who are less fortunate than many. One woman, a nun, Dr. Anne Brooks, established a medical clinic for the people of an impoverished town in Mississippi; she is still taking care of more than 1,200 people with the help of her clinic staff and volunteers. Frank Trejo uses his talents as a karate instructor to help special education students. Mary Jane Willard helped hundreds of quadriplegics when she developed the idea of using capuchin monkeys as family living aides to quadriplegics. Others have started a hospice for AIDS patients, founded outreach programs, or established model schools for inner-city students. These 14 people are meeting personal challenges and in doing so are inspiring others to contribute what they can to their communities.

Connections: Learning About Those Who Help Others

Fourteen people, 14 stories, each inspiring others to consider what they can do to improve their schools, neighborhoods, or cities. More about some of these people can be found in "Sister Anne Brooks, Doctor and Nun, Practices Without Preaching to the Poor," by Bill Shaw (*People Weekly,* March 23, 1987); "Educated Monkeys Help the Disabled to Help Themselves," by J. Tevere MacFadyen (*Smithsonian Magazine,* October 1986); and "Detroit's Beacon of Achievement," by Renée D. Turner (*Ebony,* August 1988). Stories about other community heroes are often included in *Reader's Digest.*

Homelessness

Greenberg, Keith Elliot. **Erik Is Homeless.** Illustrated with photographs by Carol Halebian. Lerner, 1992. 40 pp. ISBN 0-8225-2551-8. (362.7 Gre).
Target Audience: Grades 4-6; Ages 9-11

Erik Justiniano is a nine-year-old boy who lives with his mother in a transitional home in the South Bronx, New York City. More than 61 children and their families live in the shelter, which was once a hospital. The building is clean and warm. Erik and his mother share a room. Most of their clothing is stored in cardboard boxes and the one dresser that they share. A small black-and-white television sits on top of a small refrigerator. The book tells how Erik and his mother became homeless and also tells about other homeless people. The text is expanded through photographs that show the shelter, Erik's mother walking him to school through the dangerous neighborhood, and scenes from their life in the shelter. Sometimes Erik walks to school with other children. He does not want the other children to know that he is homeless. Erik's story can be a lead-in for sharing statistics about the number of homeless people in New York City and throughout the United States.

Connections: Books About the Homeless

Several novels for older intermediate readers present views of homelessness. Eric's situation is relatively safe and secure, especially when compared to the plight of a young man, Clay, who finds himself deserted by his parents and all alone in the world. The situation is described by Paula Fox in *Monkey Island* (Orchard, 1991). Clay is befriended by two older men, and the three sleep on cement, under trees, or anywhere they can in a New York City park. Clay eventually finds his mother, and they are given a new chance at having a home. In *The Leaves of October* (Atheneum, 1991), Karen Ackerman writes about a nine-year-old girl, Libby, and her younger brother, who live in a shelter with their father. Because their father must care for them in the home, the children fear that they will have to go to a foster home so that their father will be able to get a job and save for the home that they all dream of having.

Books for middle-grade readers that focus on the plight of the homeless include Mary Downing Hahn's *December Stillness* (Avon, 1988) and Jonathan Kozol's *Rachel and Her Children* (Crown, 1988).

In Eve Bunting's picture book, *Fly Away, Home* (Clarion, 1991), a homeless boy and his father live in an airport, where they move from terminal to terminal to avoid being noticed. A bird who is set free to "fly away, home" represents the only hope the boy has that someday he too might leave the airport and "fly away, home."

After reading these stories, discuss ways that homeless people could be helped. Those who want to read about helping the homeless from the perspective of a person who has been homeless may read "Wrong Way to Help the Homeless" by Dwight Hobbes (*Reader's Digest*, May 1993).

Hopscotch

Lankford, Mary D. **Hopscotch Around the World.** Illustrated by Karen Milone. Morrow, 1992. 48 pp. ISBN 0-688-08419-2. (796.2 Lan).
Target Audience: Grades 4-6; Ages 9-11

On the small island of Aruba, off the coast of Venezuela, the children play *Pele*. Children in India play *Chilly*, and in some parts of the United States they play *potsy*. In these and other countries from Nigeria to China to the former Soviet Union, children play variations of the age-old game commonly called hopscotch. In one variation of the game, players hop in a snail-like spiral; other variations use circles, squares, and unconnected circles. This book describes 19 variations of the game. For each variation is given instructions, the origin of the game, and an illustration of the hopscotch pattern used. A two-page world map shows the region in which each version is played.

Connections: Games People Play

Traditional games are great to play during recess or in the neighborhood. Twenty-two games and activities are included in *Simon Says—Let's Play* by Sally Foster (Cobblehill, 1990). Foster's photographs clarify her explanations of the motion, concentration, and enjoyment of games. Street rhymes, ball-bouncing activities, just-for-fun counting games, and teasing rhymes are included in *Miss Mary Mack and Other Children's Street Rhymes* by Joanna Cole and Stephanie Calmenson (Morrow, 1990) and in *The Playtime Treasury: A Collection of Playground Rhymes, Games, and Action Songs* by Pie Corbett (Doubleday, 1990).

Horses

Ancona, George. **Man and Mustang.** Illustrated with photographs by George Ancona. Macmillan, 1992. n.p. ISBN 0-02-700802-9. (636.1 Anc).
Target Audience: Grades 4-6; Ages 9-11

More than 20 years ago, a young girl who would come to be known as Wild Horse Annie learned that paid hunters were rounding up wild horses by plane, pelting them with buckshot, and selling them to slaughterhouses for dog food. Annie campaigned to have Congress pass a law that would protect the wild mustang. In 1971 Congress passed the Wild Free-Roaming Horse and Burro Act to protect the mustangs. Eventually the mustangs' natural predator, the wolf, was almost eradicated; that left the mustangs to flourish. Now there are so many mustangs roaming western lands that the Bureau of Land Management must evaluate how many mustangs can be supported on the land they inhabit. Where mustangs are too plentiful the government rounds them up and offers them to buyers through the Adopt-A-Horse program.

Ancona followed some of the mustangs first to the New Mexico State Penitentiary, where prisoners worked with the horses to tame them and ready them for adoption, and then to the families that adopted them. Photographs show every stage of the program: round-up; branding; training; the New Mexico State Fair, where the horses are shown to potential owners; and finally the adoption.

Connections: Protecting the Mustang

Jay Featherly speaks about the plight of the mustang in *Mustangs: Wild Horses of the American West* (Carolrhoda, 1986). The plight of the mustang is not nearly so devastating now as it was when Wild Horse Annie first learned that they were hunted for dog food. The story of Wild Horse Annie is told in Marguerite Henry's *Mustang: Wild Spirit of the West* (Rand McNally, 1966). Henry tells the story of Annie's fight to protect the mustang. Annie fought the professional hunters who didn't want *a girl* interfering in their business, and she fought angry sheep and cattle ranchers who accused the mustang of eating all the range grass. She even fought the Bureau of Land Management (BLM), which did not at first agree that the wild mustang had to be saved from extinction. She took her case from her county courthouse to the White House. She succeeded in getting a federal protection law passed and signed by President Dwight Eisenhower. Later Annie found three men violating the law. They were rounding up mustangs using airplanes to "buzz" the herds and portable screaming sirens. They drove the horses at heart-aching speed for more than eight miles to a corral built of bulldozed cedar trees. The hunters were captured but not before many of the horses were shot. Annie set out to see that the law was enforced. She asked readers of *Mustang: Wild Spirit of the West* to write to the BLM to remind officials that federal law protected the animals. So many letters flooded the BLM that it could not ignore the situation. Eventually the BLM set up the Adopt-A-Horse program to help control the overpopulation of mustangs. This Adopt-A-Horse program is detailed in Ancona's book.

Houses

Bare, Colleen Stanley. **This Is a House.** Illustrated with photographs by Colleen Stanley Bare. Cobblehill, 1992. 32 pp. ISBN 0-525-65090-3. (690 Bar).
Target Audience: Grades K-3; Ages 5-8
From start (architect's blueprint) to finish (completed house), this photo-essay shows the building of a house. The bulldozer is called in to clear the land and to make the site smooth and level. Then the builders begin their work, building the forms, pouring concrete for the foundation and footings, building the foundation and subfloor, putting up the frame, and adding the siding and roof. Then the interior work begins, including the plumbing, electrical, heating, and cabinetry. The last step is to move in.

Connections: A House Is a House for Me

Gail Gibbons's heavily illustrated survey of the construction of a house is presented in *How a House Is Built* (Holiday, 1990). The book begins with the architect's plan and includes the surveyor's work, heavy-equipment operators, plumbers, and carpenters. The finishing touches are put into place by the landscapers.

Many needy families have helped to build their own homes through a program called Habitat for Humanity. Former President Jimmy Carter and his wife Roslyn Carter volunteer for this group's projects. Tom Shachtman chronicles the work of Habitat volunteers as they build 20 houses in five days near Atlanta, Georgia. The message in Shachtman's *The President Builds a House: The Work of Habitat for Humanity* (Simon, 1989) is humanitarianism, but the photographs by Margaret Miller convey much information about building a house.

Ice Cream

Peeples, H. I. **Where Does This Come From? Ice Cream.** Illustrated by David Garner. Calico, 1988. 24 pp. ISBN 0-8092-4466-7. (633.1 Pee).
Target Audience: Grades K-3; Ages 5-8

The story begins on a farm, where the cows are milked twice a day and the milk is trucked to the ice cream plant. The cream is separated from the milk, pasteurized (that is, heated to kill germs), and then combined with emulsifiers and chemicals to make a smooth, creamy mixture. The mixture is sweetened, homogenized, and cooled. After the basic ice cream is created flavor is added. In some cases fruit and nuts are added. Most ice cream producers keep their recipes secret. Taste testers test every batch of ice cream, and then the ice cream gets packaged. All the packages are kept frozen until they are delivered to ice cream parlors, restaurants, and other customers.

Connections: Origins and Uses of Food Products

Most food comes from agricultural areas, and ice cream is just one of those foods. Other books explain the origin of various foods. *Corn: What It Is, What It Does* by Cynthia Kellogg, illustrated by Tom Huffman (Greenwillow, 1989), tells about the uses of corn as a food and for many other products. *Milk from Cow to Carton* by Aliki (HarperCollins, 1992) tells about cows, milking, and milk processing. *The Victory Garden Alphabet Book* by Jerry Pallotta and Bob Thomson (Charlesbridge, 1992) shows vegetables, from asparagus to zucchetto, growing in a garden. *The Amazing Potato: A Story in Which the Incas, Conquistadors, Marie Antoinette, Thomas Jefferson, Wars, Famines, Immigrants, and French Fries All Play a Part* by Milton Meltzer (HarperCollins, 1992), offers 105 pages of information about the history and uses of potatoes as well as some nutritional and botanical facts. General information about a variety of foods, including ethnic and vegetarian dishes, and a diagram of the food pyramid are included in Dorothy Hinshaw Patent's *Nutrition: What's in the Food We Eat?* (Holiday, 1992).

Immigrants

O'Connor, Karen. **Dan Thuy's New Life in America.** Illustrated with photographs by Phillip C. Roullard. Lerner, 1992. 40 pp. ISBN 0-8225-2555-0. (325 O'Co). (Photograph of the jacket is courtesy of the publisher and is reprinted with the permission of Lerner Publications/Carolrhoda Books.)
Target Audience: Grades 4-6; Ages 9-11

At the time this book was written, 13-year-old Dan Thuy Huynh had lived in the United States just four months. She and her family came to San Diego after fleeing Vietnam by boat and spending three years in a refugee camp in Thailand. One of Dan Thuy's uncles and his wife, who were already in the United States, sponsored Dan Thuy's family. The family was among more than 370,000 people who fled Vietnam on boats. Although the family members enjoy their new life in the United States, they don't want to forget their friends and family in Vietnam. Dan Thuy still wears her traditional dress on special occasions, such as the Tet festival (the Vietnamese new year) or at weddings and other celebrations. However, most days she dresses in an oversized T-shirt and leggings, like other American teenagers. The family eats coffeecake and cinnamon rolls but also enjoys favorite foods from Vietnam, such as noodles and meat in a hot broth. A bibliography is included.

⚜ Connections: Coming from Vietnam

Diane Hoyt-Goldsmith has written about another young person and his family's escape to the United States in *Hoang Anh: A Vietnamese-American Boy* (Holiday, 1992). Hoang Anh Chau's parents and 24 other refugees fled from Vietnam on Hoang Anh's father's fishing boat. They reached Malaysia and lived in a crowded refugee camp, where Hoang Anh was born. Hoang Anh was a few months old when the family emigrated to the United States under the sponsorship of a church in Oregon. Later the family moved to San Rafael, California, where Hoang Anh's father fishes for a living. Hoang Anh's words are used to tell about his family's life in America. The book concludes with Hoang Anh's description of activities during the three-day new year (Tet) celebration.

Two writers have written novels involving immigrants from southeast Asia. Jamie Gilson interviewed many refugees and used their experiences in her novel *Hello, My Name Is Scrambled Eggs* (Lothrop, 1985). In Gilson's story Tuan Nguyen comes to America with his family when a church group sponsors the family. Tuan Nguyen and Harvey, a character in other books by Gilson, become friends, and Harvey introduces Tuan Nguyen to many new experiences. Jayne Pettit writes about another immigrant in *My Name Is San Ho* (Scholastic, 1992). San Ho lives in much danger in the Vietnam countryside until his mother takes him to the city of Saigon to live with a friend. San Ho's mother meets an American serviceman, and after they are married she travels to America with her new husband. Later San Ho's mother is able to send for San Ho. Life in America seems good, but San Ho finds that he and his mother are not always welcome; together they face racist remarks and prejudice.

Many people from Laos, Thailand, and Vietnam bring with them traditions and stories from their homelands. Norma J. Livo and Dia Cha have collected many of those stories in *Folk Stories of the Hmong: Peoples of Laos, Thailand, and Vietnam* (Libraries Unlimited, 1991). In addition to 27 stories, the book describes Hmong history, culture, and folklore, and it includes 16 pages of color photographs of Hmong dress and needlework. The collection, designed for high-school or adult readers, provides stories that are appropriate to read aloud to intermediate-age children. Any of the books listed here could be used to begin a focus on family history or ancestors.

Insects

Bernhard, Emery. **Dragonfly.** Illustrated by Durga Bernhard. Holiday, 1993. n.p. ISBN 0-8234-1033-1. (595.7 Ber).
Target Audience: Grades K-3; Ages 5-8

The dragonfly's face is sometimes thought to look fierce, somewhat like a little dragon. Dragonflies are thought to have been on earth since millions of years before dinosaurs. Ancient dragonflies' wingspans measured up to 33 inches. Today's dragonflies are much smaller, with wingspans of 1-7 inches. Of the more than 5,000 kinds of dragonflies in existence, more than 400 types live in the United States. Bernhard does an excellent job of describing the physical characteristics of the dragonfly and its activities. Information about how a dragonfly avoids its predators and how it develops from egg to nymph to adult is given. The lives of adult dragonflies are short; they mate a few weeks after they emerge with wings and die soon after. During its short life each dragonfly eats thousands of mosquitoes and flies. They help to keep the water clean in wetlands. Legends from Japan, Great Britain, and Native American tribes from the Southwest are included in the final pages of *Dragonfly*.

Connections: Insects

More information about the dragonfly can be found in *Dragonfly* by Barrie Watts (Burdett, 1989). Watts's book is a simple photo-essay about the life cycle of the dragonfly; it focuses on both the annoying characteristics and the helpful aspects of dragonflies.

The roles of other insects and bugs are depicted in fiction and in information books. Eric Carle's *The Grouchy Ladybug* (Crowell, 1977) is a tale about an ill-tempered ladybug who does not want to share anything. In telling the story Carle includes information about the ladybug's role in eating aphids and shows its body. An information book by Emery Bernhard, *Ladybug* (Holiday, 1992) describes the facts and fables surrounding the ladybug. Included are information about the ladybug's usefulness to humans, superstitions and rhymes about the insect, and information about its physical characteristics.

Another of Carle's books, *The Very Hungry Caterpillar* (Collins, 1969) depicts the life cycle of a butterfly in a tale about a caterpillar who eats unusual foods during the seven days before it spins its cocoon and some days later emerges as a beautiful butterfly.

One beautiful butterfly is the monarch, and it is the subject of several information books. Mary Ling's *Butterfly* (Dorling, 1992) uses photographs and a very simple text to emphasize the growth of a butterfly from hatching to maturity. A more detailed but straightforward and easy-to-understand introduction to the monarch butterfly is Gail Gibbons's *Monarch Butterfly* (Holiday, 1989). Ethan Herberman tells about the migratory habits of the monarch butterfly in *The Great Butterfly Hunt: The Mystery of the Migrating Monarchs* (Simon, 1990).

Other writers offer more scientific explorations of insects. Chris Van Allsburg gives readers an ant's-eye view of a kitchen in his *Two Bad Ants* (Houghton, 1988). The illustrations show sugar crystals and other common household objects close-up. Laurence Pringle discusses the dreaded African bees' arrival in Texas in *Killer Bees* (Morrow, 1990). His research includes information about the bees' migration from Brazil to Mexico to the United States. Life cycles of insects are the focus in several books, including *Insect Metamorphosis: From Egg to Adult* by Nancy Goor and Ron Goor (Atheneum, 1990); *The Housefly* by Heiderose Fischer-Nagel and Andreas Fischer-Nagel (Carolrhoda, 1990); *The World of Honeybees* adapted by Virginia Harrison (Gareth, 1990); *The Honeybee in the Meadow* by Christopher O'Toole (Gareth, 1990); *Amazing Spiders* by Alexandra Parsons (Eyewitness Junior series, Knopf, 1990); and *Insect* by Laurence Mound (Eyewitness series, Knopf, 1990).

Maria M. Mudd uses a pop-up format to capture young readers' interest in two 14-page books, *The Beetle* (Stewart, 1992) and *The Spider* (Stewart, 1992). Each features a large, three-dimensional insect in the center of the book and many smaller pop-ups and moving parts. The text gives much information about the physical aspects of the creatures and details of their life cycles.

Use Joan Irvine's *How to Make Pop-Ups* (Morrow, 1988) and *How to Make Super Pop-Ups* (Morrow, 1992) to make your own insect pop-up books. Irvine gives step-by-step instructions with clear diagrams for making many different types of pop-ups and special-effects books.

Inventions, Accidental

Jones, Charlotte Foltz. **Mistakes That Worked.** Illustrated by John O'Brien. Doubleday, 1991. 82 pp. ISBN 0-385-26246-9. (609 Jon). (Photograph of the jacket is courtesy of the publisher and is reprinted with the permission of Bantam Doubleday Dell.)

Target Audience: Grades 4-6; Ages 9-11

Some say that necessity is the mother of invention, but in the cases chronicled in this book much of the credit goes to accidents. Forty short (one-page) stories recount the mistakes that resulted in some of our favorite products. George Crum, a Native American chef, was trying to please a difficult customer when he created the potato chip. Ruth Wakefield, the proprietor of the Tollhouse Inn, was making chocolate cookies when she ran out of chocolate. She added chocolate bits to the batter, thinking they would melt and make chocolate cookies. Instead she created the first chocolate chip cookies. James Gamble and David Gamble developed a formula for a high-quality, affordable soap they called White Soap. One day a workman accidently mixed the soap mixture for too long, and when the soap was formed and hardened the bars floated. The Gamble brothers' partner, Harley Procter, called the new soap Ivory. To date more than 30 billion bars of Ivory soap have been sold. These are just a few of the "mistakes that worked" that are part of this book. Other inventions in this book include Coca-Cola, Popsicles, aspirin, Silly Putty, paper towels, Scotchgard, Levi jeans, and Post-it notes. A selected bibliography and an index are included.

Connections: National Inventors Day

The Patent and Trademark Office in Arlington, Virginia, inducts inventors into the National Inventors Hall of Fame, which is part of the National Inventors Center in Akron, Ohio. The inductees are honored on National Inventors Day, February 8. The first honoree was Thomas A. Edison, who was inducted in 1973. Information about other inventions and inventors is included in *Dreamers and Doers: Inventors Who Changed Our World* by Norman Richards (Atheneum, 1984), *Weird and Wacky Inventions* by Jim Murphy (Crown, 1978), *Guess Again: More Weird and Wacky Inventions* (Bradbury, 1986), *The Story Behind Great Inventions* by Elizabeth Montgomery (Dodd, 1944), *Inventions That Made History* by David Cooke (Putnam, 1986), *Inventors of the World* by I. O. Evans (Warne, 1962); and *Better Mousetraps: Product Improvements That Led to Success* by Nathan Aaseng (Lerner, 1990).

Inventions and Inventors

Aaseng, Nathan. **Better Mousetraps: Product Improvements That Led to Success.** Illustrated with photographs. Inside Business series. Lerner, 1990. 80 pp. ISBN 0-8225-0680-7. (658.5 Aas).
Target Audience: Grades 4-6; Ages 9-11
This book describes how eight inventions were improved and became nationally known products. The products discussed are Otis elevators, Eastman Kodak photography equipment, Gillette razors, Rolls-Royce automobiles, Caterpillar equipment, Pepperidge Farm bread, Tupperware®, and Zamboni ice-resurfacing machines. Each 6-8 page chapter discusses the original product, how it was improved,

and the effect the improvement had on the success of the product. A bibliography and an index are included.

Connections: Inventors

People who have improved our lives through their inventions or improvements to inventions are discussed in *Entrepreneurs: The Men and Women Behind Famous Brand Names* by J. J. Fucini and S. Fucini (Hall, 1985); *The Entrepreneurs: An American Adventure* by R. Sobel and D. B. Sicilia (Houghton, 1986); and *Mistakes That Worked* by Charlotte Foltz Jones (Doubleday, 1991). Jones's book includes interesting accounts of the invention of Liquid Paper, Ivory soap, and other products that resulted from accidents.

Karate

Goedecke, Christopher J. **The Wind Warrior: The Training of a Karate Champion.** Illustrated with photographs by Rosmarie Hausherr. Four Winds, 1992. 64 pp. ISBN 0-02-736262-0. (796.8 Goe).

Target Audience: Grades 4-6; Ages 9-11

Nicholas Armitage is a 13-year-old *karata-ka* (student). He has been attending karate classes since he was seven years old, the minimum age for enrolling at the Madison, New Jersey, club he attends. After six years of training he has earned a dark-brown belt. The coveted black belt, which indicates expert status, is three promotions away. The book takes us with Nicholas to the *dojo* at the local YMCA. (*Dojo* means way place and is the name of the karate practice area.) Nick's teacher has been studying karate for 24 years and is a master of *isshinryu,* the "one-heart" method. *Isshinryu* is a popular Okinawan karate that has become popular in New Jersey. Many photographs help young readers visualize the exercises described and understand the rigorous activities that karate students must undertake to reach their goal.

Connections: Martial Arts in Fiction

Gary Soto uses the martial arts to bring together Mexican-American and Japanese children. Lincoln Mendoza and Tony Contreras, from the San Francisco barrio, go on a summer-exchange visit to Japan. There they develop a warm relationship with their Japanese hosts when they discover that they have a mutual interest in the martial art of *shorinji kempo.* Lincoln and Tony first appeared in *Taking Sides* (Harcourt, 1991), and their story of travel to Japan is continued in *Pacific Crossing* (Harcourt, 1992). Another author, Patricia Rhodes Mauser, uses the martial arts as a key component in *A Bundle of Sticks* (Macmillan, 1982). Mauser's protagonist finds that studying the martial arts gives him the confidence to deal with a class bully without resorting to physical fighting.

Kites

Gibbons, Gail. **Catch the Wind! All About Kites.** Illustrated by Gail Gibbons. Little, Brown, 1989. n.p. ISBN 0-316-30955-9. (629.133 Gib).

Target Audience: Grades K-3; Ages 5-8

Woven into a story about two young children who visit Ike's Kite Shop is information about the history of kites and the people who fly them. Types of kites are explained and shown in bright, graphic illustrations. Parts of a flat kite are labeled and illustrated, and a visit to Ike's kite-making workshop is highlighted. The final pages of the book explain how to make your own flat kite, how to launch a kite, and how to bring a kite down.

Connections: Kites Everywhere

Another book with instructions for making a variety of kites is Barrie Caldecott's *Kites* (Watts, 1990).

In the Chinese tradition, Kite Day is observed on the ninth day of the ninth month. Thousands of kites shaped like dragons, fish, birds, and butterflies are flown over the cities and the countryside. A picture book that shows the beauty of a dragon kite is Valerie Reddix's *Dragon Kite of the Autumn Moon,* illustrated by Jean Tseng and Mou-Sien Tseng (Lothrop, 1992). The story tells of a boy's love for his grandfather and for the ancient traditions of Taiwan. The Tsengs's watercolors capture the gloriousness of the dragon kite that Tad-Tin loves but is willing to give up to restore his grandfather's health.

Kites are treasured gifts for children in China and Japan. Allen Say's fictionalized account of the first Christmas he celebrated as a young child in Japan is an episode in which the first Christmas gift a small Japanese boy receives from his parents is a very special kite. The story is told in Allen Say's *Tree of Cranes* (Houghton, 1991).

Kwanzaa

Pinkney, Andrea Davis. **Seven Candles for Kwanzaa.** Illustrated by Brian Pinkney. Dial, 1993. 32 pp. ISBN 0-8037-1292-8. (394.2 Pin).
Target Audience: Grades K-3; Ages 5-8
Brian Pinkney's magnificently rendered scratch board illustrations complement Andrea Pinkney's story of a family's ritual as they light each of the candles in the kinara during the week of Kwanzaa. Andrea Pinkney's simple but concise text explains the seven principles and provides practical applications of the principles. Borders with motifs of African designs surround the illustrations on each page.

Connections: More About Kwanzaa

The seven principles of Kwanzaa are *imani* (faith), *kujichagulia* (self-determination), *kuumba* (creativity), *nia* (purpose), *ujamaa* (cooperative economics), *ujima* (collective work and responsibility), and *umoja* (unity). Kwanzaa is an African American holiday that begins on December 26 and ends January 1. The holiday was founded in 1966 by Dr. Maulana Karenga as a gathering of African Americans to celebrate their history. A beginning reader's explanation of how this ethnic holiday got its start and how it is celebrated is given in *Kwanzaa* by A. P. Porter, illustrated by Janice Lee Porter (Carolrhoda, 1991). Diane Hoyt-Goldsmith takes a look at the holiday in *Celebrating Kwanzaa,* photographs by Lawrence Migdale (Holiday, 1993). In Goldsmith's book a child tells the story of an African American family from Chicago that celebrates Kwanzaa. The festival, name philosophy, and meaning of each day are explained.

Deborah M. Chocolate explains the traditions of Kwanzaa in *Kwanzaa* (Children's Press, 1993). Virginia Kroll's story, *Wood-Hoopoe Willie,* illustrated by Katherine Roundtree (Charlesbridge, 1992), tells the story of Willie, who uses forks, pencils, and hot pepper shakers to play rhythms that he feels. He dreams of using the instruments used by his African ancestors: *guedras, ecasa, atumpan,* and *dundun* drums. His dreams become a triumphant day of glory on the final day of Kwanzaa.

A novel that uses Kwanzaa as a story element is Mildred Pitts Walter's *Have a Happy...,* illustrated by Carole Byard (Lothrop, 1989). Walter tells the story of Chris as he celebrates his birthday during Kwanzaa. The story is a realistic tale of a warm, loving family enjoying the holiday and one another.

Letter Writing

Leedy, Loreen. **Messages in the Mailbox: How to Write a Letter.** Illustrated by Loreen Leedy. Holiday, 1991. 32 pp. ISBN 0-8234-0889-2. (395.4 Lee). (Photograph of the jacket is courtesy of the publisher and is reprinted with the permission of Holiday House, Inc.)
Target Audience: Grades K-3; Ages 5-8

Mrs. Gator (an alligator) gives her students information to help them correspond with friendly letters, postcards, invitations, thank-you notes, get-well letters, love letters, sympathy letters, notes of apology, congratulatory letters, form letters, fan letters, business letters, requests, protests, and letters to the editor. The human and animal students add information to the discussions. The first section on friendly letters sets the stage for the entire book. Parts of the letter are shown, and alternative closings and possibilities for postscripts are discussed. Reasons and topics for writing are suggested, and several recipients are suggested, from pen pals to famous people and characters, such as Santa Claus. The friendly letter section is followed by information about addressing the envelope and an explanation of the need for appropriate postage. Leedy also presents information about creating shape letters, making puzzle letters, and writing in invisible ink. Double-page spreads illustrated in comic-book format can be used as posters in a writing center to motivate experimentation in various forms of letter writing.

Connections: Letter Writing in Fiction

Writing postcards is the focus of a story of a trip to the sea as Stringbean Coe and his brother Fred set off in a pickup truck to travel across the country to the Pacific Ocean. While Stringbean and Fred are on the trip they send unique and unusual postcards to their family at home. The postcards chronicle their trip. *Stringbean's Trip to the Shining Sea* by Vera B. Williams and Jennifer Williams (Greenwillow, 1988) will inspire students to create their own postcard designs.

Williams designed special stamps for each of the postcards in *Stringbean's Trip to the Shining Sea*. The stamps reflect the theme of the postcard's design. Many special stamp designs are available from the U.S. Postal Service. Information about stamps is available at your local post office. Information about stamps may spark an interest in stamp collecting.

Lighthouses

Gibbons, Gail. **Beacons of Light: Lighthouses.** Illustrated by Gail Gibbons. Morrow, 1990. n.p. ISBN 0-688-07379-4. (387.1 Gib).
Target Audience: Grades 4-6; Ages 9-11

Several existing lighthouses are shown in accurate drawings against a background of spattered watercolor waves. The lighthouses include eight from Maine, six from Massachusetts, six from other states, and one historical lighthouse: a stone tower with fires burning at the top in Alexandria, Egypt. Lighthouses served an important role in ensuring the safety of ships by warning of rocks, ledges and hidden dangers. The first lighthouse in America was built of masonry in 1716. It was erected on Little Brewster Island at the entrance to Boston Harbor. Spermaceti oil was used to fuel the light, and a special levy of one penny per ton was charged to all incoming and outgoing vessels to fund the operation of the lighthouse. Another early lighthouse was the Boston Light, which was built in 1716.

Lighthouses were usually round, narrow, and tall. Wick lamps, which burned whale oil or fish oil, were used in the earliest lighthouses. Later a lamp with a circular wick that burned kerosene was used. By 1822 a Frenchman developed a prism lens that reflected the light and made it visible from a much greater distance. A lighthouse keeper was responsible for keeping the wicks trimmed and the windows clean of soot. He or she often lived in a house near the lighthouse or right inside the lighthouse. Many lighthouses were built on islands or in other remote locations, requiring the lighthouse keeper to maintain the grounds and stock provisions. During storms the lighthouse keeper was sometimes the only person who could rescue people who were caught at sea.

Contemporary lighthouses are powered by electricity, and their beams can be seen for many miles. Bells, foghorns, or other warning sounds are used in addition to the lights. Contemporary lighthouses take many distinctive shapes and for the most part are not tall, round, and narrow. Some of the newer lighthouses stand on stilts and do not even vaguely resemble a traditional lighthouse.

Gibbons's book is filled with information about the history of lighthouses, and the final page includes facts about the tallest, oldest, and the first electrified lighthouse: the Statue of Liberty.

Connections: Brave Deeds and Lighthouse Organizations

General encyclopedias like the *World Book Encyclopedia* are good sources for more information about lighthouses in the United States and in other countries.

One of the bits of information included on the final page of Gibbons's book tells about Abbie Burgess, who kept the lights burning for four weeks during a storm at Matinicus Rock Lighthouse off the coast of Maine. Abbie's father was away from the lighthouse getting supplies, and her mother became very ill. The storm prevented anyone from coming to the island, but the danger to ships was still there. Abbie saved many lives because of her courageous act. Her story is told in *Keep the Lights Burning, Abbie* by Peter Roop and Connie Roop (Carolrhoda, 1985). Abbie's courage can be compared to the courage and persistence of Kate Shelley, a 15-year-old girl who in 1881 crawled across a broken bridge during a fierce storm to reach a railroad depot and warn the conductor of a passenger train that the bridge was out. Her story is told in *Kate Shelley and the Midnight Express* by Margaret K. Wetterer (Carolrhoda, 1990).

The preservation and restoration of more than 200 lighthouses on the five Great Lakes is the goal of the Great Lakes Lighthouse Keepers Association. The nonprofit group sponsors historic tours and publishes a quarterly newsletter. Those interested in the work of this association may write to Great Lakes Lighthouse Keepers Association, P.O. Box 580, Allen Park, MI 48101. Another organization interested in lighthouses is the U.S. Lighthouse Society, 244 Kearmy Street, 5th Floor, San Francisco, CA 94108.

Hand-painted, cast-iron scale models of dozens of real lighthouses are available from Original Lighthouse Collection, 109 Davis Street, Monroe, GA 30655.

Machines

Horvatic, Anne. **Simple Machines.** Illustrated with photographs by Stephen Bruner. Dutton, 1989. n.p. ISBN 0-525-44492-0. (531 Hor).
Target Audience: Grades K-3; Ages 5-8

An excellent introduction to the five simple types of machine: lever, wheel, inclined plane, wedge, and screw. Each are described and explained in simple text accompanied by black-and-white photographs.

Examples of each type of machine are shown in settings that are familiar to most young readers. For example, using a screwdriver to open a paint can, the claw of a hammer to remove a nail, and lifting the pop-top of a soda can are shown as examples of a lever at work. A potter's wheel, a tractor's wheel, and a doorknob are shown as wheels in action, and roofs and ramps used for skate board stunts or car lifts are examples of the inclined plane. Wedges depicted include nails, axes, and teeth (when biting food). The final type of machine discussed is the screw. A screw is used to hold things together or to move things along a threaded path. Screws combine with other simple machines to form more complex machines, for example, a screw and wheel combine to make a mechanism that grinds wheat into flour.

Connections: More Machines

A novelty book that might help to motivate interest in machines is Lisa Rojany's *The Hands-On Book of Big Machines* (Little, Brown, 1992). The book is illustrated with watercolors and simple pop-ups showing how monster-size machines work. Another simple introductory book to machines is *The Science Book of Machines* by Neil Ardley (Gulliver Green, 1992). The book uses photographs to demonstrate uses of machines.

More details about machines are included in books by Christopher Lampton, who uses an elephant and a worm to explain how pulleys work in his *Sailboats, Flagpoles, Cranes: Using Pulleys As Simple Machines* (Millbrook, 1991). Other titles by Lampton that explain machines include *Bathtubs, Slides, Roller Coaster Rails: Simple Machines That Are Really Inclined Planes* (Millbrook, 1991); *Marbles, Roller Skates, Doorknobs: Simple Machines That Are Really Wheels* (Millbrook, 1991); *Seesaws, Nutcrackers, Brooms: Simple Machines That Are Really Levers* (Millbrook, 1991); and *Simple Machines Made Simple* (Teacher Ideas Press, 1993).

The Random House Book of How Things Work by Steve Parker (Random, 1991) includes explanations (descriptions and cut-away illustrations) of the inside workings of everything from kitchen appliances to the human body. With older intermediate readers in mind, Robert Gardner presents *Forces and Machines* (Messner, 1992), a book suggesting experiments requiring only basic materials. The information is followed by suggestions for further investigation. David Macaulay's *The Way Things Work* (Houghton, 1988) uses detailed drawings to show hundreds of machines, mechanisms, and processes that affect our daily lives.

Meteors

Branley, Franklyn M. **Shooting Stars.** Illustrated by Holly Keller. Let's-Read-and-Find-Out Science Book series. Crowell, 1989. 32 pp. ISBN 0-690-04701-0. (523.5 Bra).
Target Audience: Grades K-3; Ages 5-8
Some people believe that the first person to spot a shooting star is entitled to make a wish that will come true. This book explains what those streaks of light really are; that a shooting star is really not a star at all but a piece of rock or ash falling to Earth. The friction generated as the fragment falls through the atmosphere makes the piece of debris hot—so hot that it actually glows. Usually the falling rock or ash burns up as it travels through the Earth's atmosphere, but sometimes it is large enough that a part of it remains and hits the Earth. Meteors that strike the Earth are called meteorites. Some of the larger meteorites create craters when they land. Specific instances of meteorites landing in the United States are listed in this book.

Connections: Watching for Shooting Stars

Patricia Polacco wrote a story, *Meteor!* (Putnam, 1987), based on the aftermath of an incident in which a meteorite landed on her grandparents' farm. Deborah Kogan Ray deals with shooting stars in her poetic tale of a little girl and her mother who make their way through the woods, up a hill, and to a meadow where they watch for shooting stars. *Stargazing Sky* (Crown, 1991) captures the quiet stillness of the night and the warm relationship between mother and daughter through gentle words and luminous illustrations. The mother and daughter spread out a blanket and look at the sky. They find the Big Dipper and the North Star, discuss the blinking lights, and describe a shooting star as "a meteor, a tiny speck of burning sky dust." Each of these books provides a fictional connection to the information about meteors and meteorites.

Mexican Americans

Hewett, Joan. **Hector Lives in the United States Now: The Story of a Mexican-American Child.** Illustrated with photographs by Richard Hewett. Lippincott, 1990. 44 pp. ISBN 0-397-32295-X. (973 Hew).
Target Audience: Grades 4-6; Ages 9-11
The day-to-day activities of 10-year-old Hector Almaraz are the subject of this photo-essay. For as long as he can remember, Hector has lived in Los Angeles, but he was born in Mexico like his parents

and his nine-year-old brother. His two younger brothers were born in Los Angeles and are citizens of the United States. Hector plays soccer and baseball, reads comic books, and collects baseball cards. Like Hector, many of his friends speak Spanish at home but speak English elsewhere. Hector's teacher encourages members of the class to find out about their ancestors. Various children in the classroom are descendants of Philippine islanders, Norwegians, Germans, Yaqui, French, Ukrainians, Italians, Irish, Spanish, and Africans. Twelve others in Hector's class have Mexican ancestors.

Many members of Hector's extended family live in the United States close to Hector's family. Some of the Mexican immigrants came with temporary work permits, and many of those permits expired a long time ago. Because of a new law, some of the immigrants on temporary permits, including Hector's parents, could apply for amnesty and permanent residency in the United States. They had to apply before May 2, 1988. Many applied, including Hector's parents. They also applied for amnesty for Hector and his brother.

Details of Hector's family's activities, the foods family members like, and traditions they enjoy are included in this account of Hector's life. One of the most exciting activities is a trip to Mexico to see the relatives they have not seen for a long time. Because the family has permanent residency cards, they were free to travel to Mexico and return to the United States. A bibliography is included.

Connections: Immigrant Experiences

Those who wish to learn more about Mexican Americans, their history, and their traditions may wish to read: *The Hispanic Americans* by Milton Meltzer (Crowell, 1982) or *Mexico: Giant of the South* by Eileen L. Smith (Dillon, 1983). Famous Mexican Americans include Gloria Molina, who was the first Mexican American state assemblywoman in California. The story of her efforts to be elected is told in *Getting Elected: The Story of a Campaign* by Joan Hewett (Lodestar, 1989). Henry Cisneros, a Mexican American, who when very young became the mayor of San Antonio, Texas, is the subject of *Henry Cisneros, Mexican-American Mayor* by Naurice Roberts (Children's Press, 1986). The story of how Cesar Chavez organized the first successful farm workers' union in the United States is told in *Cesar Chavez: Man of Courage* by Florence M. White (Garrard, 1973).

Of the more than 1.6 million aliens who were granted legal residence as a result of the 1988 opportunity for amnesty, most were from Mexico. But of course, not all immigrants have come from Mexico. A book by Melvin Berger and Gilda Berger, *Where Did Your Family Come From? A Book About Immigrants* (Ideals, 1993) can help students identify other countries of origin. It could be used to introduce a focus on immigration as it relates to individual families. Stories of immigrant families are told in Diane Hoyt-Goldsmith's *Hoang Anh: A Vietnamese-American Boy* (Holiday, 1992) and Riki Levinson's *Soon, Annala* (Orchard, 1993).

Mexican Americans, Achievers

Morey, Janet, and Wendy Dunn. **Famous Mexican Americans.** Illustrated with photographs. Cobblehill, 1989. 176 pp. ISBN 0-525-65012-1. (920 Mor).

Target Audience: Grades 4-6; Ages 9-11

Fourteen prominent Mexican Americans and their accomplishments are detailed in this book. The people profiled are Cesar Chavez, president of the United Farm Workers; Henry Cisneros, mayor of San Antonio, Texas; Patrick Flores, an archbishop in San Antonio, Texas; Dolores Huerta, vice-president of the United Farm Workers; Nancy Lopez, golfer; Vilma Martinez, attorney; Luis Nogales, business executive; Edward James Olmos, actor; Katherine Davalos Ortega, treasurer of the United States; Blandina Cardenas Ramirez, member of the U.S. Commission on Civil Rights; Edward R. Roybal, United States congressman; Dan Sosa, Jr., justice on the New Mexico State Supreme Court; Luis Valdez, writer and film director; and William Velasquez, former president of the Southwest Voter Registration Education Project.

Connections: The Mexican-American Experience

Many Mexican Americans have become famous in the United States. Lee Trevino is a successful golfer. Thomas W. Gilbert has profiled Trevino in a book in the Hispanics of Achievement series, *Lee Trevino* (Chelsea, 1991). Another title in the series is *Jorge Luis Borges* by Adrian Lennon (Chelsea, 1991). Bruce W. Concord writes a full-length account of the life of Cesar Chavez in *Cesar Chavez* (Chelsea, 1992). Conord's book is a title in Chelsea's Junior World Biographies series.

Joan Hewett has written about a 10-year-old boy who as a very young child came to the United States with his family in *Hector Lives in the United States Now: The Story of a Mexican-American Child* (Lippincott, 1990). The photographs by Richard Hewett take us through a day with the young boy.

Information about culture and lifestyle can be gleaned from fictional accounts of life as a Mexican American. Gary Soto, a Mexican American, has written a picture book and several novels incorporating information about Mexican Americans. His picture book, *Too Many Tamales,* illustrated by Ed Martinez (Putnam, 1993), presents a girl with a dilemma: Maria tries on her mother's wedding ring while helping make tamales for a Christmas celebration. After the ring slips off, Maria discovers that she does not know where the ring is, so she and her cousins eat all of the tamales in an effort to find the ring. Soto's junior novel, *The Skirt* (Delacorte, 1992), is a pleasant glance at the life of a Mexican-American family in California. In this short chapter book, Miata attempts to retrieve her *folklorico* skirt from the school bus, where she left it. Soto's *Taking Sides* (Harcourt, 1991), a book for intermediate readers, features Lincoln Mendoza and Tony Contreras. In a sequel, *Pacific Crossing* (Harcourt, 1992), Soto tells of Mendoza's and Contreras's participation in a summer-exchange program in Japan. They both have an interest in the martial arts and are able to learn more about the art of *shorinji kempo*. Lincoln develops a special fondness for his host family and is able to re-examine his own attitudes as he tries to explain to his hosts what being Mexican American means. Soto's *Baseball in April and Other Stories* (Harcourt, 1990) is a collection of 11 vignettes featuring Mexican-American families.

Money

Schwartz, David M. **If You Made a Million.** Illustrated with drawings by Steven Kellogg. Lothrop, 1989. n.p. ISBN 0-688-07017-5. (332.024 Sch).

Target Audience: Grades 4-6; Ages 9-11

Which would you rather have: a 5-foot stack of pennies, a 15-inch stack of nickels, a 5-inch stack of dimes, or a 3¼-inch stack of quarters? That would be 1,000 pennies, 100 nickels, 100 dimes, or 40 quarters. Each of these stacks is worth $10, so whichever stack you chose, your reward will be the same. This fact and many others involving money are presented by Marvelosissimo the Mathematical Magician in *If You Made a Million*. The illustrations help those reading the book understand the transactions that are described in the text. However, because Kellogg's illustrations are very intricate and detailed, they are best shared with small groups or individuals. A lengthy author's note at the end of the book gives more information about the topics introduced in the body of the book. Schwartz expands on topics in note sections titled "What Would We Do Without Money?" "Banks: They Don't Work Like Piggybanks"; "Interest and Compound Interest"; "Checks and Checking Accounts"; "Loans"; "Income Tax"; and "Will a Million Dollars in Pennies Really Stack Up 95 Miles High?"

Connections: Money and Millions

Additional books that focus on money include *The Hundred Penny Box* by Sharon Bell Mathis (Viking, 1975) and *Alexander Who Used to Be Rich Last Sunday* by Judith Viorst (Atheneum, 1978). Shel Silverstein has written a delightful poem about the exchange of money. That poem, "Smart," can be found in *Where the Sidewalk Ends* (Harper, 1974). But for most students the real intrigue is with the concept of a million (or a billion). The concept of a million is treated in Wanda Gág's *Millions of Cats* (Coward, 1928); Bernice Myers's *The Millionth Egg* (Lothrop, 1991); and another title by David M. Schwartz, *How Much Is a Million?* (Lothrop, 1985).

A focus on money could lead to an investigation of careers in banking and investing. Read *Careers in Banking and Finance* by Patricia Haddock (Rosen, 1990). In addition to reading about careers in banking, investigate careers by interviewing people who currently work in banking and finance occupations.

Museums

Gibbons, Gail. **Dinosaurs, Dragonflies & Diamonds: All About Natural History Museums.** Illustrated by Gail Gibbons. Four Winds, 1988. n.p. ISBN 0-02-737240-5. (508 Gib).
Target Audience: Grades K-3; Ages 5-8

The history and purpose of natural history museums are presented, from the first natural history museum in South Carolina, founded in 1773, to special small museums established throughout the country to display birds, plants, fish, and wild animals. Many are displayed in habitat groups, showing animals in their natural environments. Other museums or displays focus on the history of human beings, gems, bugs, dinosaurs, and special topics, such as gold and the California gold rush. In addition to arranging exhibits, employees of a natural history museum give lectures; help scientists study the materials in the museum's collection; label, tag, and record items received by the museum; and do their own research related to the museum's specialty. The final pages describe the steps involved in creating a rattlesnake exhibit. The process begins when the museum sends a curator to a site where rattlesnakes are found.

Connections: Visiting Museums

Lisl Weil uses simple language and two-color illustrations to explain the history of museums in *Let's Go to the Museum* (Holiday, 1989). Weil's book will augment Gibbons's introduction to natural history museums. Daniel Cohen and Susan Cohen have produced an extensive guide to museums, parks, and quarries in the United States where information about dinosaurs can be found. In *Where to Find Dinosaurs Today* (Cobblehill, 1992), the Cohens describe various monuments, specialty shops, and permanent exhibits for those interested in visiting exhibits featuring dinosaurs.

Caroline Arnold and photographer Richard Hewett give us information about a traveling exhibit from Australia shown in Los Angeles in 1988. Arnold's book, *Dinosaurs Down Under and Other Fossils from Australia* (Clarion, 1990) is a photo-essay depicting the behind-the-scenes action at a museum and giving intriguing details about the unique fossils of prehistoric Australia. Part of the text details how an exhibit is put together.

Ruth B. MacFarlane tells how to collect, prepare, preserve, and display natural history items in *Making Your Own Nature Museum* (Watts, 1989). She details how to work with plants, insects, bones, minerals, and fossils. MacFarlane also discusses the safety and legal aspects of collecting artifacts.

Music, Origin of Hymns

Haskins, Jim. **Amazing Grace: The Story Behind the Song.** Millbrook, 1992. 48 pp. ISBN 1-56294-117-8. (264 Has). (Photograph of the jacket is courtesy of the publisher and is reprinted with the permission of The Millbrook Press.)

Target Audience: Grades 4-6; Ages 9-11

The story of John Newton, slave trader turned minister, is truly amazing. When he was a young man, Newton's mother taught him Bible stories, but after she died John became a somewhat rebellious young man. He was sent off to sea by his father. When Newton missed the boat he was supposed to take, he was kidnapped by the British Royal Navy, which was allowed to take him to sea as a member of a ship's crew. Still rebellious, the navy traded Newton to a slave trader to be a member of that ship's crew. Eventually, Newton became a slave trader himself. Over a period of time Newton began to recognize that he was not invincible.

On several occasions Newton felt that his life was saved by the grace of God. After three trips to take slaves to America, Newton became ill and quit the slave trade. He returned to England and settled in the town of Olney, where he met a poet named William Cowper. The two men became quite close and composed some songs together. "Amazing Grace" was one of those songs.

That was in the late 1600s. The song survives and is often sung at special events. Metropolitan Opera soprano Jessye Norman sang the song in concert in London in 1990 to honor Nelson Mandela, who had been released after spending 25 years in prison because he worked for freedom for black South Africans. The families of soldiers who served in the Gulf War in 1991, sang the song at prayer meetings. When Johnny Cash, a country singer, sings the song, he includes a verse that he remembers hearing as a child.

The song reflects the story of a man who started as a rebellious teenager, became a slave trader, and finally became a minister who wrote many letters and talked to many people about the evils of slave trade. John Newton was 82 years old when he died in 1807, 27 years before slavery was abolished in England. In addition to the song "Amazing Grace," John Newton left behind many writings, including one of the most detailed records of the slave trade that exists. A good index is appended at the end of this book.

Connections: Amazing Grace and Other Musical Origins

Mary Hoffman wrote a picture book that plays on the title of the song. Hoffman's *Amazing Grace,* illustrated by Caroline Binch (Dial, 1991), tells the story of Grace, who wants very much to be Peter Pan in a school play. Her schoolmates tell her that she cannot play the part because she is a girl and because she is African American. Grace's mother and grandmother assure her that she can do anything she wants to do. Grace steps forward with self-assurance and indeed, earns the part of Peter Pan. Hoffman's book puts a different perspective on and establishes a multiple meaning for the term *amazing Grace.*

Many references to history (historical allusions and literary allusions) appear in books for young people. The stories behind other songs are told in *Climbing Jacob's Ladder: Heroes of the Bible in African-American Spirituals* by John Langstaff, illustrated by Ashley Bryan (McElderry, 1991); *Gonna Sing My Head Off! American Folk Songs for Children* by Kathleen Krull, (Knopf, 1992); and Robert Quackenbush's songs in *Go Tell Aunt Rhody* (Lippincott, 1973); *Clementine* (Lippincott, 1974); *Pop! Goes the Weasel and Yankee Doodle* (Lippincott, 1976); *The Man on the Flying Trapeze* (Lippincott, 1972); *She'll Be Comin' 'Round the Mountain* (Lippincott, 1973); *Skip* to My Lou (Lippincott, 1975); and *There'll Be a Hot Time in the Old Town Tonight* (Lippincott, 1974). Most of Quackenbush's books feature songs popular during the American Revolution; one chronicles the famous Chicago fire of 1871.

Native Americans

Sewall, Marcia. **People of the Breaking Day.** Illustrated by Marcia Sewall. Atheneum, 1990. 48 pp. ISBN 0-689-31407-8. (305.8 Sew).
Target Audience: Grades 4-6; Ages 9-11

In a first-person narrative Sewall tells about the Wampanoag Native Americans, who were in the area later called Plymouth, Massachusetts, when the Pilgrims arrived. The traditions of the tribe are described. During peaceful times the Wampanoag traded with the Narragansett and with the Abanaki. From the Narragansett they got soapstone pipes, bowls, and wampum. Wampum was delicate purple and white beads made from quahog shells, which were found in waters near Narragansett villages. From the Abanaki the Wampanoag obtained birch bark, which they used to make lightweight canoes. From tribes farther away the Wampanoag traded for copper and sharp-cutting flint. They played games with other tribes and matched skills. The men hunted, trapped, and fished. The wild game was often smoked in the village smokehouse. The women planted gardens with the help of the children. The Wampanoag are portrayed as gentle, thoughtful, and hard-working people who were very self-sufficient. This is the story of the Wampanoag before the coming of the Pilgrims to Plymouth.

Connections: Pilgrims and Native Americans

Marcia Sewall's *Pilgrims of Plimoth* (Atheneum, 1986) tells the story of the Pilgrims who landed near Plimoth (Plymouth), Massachusetts. Jean Craighead George tells about the Wampanoag and their encounters with the first Pilgrims during *The First Thanksgiving* (Philomel, 1993).

Native Americans, History

Goble, Paul, and Dorothy Goble. **Brave Eagle's Account of the Fetterman Fight: 21 December 1866.** Illustrated by Paul Goble. Pantheon, 1972; University of Nebraska, 1992. 64 pp. ISBN 0-8032-7032-1. (970.004 Gob).
Target Audience: Grades 4-6; Ages 9-11

On December 21, 1866, three officers and 76 privates of the 18th Infantry of the Second Calvary and four civilians under the command or protection of Captain William J. Fetterman were killed by overwhelming forces of Sioux and Cheyenne warriors. The Native Americans were lead by the chief of the Oglala Sioux, Red Cloud. The fight resulted from the U.S. government's insistence on establishing a right of way for travelers through Indian land. The Bozeman Trail would have provided the shortest route west from settled lands to Virginia City, where gold had been discovered. Because the trail cut across the tribe's best hunting ground, Red Cloud rejected the plan, and when soldiers built forts along the trail, Red Cloud and his warriors kept the soldiers busy protecting themselves and the forts; too busy to protect travelers. Eventually the soldiers and Red Cloud's warriors engaged in a battle. Fetterman and his entire command were killed. As a result of this defeat, the U.S. government abandoned the Bozeman Trail.

Connections: Red Cloud and Other Native Americans

Red Cloud was just one Native-American leader who tried to protect Native-American land from encroachment by settlers. A short biography of this great leader is included in *Indian Chiefs* by Russell Freedman (Holiday, 1987). Other leaders included in the book are Satanta, a Kiowa chief who attempted to defend Kiowa territory against emigrants bound for California; Quanah Parker, the son of a Comanche warrior, Peta Nacona, and a white woman, Cynthia Ann Parker, who as a child was kidnapped by the Comanche; Washakie, a Shoshoni chief who tried to promote peace between the Native Americans and the government; Chief Joseph, the chief of the Wallowa Valley band of the Nez Perce tribe; and Sitting Bull, a leader of the Hunkpapas, one of the seven tribes that made up the Teton Sioux nation. Sitting Bull refused to sign the treaty that provided for the Great Sioux reservation and eventually traveled with Buffalo Bill in his wild west shows.

Native Americans, Navajos

Sneve, Virginia Driving Hawk. **The Navajos: A First Americans Book.** Illustrated by Ronald Himler. Holiday, 1993. 32 pp. ISBN 0-8234-1039-0. (973 Sne).
Target Audience: Grades 4-6; Ages 9-11

The Navajo is the largest of all North American Indian tribes. The tribe's reservation covers parts of Arizona, Utah, and New Mexico. Beginning with a version of the Navajo creation tale, Sneve tells the history of "the People," the *Dineh,* who later became known as the Navajo. The tribe's migration to the Southwest, sometime between 1300 A.D. and 1600 A.D., is discussed, as are the tribe's relationships with its neighbors, the Pueblo, and with the Spaniards who arrived around 1600. During the eighteenth century, the Navajo became more involved in raising livestock and planting crops in "great planted fields." According to Sneve those fields were called *Nabaju* by the Spanish. That word became *Navajo,* and eventually became the name the Spaniards associated with Dineh, the people. Sneve summarizes Navajo family life; ceremonies; history, including battles to defend land and property, resettlement, and the problems the Navajos had in maintaining their traditions while living on the settlement; and life today.

Connections: Native Americans

The Navajo tribe is just one of the many tribes of Native Americans that played important roles in the history of the United States. Virginia Driving Hawk Sneve's book summarizes the history of the Navajo and discusses information about its culture and family life today. More information is available from the Navajo Curriculum Center, Rough Rock Demonstration School, Rough Rock, AZ 86503.

Sneve has written a similar title chronicling the history and present life of the Sioux. That title, *The Sioux: A First Americans Book,* illustrated by Ronald Himler (Holiday, 1993), explains the migration of the Dakota Sioux from Minnesota to the Great Plains in the 1700s. At that time some of the Sioux formed the Lakota or Nakota tribes. Sneve shows how their survival depended on the buffalo, describes their roles as hunters and warriors, and explains the traditions embodied in their dances and ceremonies. When whites encroached on Sioux territory and killed many buffalo, many Sioux starved to death. The Sioux were involved in the Battle of Little Big Horn in 1876; after that battle they were forced to move to reservations in South Dakota, North Dakota, Montana, and Minnesota, where many still live today. Additional titles in this series by Sneve include *The Seminoles: A First Americans Book* (Holiday, 1994) and *The Nez Perce: A First Americans Book* (Holiday, 1994). *The Seminoles* chronicles the story of that tribe's history in Oklahoma and Florida in a manner similar to Sneve's previous titles in the series. *The Nez Perce* includes a retelling of the creation myth of the Nez Perce Indians and relates their history, customs, and facts about the tribe today. The Nez Perce originally lived in Washington, Oregon, Idaho, and Montana, but in the 1870s they were forced onto a single reservation in Idaho.

Native Americans, Pueblo

Hoyt-Goldsmith, Diane. **Pueblo Storyteller.** Illustrated with photographs by Lawrence Migdale. Holiday, 1991. 28 pp. ISBN 0-8234-0864-7. (978.9 Hoy). (Photograph of the jacket is courtesy of the publisher and is reprinted with the permission of Holiday House, Inc.)
Target Audience: Grades 4-6; Ages 9-11

April Tujillo is a 10-year-old girl who lives with her grandparents in the Cochiti Pueblo near Santa Fe, New Mexico. In telling about April's life in the pueblo, Hoyt-Goldsmith recounts the history of the Pueblo from its beginnings along the Rio Grande River. Much of the tribe's life today is rooted in the past. For example, many tribe members' homes are still made of adobe clay; they still plant and harvest corn, beans, and squash; and they make beautiful pottery and drums. Many traditional songs are sung and dances performed. Children no longer have to go away to boarding schools, they can attend schools in their pueblo. Children learn to speak their native language, *Keres*.

April's life is a mixture of the past and the present. With her grandmother she bakes traditional loaves of *báa*, round loaves of bread made from flour, lard, yeast, and water. With her friends, April plays the basketball game called Horse. April works with her grandparents to gather clay that they will use to make pottery or storytelling figures. April learns how to work with the clay by watching her grandparents and helping them. Her grandfather kneads the clay with water and sand; her grandmother forms the storyteller; April helps her grandfather sand the pottery or figures to prepare them for her grandmother, who paints them. April hones her skills by making a small turtle, an important creature in pueblo legends.

Readers also learn about April's uncle, who makes Cochiti drums using aspen or cottonwood. The head of the drum is made of cowhide. Many of the drums are used in conjunction with the Buffalo Dance, which is another tradition that April explains. The final pages of the book feature a favorite story told to April by her grandparents. The story is the Pueblo legend of "How the People Came to Earth." April's grandparents are storytellers, much like the figures they often create. They bring the past into their lives through their language, their pottery, and the food they eat. Color photographs of April and the people and activities in her life help to present the information. A glossary of terms and an index help the reader locate information.

Keegan, Marcia. **Pueblo Boy: Growing Up in Two Worlds.** Illustrated with photographs by Marcia Keegan. Cobblehill, 1991. n.p. ISBN 0-525-65060-1. (978.9 Kee).
Target Audience: Grades 4-6; Ages 9-11

Timmy Roybal is a 10-year-old boy who lives in the San Ildefonso Pueblo in New Mexico. Tribal traditions are part of his modern world of school, baseball, and computers. Timmy is proud of his heritage and participates in traditional dances and rituals. He watches his grandmother make some of the pottery for which his pueblo is famous, and he learns the customs and prayers of his people from his father. Many other relatives are involved in traditional activities. His mother, who is a computer programmer, spends many evening hours weaving traditional ceremonial belts on a handmade wooden loom. Timmy's uncle carves *kachinas,* dolls that represent spirits who serve as messengers to the gods. Women in Timmy's pueblo still bake bread in outdoor ovens, called *hornos,* much as their ancestors did. Timmy speaks English, as does his family, but the language of their ancestors, *Tewa,* is also spoken in the pueblo. Photographs are included on every page.

Connections: Life in the Pueblo

Keegan's book describes the life of a 10-year-old boy, Timmy, who lives in the San Ildefonso Pueblo in New Mexico, north of Santa Fe. In *Pueblo Storyteller* (Holiday, 1991) Diane Hoyt-Goldsmith describes the life of a 10-year-old girl, April, who lives with her grandparents in the Cochiti Pueblo, south of Santa Fe. The traditions of the pueblo are inherent in the lives of both children. Use the books to introduce the culture of the Pueblo. The San Ildefonso and Cochiti pueblos are just two of eighteen pueblos in New Mexico. The Hopi Pueblo is located in Arizona. The San Ildefonso Pueblo is a Tewa pueblo, while the Cochiti Pueblo is a Keresan pueblo.

The figurines known as Storytellers first appeared in the Cochiti Pueblo which was already known for its fine, large drums. The potters of San Ildefonso were known for a matte black finish on polished blackware pottery. World-famous potter Maria Martinez and her husband, Julian, are credited with reviving the art of making blackware. San Ildefonso potters also produce a polished redware and some polychrome work. Resources that will help readers learn more about Storyteller figurines and other traditions in the Pueblo culture include *Pueblo Stories and Storytellers* by Mark Bahti (Treasure Chest, 1988) and several articles in the November 1982 issue of *National Geographic* (vol. 162, no. 5). The articles include "The Anasazi" (pp. 554-592), which tells about the intricate, lost society that built giant pueblos and irrigation works. Photographs accompanying the article show the kiva and the other day-to-day events of life in an Anasazi pueblo. Another article, "Pueblo Artistry in Clay" (pp. 593-606), discusses the traditional and contemporary creations made from clay, including pottery and storytellers, from various pueblos throughout New Mexico. A chart showing traditional pottery from specific pueblos will help readers identify traditions in each pueblo. Information about the Hopi, "Inside the Hopi Homeland" (pp. 607-629), discusses the pressures the Hopi feel from their Navajo neighbors and the dominant society.

Diane Hoyt-Goldsmith has also written about the Cherokee in *Cherokee Summer* (Holiday, 1993). That book tells about the Cherokee nation from the perspective of a young member of the tribe. Just as April's story involves the past, so does the story of the Cherokee. Another tribe's story is told in Hoyt-Goldsmith's *Arctic Hunter* (Holiday, 1992). In this book, the author relates the story of Reggie, an Inupiat living in Alaska. The focus is on the summer months spent at camp, when Reggie and others in his tribe spend much of their time hunting and fishing—gathering food for their families to eat during the rest of the year. Many books written about Native Americans emphasize the past and do not leave lasting images of the contemporary Native American. Hoyt-Goldsmith's books put the contemporary images up front but do not abandon information about the past. Her books are enhanced by ample color photographs that show life as it is today.

Another author, Virginia Driving Hawk Sneve, has created a series called First Americans. The first three titles in the series are: *The Navajos: A First Americans Book* (Holiday, 1993); *The Sioux: A First Americans Book* (Holiday, 1993); and *The Seminoles: A First Americans Book* (Holiday, 1994). The books depict the history of each tribe and relate their history to contemporary life. The titles are illustrated in realistic paintings by Ronald Himler.

New York City

Jakobsen, Kathy. **My New York.** Illustrated by Kathy Jakobsen. Little, Brown, 1993. 32 pp. ISBN 0-316-45653-5. (974.7 Jak).

Target Audience: Grades K-3; Ages 5-8

Kathy Jakobsen offers a sentimental account of a young girl's vision of New York City. A young girl, Becky, describes the city in a letter to her friend Martin. Accompanying her letter are pictures that depict each of the scenes she describes. The pictorial tour takes readers from the Sixth Avenue flea market at Sixth Avenue and Twenty-sixth Street to the subway tunnels, the Empire State Building, Central Park Zoo, F. A. O. Schwarz (a magnificent toy store), Plaza Hotel, the route of the famed New York City Marathon, Chinatown, the home of Baby Watson Cheesecake, American Museum of Natural History, Madison Square Garden, *Intrepid* Sea-Air-Space Museum on Pier 86 on the Hudson River, Statue of Liberty, and Ellis Island. Some pages fold out and some fold up to show wide scenes or tall buildings. Endpapers are illustrated with a map of the Manhattan area from Central Park to Staten Island. The map also shows the route of the New York City marathon through Brooklyn, Queens, and over the Queensboro Bridge.

Connections: Information and Letters

Several authors have used the technique of imparting information through letters. Jakobsen does it admirably in *My New York*; a letter between friends gives chatty information about the tourist sites in a city that many people will enjoy visiting, especially after reading her book. Another writer, Loreen Leedy, used a similar technique in *Postcards from Pluto: A Tour of the Solar System* (Holiday, 1993). In Leedy's book Dr. Quasar gives a group of children a tour of the solar system. He describes each of the planets from Mercury to Pluto. Throughout their trip in space, the students write postcards to people on Earth, summarizing the facts they are learning. Text and illustrations are combined to show the children's postcards home. Jean Craighead George used the letter format in *Dear Rebecca, Winter Is Here* (HarperCollins, 1993), in which a grandmother writes a letter to her granddaughter, telling her about the winter season. The letter is written on the shortest day of the year, December 21. Grandmother shares her view of the season, calls up images from summer, and shows the events that occur during winter.

Ocean

Cole, Joanna. **The Magic School Bus on the Ocean Floor.**
Illustrated by Bruce Degen. Scholastic, 1992. n.p. ISBN 0-590-41430-5. (591.92 Col).
Target Audience: Grades K-3; Ages 5-8

Ms. Frizzle is known for the wacky field trips that she and her class take. Each trip begins as an ordinary field trip, but when Ms. Frizzle is in charge the trip takes crazy turns. In this account of the class's field trip to the ocean, the children dress in swimsuits and board the bus to begin their trip. When Ms. Frizzle (who is driving the bus) arrives at the beach, she does not stop at the parking lot but continues to the water's edge. Ms. Frizzle does not even stop there. Before anyone can jump out of the bus, they are *in* the ocean. The bus turns into a submarine, and everyone is wearing a diving suit. The children are on another one of Ms. Frizzle's class trips. They learn about the continental shelf and explore the ocean and its plants and animals. They use a microscope to examine plankton and swim away from shark-infested waters. Degen's illustrations show what the children see under the microscope and give other information. For example, a panel across the bottom of one page illustrates the food chain from large fish to microscopic plankton. The children see tiger sharks, whale sharks, and glow-in-the-dark fish. As the bus rises to the surface, it becomes a glass-bottomed boat that allows the children to see the coral reef. They dive into the water to explore the reef close up, but must scramble aboard the boat/bus when Ms. Frizzle begins to move it away from the reef and into an ocean current, where they are swept into fast-moving water. At this point their vehicle becomes flat like a surfboard. Before they know it, they are surfing through the waves on their giant surfboard. Soon they are washing up on shore, their diving suits are gone, and the bus is its old self, parked in the parking lot.

Connections: Class Trips

Trina Hakes Noble writes about a crazy field trip in a picture book titled *The Day Jimmy's Boa Ate the Wash* (Dial, 1980). Just as Degen's illustrations add to the fun in Cole's books, Steven Kellogg's illustrations in Noble's title bring hilarious images to the account of a group of children who take a field trip to a farm. Noble imparts some facts about farms and animals, but the thrust of the book is humor and lighthearted fun.

Cole's Magic School Bus titles are both humorous and full of facts. In her first Magic School Bus title, *The Magic School Bus at the Waterworks* (Scholastic, 1986), Ms. Frizzle conducts a field trip to the waterworks plant, and children learn all about a city's water department. Similarly, in *The Magic School Bus Inside the Earth* (Scholastic,

1987); *The Magic School Bus Inside the Human Body* (Scholastic, 1989); and *The Magic School Bus Lost in the Solar System* (Scholastic, 1990) Ms. Frizzle and her class learn all about their topic through exploration and extra-special experiences. Ms. Frizzle is known not only for her crazy field trips but also for her unusual clothing. In each book the fabric of her dresses is patterned to reflect the action. At the end of each field trip, Ms. Frizzle's clothes hint at the topic of the next Magic School Bus book. For example, at the end of *The Magic School Bus Lost in the Solar System* Ms. Frizzle is shown getting ready to go home. The fabric of her coat is blue with a pattern of sea creatures. Her purse is shaped like a fish, and close by on the floor are two books, *Our Fish Friends* and *Oceans & Seas*. Of course, the next Magic School Bus book was *The Magic School Bus on the Ocean Floor*. At the end of the ocean book Ms. Frizzle is wearing a dress covered with images of jungle animals. Observant readers are looking forward to accompanying Ms. Frizzle and her class to the rain forest.

Pandas

Irvine, Georgeanne. **The Visit of Two Giant Pandas at the San Diego Zoo.** Illustrated with photographs. Simon, 1991. 45 pp. ISBN 0-671-73922-0. (599.74 Irv).
Target Audience: Grades K-3; Ages 5-8

Illustrated with color photographs, the visit of Basi and Yuan Yuan, two giant pandas from China, is covered from their arrival at the San Diego Zoo to their departure at the end of the goodwill trip. Giant pandas are a rare species. They are native only to China's interior mountain ranges. In recent years they have become endangered because of the destruction of their habitat, poaching, and bamboo die-offs. In 1984 peasant field workers rescued a starving young female panda. She was starving because the bamboo died in the Baoxing country and in other regions of the Qionglai Mountains. She was named Basi after the Basi Gou (Basi Gully), where she was found. Instead of being returned to the wild, as many other rescued pandas are, Basi was sent to the Fuzhou Zoo in southeastern China, where she became part of a panda conservation and breeding program. About the same time that Basi arrived at the zoo, a young male panda also arrived. Yuan Yuan had also been rescued by a panda patrol. Yuan Yuan had been found in the region of the Yuantuo Shan (Round Head Hill), where he had been starving.

In 1987 China decided to publicize the plight of the panda to the people of the United States. Basi and Yuan Yuan were selected to travel as goodwill ambassadors to the United States for 200 days. Panda preservationists hoped that Americans would donate money

110 / Seeking Information

to help China save the giant pandas and other endangered species. During the pandas' visit, more than two million visitors visited the San Diego Zoo. On February 9, 1988, the two pandas returned to China with their caretakers, Xiao Ling and Mei Lin, aboard the same United Airlines jet on which they had arrived. As they left, Basi held up a sign that read, "Basi and Yuan Yuan bid a fond farewell to San Diego." It was time for the giant pandas to return to the Fuzhou Zoo, where Basi became a mother and Yuan Yuan became a father.

Connections: More Pandas

Many animals are endangered but none so endearing as the giant pandas, who are known as the clowns of the bamboo forest. Irvine's book not only details the lives of Basi and Yuan Yuan during their visit to the United States but explains why the species became endangered and what the Chinese government is doing to protect it. Other books about pandas include *Picture Library: Pandas* by Norman Barrett (Watts, 1988); *Ling-Ling and Hsing Hsing: Year of the Panda* by Larry R. Collins and James K. Page, Jr. (Doubleday, 1973); *Lili, a Giant Panda of Sichuan* by Robert M. McClung (Morrow, 1988); *Giant Pandas* by Barbara Radcliffe Rogers (Mallard, 1990); *Pandas* by Miriam Schlein (Atheneum/Byron Preiss, 1989); and *Panda* by Caroline Arnold (Morrow, 1992).

Books about endangered animals are a natural connection to the story of the pandas' plight. Begin by reading a picture book by John Burningham, *Hey! Get Off Our Train* (Crown, 1990). During a dream journey, a boy and his dog encounter several endangered animals who are seeking sanctuary. Then proceed to Victor H. Waldrop's *Endangered Animals* (National Wildlife, 1989). This Ranger Rick title is filled with color photographs. It is well organized and presents a wide selection of endangered species; it also includes stories of conservation, breeding in captivity, and preservation. As more endangered species are identified, locate additional titles about those species.

Pirates

Gibbons, Gail. **Pirates: Robbers of the High Seas.** Illustrated by Gail Gibbons. Holiday, 1993. n.p. ISBN 0-316-30975-3. (910.45 Gib).
Target Audience: Grades K-3; Ages 5-8

This book offers a simple explanation of the roles that pirates played on the high seas while explorers were traveling across unknown oceans and entering new lands. The first pirates were Greeks and Romans. They attacked ships, stole cargo, and even captured prisoners. Bands of pirates sailed the seas, raiding and stealing from ships that sailed from the African coast, Spain, and other European countries. Few ships were safe from pirates. Pirate ships were small, armed, and easy to maneuver. Often pirates were able to disable galleons and jump aboard. Once on board the pirates attacked the crew and robbed the cargo. After the ship was plundered it was set afire, and the pirates returned to their ship to divide up the treasure. If the treasure was too heavy to carry around, the pirates spent it quickly or buried it in a secret place. To help them return to the spot where they buried the treasure, pirates drew maps, some of them very detailed. Some pirates worked for kings and queens, who hired the pirates to rob the ships of their enemies. These pirates were considered heroes in their countries. Eventually pirates were captured or conquered in battle. It has been hundreds of years since old-time pirates sailed the seas. Some think the treasure of many pirates' remains buried and lost forever.

Connections: More Pirates

The final pages of Gibbons's book list eight notorious pirates who lived in the seventeenth and eighteenth centuries. They are Sir Henry Morgan, Captain Kidd, Edward "Blackbeard" Teach, Anne Bonney, Mary Read, John Avery, Bartholomew "Black Bart" Roberts, and Captain Hook. The book offers enough information to allow students to plot the general location of each pirate's activities and to find additional information about each pirate. Additional pirates are Sir Francis Drake, William Dampier, Captain Jack "Calico Jack" Rackham, Stede Bonnet, and Captain Greavs.

Older intermediate readers will enjoy reading more about pirates in *Pirates* by Karen McWilliams (Watts, 1989). The author takes a look at who pirates were, how they lived, and why filmmakers do not always depict pirates accurately. McWilliams researched the book in the Caribbean, where many pirates sailed during the seventeenth and eighteenth centuries. A book that will help readers explore the subject of pirates through creative activities is *Pirates* by Rachel Wright (Watts, 1991). Wright focuses on pirate stories from the sixteenth century through the eighteenth century and makes the stories come alive with instructions for drawing maps, making disguises, building treasure chests, and making a pirate island.

Fictional pirates are featured in several excellent read-alouds. One of the best is *T. J. and the Pirate Who Wouldn't Go Home* by Carol Gorman (Scholastic, 1990), a contemporary story about T. J., a sixth-grader, and his Uncle Ainsley, who use a time machine to bring Captain Billy from the past into the twentieth century.

112 / Seeking Information

Connect prose books with poetry about pirates. Start with "The Pirate Don Durk of Dowdee" by Mildred Plew Meigs in May Hill Arbuthnot's *The Arbuthnot Anthology of Children's Literature* (Scott, Foresman, 1971). Look for other pirate poems in other anthologies.

Poets

Janeczko, Paul B., ed. **The Place My Words Are Looking For: What Poets Say About and Through Their Work.** Bradbury, 1990. 150 pp. ISBN 0-02-747671-5. (811.008 Jan). (Photograph of the jacket is courtesy of the publisher and is reprinted with the permission of Macmillan Children's Book Group.)

Target Audience: Grades 4-6; Ages 9-11

Well-known poets talk about their poetry and what it means to them or how incidents from their lives become part of their poetry. Poets represented are Gwendolyn Brooks, William Cole, Paul Fleischman, Michael Patrick Hearn, Margaret Hillert, Russell Hoban, Bobbie Katz, X. J. Kennedy, Steven Kroll, Maxine Kumin, Karla Kuskin, Myra Cohn Livingston, Eve Merriam, Naomi Shihab Nye, Jack Prelutsky, Joanne Ryder, Cynthia Rylant, Gary Soto, Nancy Willard, Valerie Worth, and 18 others.

Connections: More Poetry

The poets represented in *The Place My Words Are Looking For* are some of the best poets for intermediate readers. Use indexes in poetry anthologies to locate more poetry by these poets. Several of the poets have produced books of poetry. Of special interest are *I Am Phoenix: Poems for Two Voices* (Harper, 1985) and *Joyful Noises: Poems for Two Voices* (Harper, 1988), both by Paul Fleischman; *4-Way Stop and Other Poems* (Atheneum, 1976) and *A Circle of Seasons* (Holiday, 1982), both by Myra Cohn Livingston; *All the Small Poems* (Farrar, 1987) and *At Christmastime* (HarperCollins, 1992) by Valerie Worth; *Blackberry Ink* (Morrow, 1985), *It Doesn't Always Have to Rhyme* (Atheneum, 1964), and *There Is No Rhyme for Silver* (Atheneum, 1962), all by Eve Merriam; and *Brickyard Summer* by Paul B. Janeczko (Orchard, 1989).

Pollution

Cone, Molly. **Come Back, Salmon: How a Group of Dedicated Kids Adopted Pigeon Creek and Brought It Back to Life.** Illustrated with photographs by Sidnee Wheelwright. Sierra, 1992. 48 pp. ISBN 0-87156-572-2. (639.3 Con).

Target Audience: Grades 4-6; Ages 9-11

Molly Cone, the author of more than 40 books for young readers, chronicles a restoration project undertaken by the students of Jackson Elementary School in Everett, Washington. The project was inspired by a Washington State Environmental Education Seminar led by Snohomish County Adopt-A-Stream Foundation Director Tom Murdoch. The author worked with the teachers and students, interviewed them, arranged for photographs, and translated the interviews and discussions into a text that explains the project and its success. The project was to reclaim a stream that had once been a spawning ground for salmon. Salmon had not been in the stream for more than 20 years. Pigeon Creek had been choked with debris, from bottles to bed springs. The first step was to clean the stream and then to patrol it daily to discourage dumping. The children's teachers helped them set up an aquarium and stocked it with salmon eggs. The eggs hatched, and the alevins grew to be fry. Eventually the young salmon were ready to be released into Pigeon Creek. From the creek the salmon would migrate to the ocean and, the students hoped, return to Pigeon Creek to spawn. The book ends on an exhilarating note when the students of Jackson Elementary find the first mature salmon that has returned to Pigeon Creek to spawn.

Connections: Taking Action

There are many books about environmental concerns, but this one should convince children that they can make a difference. One book that might help youngsters take on smaller projects is *Save the Earth: An Action Handbook for Kids* by Betty Miles (Knopf, 1991). Miles talks about projects involving land, atmosphere, water projects, energy, and plants and animals. She describes projects that take one, two, or more hours to complete.

Brother Eagle, Sister Sky: A Message from Chief Seattle by Susan Jeffers (Dial, 1991) is often mentioned when books about saving the environment are discussed. While Jeffers's book presents a message that many want to hear, the story is basically a hoax that is revealed in "The Little Green Lie," (*Reader's Digest,* July 1993, pp. 100-104). Read Jeffers's book, and then read the *Reader's Digest* article. Discuss the book and article in relation to one another.

Ponds

Taylor, Barbara. **Pond Life.** Illustrated with photographs by Frank Greenaway. Dorling, 1992. 29 pp. ISBN 1-879431-94-7. (591.92 Tay).
Target Audience: Grades K-3; Ages 5-8
Large photographs and informative captions examine and explain the various animals and plants that are found in ponds. Included is information about fringed flowers, newts, water boatmen, stickleback fish, frogs, diving beetles, a caddis fly, and a pond snail.

Connections: Rivers, Ponds, and Streams

A very simple pictorial introduction to creatures who live in or near a river— a turtle, frog, fish, eel, salamander, dragonfly, muskrat, water beetle, duck, and crayfish—are included in *My River* by Shari Halpen (Macmillan, 1992), which is illustrated with collages. Other titles that contain information about animals and plants that live near the water include *Fish Do the Strangest Things* by Leonora Hornblow and Arthur Hornblow, illustrated by John F. Eggert (Random, 1990), and *Life in a Tidal Pool* by Alvin Silverstein and Virginia Silverstein, illustrated by Pamela Carroll and Walter Carroll (Little, Brown, 1990). Books about whales and other sea creatures are listed in this book under the headings Whales, Sharks, and Dolphins.

A natural follow-up to reading the books is a visit to a nearby pond, stream, or creek. Record the animals, insects, and other life that are found. Water from the pond, stream, or creek could be brought back to the classroom to be examined under a microscope.

Postal Service

Skurzynski, Gloria. **Here Comes the Mail.** Illustrated with photographs by Gloria Skurzynski. Bradbury, 1992. n.p. ISBN 0-02-782916-2. (383 Sku).
Target Audience: Grades K-3; Ages 5-8
Full-color photographs and explanatory text depict the journey of an envelope containing a picture that is being sent from Stephanie, who lives in Santa Fe, New Mexico, to her cousin Kathy, who lives in Salt Lake City, Utah. Behind-the-scenes photographs show the sorting, transporting, and delivery of the envelope from one city to the other. The book begins as Stephanie's mother helps Stephanie prepare the envelope; it ends as the letter carrier delivers the envelope to Kathy. The final pages show the proper way to address mail.

Connections: Writing Letters and Sending Mail

The straightforward language and clear, informative photographs in Skurzynski's book explain a process that is addressed in two other titles. Gail Gibbons's simple illustrations help to explain how letters are collected, stamped, sorted, transported, and delivered in *The Post Office Book: Mail and How It Moves* (HarperCollins, 1982). Harold Roth's photo-essay, *First Class! The Postal System in Action* (Pantheon, 1983), follows the paths of letters and packages through the postal system from the point of being postmarked to their destination. Young readers will enjoy Cynthia Rylant's *Mr. Griggs' Work*, illustrated by Julie Downing (Orchard/Richard Jackson, 1989). Mr. Griggs is a postman who loves his work, and Rylant's book helps to capture his enthusiasm for what he does.

How to write letters and notes are shared in Loreen Leedy's *Messages in the Mailbox: How to Write a Letter* (Holiday, 1991). Leedy's illustrations include examples to share with small groups or individuals. (See p. 90 for a full description of this title.)

Pussy Willow

Wexler, Jerome. **Wonderful Pussy Willows.** Illustrated by Jerome Wexler. Dutton, 1992. n.p. ISBN 0-525-44867-5. (583 Wex).
Target Audience: Grades K-3; Ages 5-8

Each spring pussy willows can be found by roadways and in fields. The soft, silky buds (catkins) are fun to touch, and the branches make nice arrangements. After picking, the branches last for months. This book offers information about the origin of the pussy willow (it is related to the weeping willow) and its name. Photographs show every stage of pussy willow development, beginning with the soft, bud-like nibs. Pussy willows produce two kinds of flowers: the pistillate (the female bloom) and the staminate (the male bloom). In clear prose Wexler explains how the blooms contribute to the reproduction of the plant, the role of bees in the process, the plant's growth cycle, and its propagation.

Connections: Growing Plants and Making a Garden

Wexler suggests that pussy willows could be cut and dried or the branches placed in water to allow roots to develop. After the roots sprout, the branch can be planted; eventually it will grow into a bush to be enjoyed by another generation.

Many plants begin from seeds. Information about planting seeds is well presented in *How a Seed Grows* by Helene J. Jordan (HarperCollins, 1992). Planting and propagating many types of plants provides practical activities to accompany a study of plants and extends the fun of favorite books. For example, find out just what is involved in planting a carrot seed (*The Carrot Seed* by Ruth Kraus, illustrated by Crockett Johnson [Harper, 1945]); grow and taste turnips (*The Great Big Enormous Turnip* by Aleksey Nikolaevich Tolstoy, illustrated by Helen Oxenbury [Watts, 1968]); and plant zucchini to save for the groundhog (*A Garden for Groundhog* by Lorna Balian [Abingdon, 1985]).

Graham Rust's illustrated *The Secret Garden Notebook: A First Gardening Book* (Godine, 1991) complements the novel by Frances Hodgson Burnett. Other books suggest gardening activities for the fledgling gardener. Much advice for raising all types of plants can be found in books. Read *A Very Young Gardener* by Jill Krementz (Dial, 1991) and *Grow It! An Indoor/Outdoor Gardening Guide for Kids* by Erica Markmann (Random, 1991). In *The Garden in the City* by Gerda Muller (Dutton, 1992), a family transforms the backyard of their new home into a garden. A photo-essay that shows just such an action plan is *Greening the City Streets: The Story of Community Gardens* by Barbara A. Huff (Clarion, 1990). Huff's book attempts to show that community gardens are not only places to grow food but also provide a place to watch nature and to involve the community in building a common area for neighborhood interaction. For a story interspersed with information and hints about planting gardens, look for *The Second Street Gardens and Green Truck Almanac* by Jacqueline Briggs Martin (Four Winds, 1995).

Those who want to preserve the beauty of their gardens may wish to use *A Child's Book of Wildflowers* by M. A. Kelly (Four Winds, 1992). Kelly discusses the blooming cycles of flowers, their size, and their color. Activities are suggested by the author.

Rain Forest

George, Jean Craighead. **One Day in the Tropical Rain Forest.** Illustrated by Gary Allen. Crowell, 1990. 56 pp. ISBN 0-690-04767-3. (508.315 Geo).
Target Audience: Grades 4-6; Ages 9-11

Tepui lives in a jungle filled with scarlet macaws, orchids, cebus monkeys, prehensile-tailed porcupines, army ants, great kiskadees, and jaguars. Tepui shares information about his forest with Dr. Juan Rivero and four other biologists. When Tepui and the biologists learn that a caravan of bulldozers and trucks will soon arrive from Caracas, Venezuela, to destroy the lush forest, they know that they must find an elusive, mysterious, butterfly immediately. If Tepui and the professor could locate and capture just one of the butterflies, the bulldozers would have to be called off. They have only one day to do it. Tepui's quest to find the butterfly takes the reader on an informative trip through the rain forest, all in one day.

Connections: More About the Rain Forest

Who Is the Beast? by Keith Baker (Harcourt, 1990); *The Great Kapok Tree: A Tale of the Amazon Rain Forest* by Lynne Cherry (Harcourt, 1990); and *Rain Forest* by Helen Cowcher (Farrar, 1988) are picture books that introduce some of the animals of the rain forest: tigers, macaws, toucans, monkeys, and jaguars.

A very basic presentation of eight jungle animals is included in one of the titles in the Eye Openers Series, *Jungle Animals* (Aladdin, 1991). More detailed information about the rain forest and its animals is included in *Chico Mendes: Fight for the Forest* by Susan DeStefano (Twenty-First Century, 1992); *Rainforest Secrets* by Arthur Dorros (Scholastic, 1990); *Rain Forest* by Billy Goodman (Little, Brown, 1991); *Tropical Rain Forests Around the World* by Elaine Landau (Watts, 1990); *Our Endangered Planet: Tropical Rain Forests* by Cornelia Mutel and Mary M. Rodgers (Lerner, 1991); and *Journey Through a Tropical Jungle* by Adrian Forsyth (Simon, 1989).

Forsyth's book is a Canadian biologist's account of a trip to the mountains of Costa Rica. The photographs and clear writing make Forsyth's book a great read-aloud title to complement George's *One Day in the Tropical Rain Forest.* Another excellent book filled with photographs and information about the plants and animals of the rain forest is *Rain Forest* by Barbara Taylor, illustrated by Frank Greenaway (Dorling, 1992). The photographs in Taylor's book give the reader close-up views of the flying gecko, the poison dart frog, and the curly-haired tarantula, along with many other inhabitants of the rain forest.

Recycling

Gibbons, Gail. **Recycle! A Handbook for Kids.** Illustrated by Gail Gibbons. n.p. Little, Brown, 1992. ISBN 0-316-30971-0. (628.4 Gib). (Photograph of the jacket is courtesy of the publisher and is reprinted with the permission of Little, Brown and Company.)
Target Audience: Grades 4-6; Ages 9-11

Trash, garbage, waste—all can be recycled. Now, most waste is hauled to landfills, where it is dumped and covered with dirt. Places to bury trash are becoming fewer and fewer, so alternatives are being sought. One solution is to reduce the amount of trash being thrown away. Reusing the objects we would normally throw away is one way to control waste. Gibbons gives suggestions for recycling paper, glass, cans, plastic, and polystyrene (Styrofoam). The final pages present statistics about garbage, including the fact that the people of the United States make enough garbage *each day* to fill 100,000 garbage trucks and that 65 billion aluminum soda cans are used each year.

Connections: Reduce, Reuse, and Recycle

Marc Brown and Laurie Krasny Brown go a step or two beyond Gibbons's plea to recycle. Their book, *Dinosaurs to the Rescue! A Guide to Protecting Our Planet* (Little Brown, 1992) gives advice about saving the environment. The Browns' suggestions are based on the "reduce, reuse, recycle" theme. Three sections are highlighted: use less, use again, and give something back. A video version of the Browns' book is available from American School Publishers.

Older students will find more in-depth information about the garbage problem in *Garbage! Where It Comes From, Where It Goes* by Evan Hadingham and Janet Hadingham (Simon, 1990) and *Recycling: Meeting the Challenge of the Trash Crisis* by Alvin Silverstein, Virginia Silverstein, and Robert Silverstein (Putnam, 1992).

Saint Lawrence Seaway

Gibbons, Gail. **The Great St. Lawrence Seaway.** Illustrated by Gail Gibbons. Morrow, 1992. n.p. ISBN 0-688-06984-3. (386 Gib).
Target Audience: Grades 4-6; Ages 9-11

Jacques Cartier was a French explorer who in 1535 sailed to North America to find a passageway to the Orient. On the feast day of Saint Lawrence, August 10, he sailed into the mouth of a river that he named the St. Lawrence River. Five hundred miles downstream, strong rapids forced the explorer to turn back. It was almost 70 years before Samuel de Champlain traveled up the St. Lawrence on a fur-trading expedition. When his crew reached the rapids, it carried the boats overland until it was safe to travel on the water. On subsequent trips de Champlain found Lake Ontario. Later traders established a fur trade along the waterways. Over the years a canal was built to bypass the rapids, settlements were established along the shore, and trade increased. After the French and Indian War, the English who had won began to encourage the use of the waterway. Locks were developed to help boats move upstream. In 1954 Canada and the United States built a continuous waterway from the Atlantic Ocean to the Great Lakes. With detailed drawings Gibbons shows how contemporary ships transport cargo through the seaway to the Midwest. The endpapers show the route through the waterways and around Niagara Falls.

Connections: Transportation—Then and Now

Many of Gail Gibbons's books deal with the development or construction of a place or building. In *The Great St. Lawrence Seaway* Gibbons chronicles the history of the development of the transportation system that evolved on the St. Lawrence River. Early overland travel is the subject of Gibbons's *From Path to Highway: The Story of the Boston Post Road* (Crowell, 1986). The history of the road begins with Native Americans who walked along paths between villages and hunting grounds. Soon colonists were walking the same trails. When horses were brought from England, the colonists begin to ride the trails. As time passed the paths were widened, and carriages and wagons began to travel on them. At this point the paths were more like dirt roads—bumpy and rough. Riders carrying mail used the roads until the American Revolution began. Bridges take the place of old ferry crossings. Farmers and tradesmen added gravel and stone to sections of land they owned—connecting the roads. During the war soldiers traveled along the roadways, and all stagecoach travel had to stop. Over the next decades railroads followed the roads on newly built tracks, automobiles chugged from village to village, stores and businesses sprang up along the roadside. Today the roads have meshed into one busy, modern four-lane highway.

Scarecrows

Littlewood, Valerie. **Scarecrow!** Illustrated by Valerie Littlewood. Dutton, 1992. 29 pp. ISBN 0-525-44948-5. (632 Lit).
Target Audience: Grades 4-6; Ages 9-11

This book offers an overview of the history of the scarecrow, which is used to protect farmers' crops from birds. Littlewood highlights the legends, fictional scarecrows, and some cultures' traditions. In some cultures human scarecrows were hired or designated to protect the fields. In ancient Japan scarecrows were burned in ceremonies at the end of each growing season. Today most cultures use figures similar to the straw-stuffed figure made popular by *The Wizard of Oz*. Over the years the stuffed scarecrow has given way, in some places, to the inflatable plastic scarecrow and other variations on the original. Other devices, such as exploding devices that activate flapping and a huge, hawk-shaped kite that looms over the field, casting a shadow of a bird of prey, are sometimes used. Scarecrows enjoyed a revival during World War II, when gardening played an important role in providing food for the nation. Myths and magic about scarecrows are included.

Connections: Scarecrows Everywhere

Scarecrows appear in movies, such as *The Wizard of Oz,* and in books and poems. While Littlewood's text will be of more interest to intermediate readers, the pictures will introduce younger readers to various types of scarecrows. To connect Littlewood's information book to other books that feature scarecrows, try some of the following titles. Eric Carle uses vibrant collages to create the scarecrow in George Mendoza's *The Scarecrow Clock* (Holt, 1971). The scarecrow's hands show the time of day and eventually signal the time "the party can begin." A scarecrow that meets a little old lady on the path to her home is the main character of Linda Williams's *The Little Old Lady Who Was Not Afraid of Anything,* illustrated by Megan Lloyd (Crowell, 1986). Williams uses the image of a pumpkin-head scarecrow; the cumulative tale begs for reader involvement. In the picture book *Jeb Scarecrow's Pumpkin Patch* (Houghton, 1992), Jana Dillon tells a tale of a scarecrow who devises a plan to keep the crows from having a party in his pumpkin patch.

A well-known scarecrow appears in the many editions of Beatrix Potter's classic titles, *The Tale of Peter Rabbit* (Warne, 1902) and *The Tale of Benjamin Bunny* (Warne, 1904). To escape from Farmer McGregor's garden, Peter has to wiggle out of his clothes. Farmer McGregor uses the clothes to make a scarecrow. When Peter and his cousin Benjamin return to get Peter's clothing, they must retrieve them from the scarecrow.

Most scarecrows depicted in picture books are more pleasant than frightening. However, scarecrows in stories for older readers may be menacing. Robert D. San Souci tells a tale in *Feathertop: Based on the Tale by Nathaniel Hawthorne,* illustrated by Daniel San Souci (Doubleday, 1992), in which a witch creates a scarecrow that looks human. The scarecrow is transformed by a young woman's love and becomes human. The tale is told in picture book format but will appeal to an older audience. All ages will enjoy Paul Fleischman's *Scarebird,* illustrated by Peter Sis (Greenwillow, 1988).

Seasons

Simon, Seymour. **Autumn Across America.** Illustrated with photographs. Hyperion, 1993. n.p. ISBN 1-56282-467-8. (508.73 Sim).
Target Audience: Grades K-3; Ages 5-8

The brilliant reds, oranges, yellows, golds, bronzes, and browns of autumn are shown in clear, well-chosen photographs. The text speaks of harvest time and the cycle of change. The seasons change because of the tilt of the Earth on its axis and the closeness of certain parts of the Earth to the Sun. Information about why leaves change color is included, along with information about the migration of birds; insects' efforts to get ready for winter; seeds that travel on the autumn breezes; and crops harvested during the autumn. A special focus on autumn activity in Yellowstone National Park and the Olympic Mountains in Washington state is included.

Connections: Autumn and Beyond

Eye-catching photographs and lyrical text introduce the concept of autumn in *Fall* by Ron Hirschi (Cobblehill, 1991). Chris Van Allsburg has written a picture book reminiscent of the legendary character, Jack Frost. Many will wonder if Jack Frost really does appear in Van Allsburg's *The Stranger* (Houghton, 1986). Autumn officially ends December 21, the first day of winter in the northern hemisphere. After autumn is gone and winter has come, read Seymour Simon's *Winter Across America* (Hyperion, 1994) and some stories from Caroline Feller Bauer's *Snowy Day: Stories and Poems,* illustrated by Margot Tomes (Lippincott, 1986). And after winter has come and most children are looking forward to spring, read Arnold Adoff's poetry in *In for Winter, Out for Spring* (Harcourt, 1991). Jerry Pinkney, who illustrates Adoff's book, presents suburban landscapes and snapshots of an African American family planting a spring garden, running barefoot through the grass, and measuring one another's height against a door.

Sharks

Cerullo, Mary M. **Sharks: Challengers of the Deep.** Illustrated with photographs by Jeffrey L. Rotman. Cobblehill, 1993. 57 pp. ISBN 0-525-65100-4. (597 Cer).
Target Audience: Grades 4-6; Ages 9-11

Are you a selachiphobic? What do you really know about sharks? Take the 12-question quiz at the front of this book, and then read on to find out the answers (or take the quick way and turn to page 53). Chapters 1 and 2 will get the attention of readers quickly. Food chains, the habitats of sharks, and other topics related to sharks—including the use of noodlelike strands of cartilage that are prized as an edible delicacy—are discussed. Interesting information about myths surrounding sharks and patterns surrounding documented shark attacks is presented in one of the final chapters of the book.

Connections: About Sharks

Cerullo's book is a very complete look at the lives of sharks. Readers who need easier-to-read titles will find an excellent introduction in Joanna Cole's *Hungry, Hungry Sharks* (Random, 1986). This is a Step 2 book in Random House's Step Into Reading series. The full-color illustrations by Patricia Wynne supplement the information presented in the text. Photographs are the highlight of *Shark* by Miranda MacQuitty (Knopf, 1992), a book in Knopf's Eyewitness series.

The danger of sharks is examined, along with other dangers, in a thrilling account of sea life authored by Russell Freedman, *Killer Fish* (Holiday, 1982). Don C. Reed was for many years a diver who scrubbed the tanks that held the sharks at a marine aquarium near San Francisco. He recounts his experiences with sevengill sharks in *Sevengill: The Shark and Me* (Knopf, 1986). His book will give a perspective on the life of a shark in captivity.

Shipwrecks

Hackwell, W. John. **Diving to the Past: Recovering Ancient Wrecks.** Illustrated by W. John Hackwell. Scribner's, 1988. 54 pp. ISBN 0-684-18918-6. (930.1 Hac).
Target Audience: Grades 4-6; Ages 9-11

How scientists locate, explore, excavate, and preserve ancient shipwrecks is the topic of this book. The use of water dredges is explained. The techniques divers use and the dangers they face as they work on an excavation are detailed and compared to methods archaeologists use on land, including methods for casting replicas of completely decayed objects by pouring plaster or fiberglass resin into cavities left by the decayed artifact. The use of computer technology, sonar devices, and magnetometers is discussed, as are the duties of the dive team. It is a fascinating account of the efforts involved in finding, excavating, reconstructing, and learning from sunken ships.

Connections: Buried Treasure

Several sunken ships have been discovered by Robert D. Ballard, who has led expeditions to excavate the treasures buried in the sea. His books, *Exploring the Titanic* (Scholastic, 1988); *Exploring the Bismark* (Scholastic, 1991); and *The Lost Wreck of the Isis* (Scholastic, 1990), a book he coauthored with Rick Archbold, tell of those expeditions. Color photographs and oil paintings help the reader see what Ballard and his crew found under the sea. An account of the sinking of the Titanic written for younger readers is Judy Donnelly's *The Titanic: Lost ... and Found,* illustrated by Keith Kohler (Random, 1987).

The *Atocha,* which sank off the coast of Florida in 1622, and its buried treasure are the subject of Gail Gibbons's illustrated information book, *Sunken Treasure* (Crowell, 1988). Gibbons's many drawings illustrate the conventional steps taken by Mel Fisher as he searched for and salvaged the treasure from the *Atocha.* Gibbons further whets the readers' interest in marine archeology in summaries of other famous shipwreck treasure hunts: the *Mary Rose,* an English warship; the *Vasa,* a Swedish warship; the *Whydah,* a pirate ship; and the *Titanic,* a luxury liner.

Those who would like to find buried treasure might get some inspiration and suggestions from James M. Deem's 192-page book *How to Hunt Buried Treasure* (Houghton, 1992). Deem combines colorful history with common sense advice about legally hunting for treasure. Deem includes puzzles to solve and codes to break. And those interested in buried treasures being found by archaeologists will want to read *Digging to the Past: Excavations in Ancient Lands* by W. John Hackwell (Scribner's, 1986).

Skeletons

Kahney, Regina. **The Glow-in-the-Dark Book of Animal Skeletons.** Illustrated by Christopher Santoro. Random, 1992. 23 pp. ISBN 0-679-81080-3. (599 Kah).
Target Audience: Grades K-3; Ages 5-8

The skeletons of 14 animals are shown in glow-in-the-dark overlays on fleshed out pictures of the animals. The first animals featured are *homo sapiens* (human beings), which are shown in a picture of a young child running toward her father, who is seated on a beach. The skeleton is a barely visible, light, yellow-green overlay on the father. The drawing can be felt as a lightly raised outline. However, if a flashlight or light bulb is held close to the figure, and then the lights are turned out, the skeleton glows in the dark. Two to three descriptive paragraphs accompany each illustration. In addition to humans, the animals included are chimpanzee, black-handed spider monkey, African elephant, bald eagle, Masai ostrich, blue whale, greater horseshoe bat, great gray kangaroo, Chinook salmon, painted turtle, house cat, cheetah, king cobra, and reticulated giraffe. Although the text is sparse, interesting facts will motivate readers to learn more about each animal. The visual representations of the skeletons are outstanding.

Connections: Skeleton and Other Body Systems

More information about human and animal skeletons is included in the Eyewitness book *Skeleton* by Steve Parker (Knopf, 1988). The book discusses the evolution, structure, and function of the human and animal skeletal systems. In addition to the skeletal system, other anatomical systems can be shared with young readers. Mary Lindsay edited a comprehensive introduction to the body, *The Visual Dictionary of the Human Body* (Dorling, 1991). The dictionary uses color photographs, anatomical terminology, and vivid illustrations to give an enthralling introduction to body parts, including the skin, eyes, and reproductive systems. A general introduction for younger students is *Outside and Inside You* by Sandra Markle (Bradbury, 1991). Markle describes the body's outer covering and its skeletal framework. Descriptions of the eyes, ears, and internal organs are also included, along with the function of many body parts.

Other books address specific systems or functions of the body. Paul Showers does an excellent job of explaining how humans hear in a book from the Let's-Read-and-Find-Out Science Books series,

Ears Are for Hearing (Crowell, 1990). Steve Parker introduces the brain and nervous system in a revised edition of a 1982 title from the Human Body series. His book, *The Brain and Nervous System* (Watts, 1990), contains one-page descriptions that are strengthened by diagrams, photographs, and experiments.

Speaking is the subject of Paul Showers's *How You Talk* (Crowell, 1992). Showers's text explains the basics of speech and how the human body produces it. Several experiments are suggested; each suggests duplicating a sound to learn how various parts of the body help to produce speech. Showers addresses the function of the skin in his book, *Your Skin and Mine* (Crowell, 1991). The sense of smell is addressed in an eight-chapter book by Alvin Silverstein, Virginia Silverstein, and Robert Silverstein. That book, *Smell, the Subtle Sense* (Morrow, 1992), not only discusses the function of smell but related disorders, pheromones, and smell communication. All five senses are introduced in Aliki's *My Five Senses* (Crowell, 1989).

A natural corollary to learning about the various systems and functions of the body is learning how some systems and functions malfunction, causing handicaps or illness. Learning more about the human body can be found by consulting indexes or library catalogs under the heading "Human Body." More information about illness and related topics can be found under the heading "Medicine and Illnesses." One particularly interesting book deals with the respiratory system and a subject not often covered: allergies. Judith S. Seixas has devoted an entire 56-page book to explaining the causes of allergies, who is affected, testing procedures, and treatments for allergies. Seixas's book, *Allergies: What They Are, What They Do* (Greenwillow, 1991), is an effective introduction for primary and intermediate readers. A general book concerned with staying healthy is Laurie Krasny Brown's and Marc Brown's *Dinosaurs Alive and Well! A Guide to Good Health* (Joy Street/Little, Brown, 1990). The Browns use dinosaurs to convey messages regarding diet, stress, and exercise.

Soccer

Grosshandler, Janet. **Winning Ways in Soccer.** Illustrated with photographs by Janet Grosshandler. Cobblehill, 1991. n.p. ISBN 0-525-65064-4. (796.334 Gro).
Target Audience: Grades K-3; Ages 5-8

Introduce the game of soccer to primary students or those who want to know more about the game. Well-drawn charts depict the field layout. Basic rules and playing techniques (using short kicks and keeping the ball close to your feet, and so forth) are discussed. Positions of the players are enumerated and shown on a position chart. Types of fouls are defined, and the play of a game is described. This book provides a good introduction to the game.

Connections: Learning the Game

Sports Illustrated offers a guide to soccer in its Make the Team series. *Soccer: A Heads-Up Guide to Super Soccer* by Richard J. Brenner (Sports Illustrated, 1990) covers attitudes and teamwork, basic information about how to play the game, equipment, rules, and drills for warming up and practicing. Black-and-white photographs illustrate the action.

Several authors have written novels about characters who play soccer. Dean Hughes's Angel Park Soccer Stars series titles include *Defense!* (Knopf, 1991); *Kickoff Time* (Knopf, 1991); *Play-Off* (Knopf, 1992); *Backup Goalie* (Knopf, 1992); *Psyched!* (Knopf, 1992); *Total Soccer* (Knopf, 1992); and *Victory Goal* (Knopf, 1992). Each title features characters from the area surrounding Angel Park, California. The focus in these books (which run slightly over 100 pages) are the players. Like Hughes, Tommy Hallowell focuses on the players in his books about four boys who participate in four different sports during their seventh-grade year. The novels mix play-by-play action with information about school and family life. The relationships among the boys are sincere and add to the development of their characters as youngsters who learn to play a game. *Shot from Midfield* by Tommy Hallowell (Viking, 1991) focuses on soccer; his other titles focus on baseball, basketball, and football: *Duel on the Diamond* (Viking, 1991); *Jester on the Backcourt* (Viking, 1991); and *Last Chance Quarterback* (Viking, 1991).

Margaret Park writes about the Houdinis soccer team's struggle to win after a long losing streak in a 64-page novel, *Harvey and Rosie ... and Ralph* (Dutton, 1992). A mysterious player named Ralph shows up and (with a little magic) helps bring the team into the winner's circle. A book of similar length is *Angel and Me and the Bayside Bombers* by Mary Jane Auch (Little, Brown, 1989). In this sports saga, Brian gets revenge for being thrown off the Bayside Bombers when he puts together a team of uncoordinated second graders and (unlikely as they are) they become winners and heroes.

An unlikely female hero is the protagonist of Sue Stops's glorious picture book story about a girl who persists in becoming part of the school's soccer team. In *Dulcie Dando, Soccer Star* (Holt, 1992), Dulcie saves the day by her expert play in a crucial game. At the end of the game she is carried off on her grandmother's motorcycle. The illustrations by Debi Gliori are lively and fun.

Solar System

Leedy, Loreen. **Postcards from Pluto: A Tour of the Solar System.** Illustrated by Loreen Leedy. Holiday, 1993. n.p. ISBN 0-8234-1000-5. (523.2 Lee).
Target Audience: Grades 4-6; Ages 9-11

Dr. Quasar welcomes Eric, Minda, Ray, Lin, Tanisha, and Simon and invites them to go on a field trip through the solar system. The children learn about the rotation and orbits of planets in the solar system. They visit the sun and each of the planets. The children learn about each of the planets and about asteroids, falling stars and other space related topics. One of the children writes a postcard to a family member or friend, describing what the group is learning. Only the very basic facts are shared, just enough to whet the reader's appetite and motivate the reader to learn more about the solar system.

Connections: Into the Solar System

Leedy's book introduces each of the planets. Other books present additional information about planets. Gail Gibbons's *The Planets* (Holiday, 1993) discusses the movements, location, and characteristics of the nine known planets of our solar system. Distance from the sun, orbits, rotation times (length of a year on that planet), and the role of the astronomer are discussed in Gibbons's book. Joanna Cole's Magic School Bus series includes *The Magic School Bus Lost in the Solar System* (Scholastic, 1990). This science adventure features Ms. Frizzle and her class, who rocket into outer space in the Magic School Bus. The pages of the book are packed with reports and information about the planets. Patricia Lauber's *Journey to the Planets* (Crown, 1982; rev. 1990) includes updated information about the moon and planets gathered on the *Voyager* explorations. Seymour Simon is the author of several books about individual planets. Each is illustrated with superb photographs that give close-up views of the planet. Titles by Simon include *Neptune* (Morrow, 1991); *Mercury* (Morrow, 1992); and *Venus* (Morrow, 1992). The sun is the topic of Franklyn Branley's *The Sun: Our Nearest Star,* illustrated by Don Madden (Crowell, 1988). This simply written explanation of the physical characteristics of the sun discusses the sun in terms of heat and light on Earth and the sun's crucial role in helping plants grow and providing warmth.

Spiders

Gibbons, Gail. **Spiders.** Illustrated by Gail Gibbons. Holiday, 1993. n.p. ISBN 0-8234-1006-4. (595.4 Gib).
Target Audience: Grades K-3; Ages 5-8

Spiders have been around since before dinosaurs, and now there are approximately 30,000 kinds of spiders. Spiders belong to a group of animals called *arachnids,* a name that originated in Greek legend. In this book, well-designed drawings help readers compare and contrast the body of a spider with the body of an insect. Following the introduction is a detailed and sequential explanation of the spider's life cycle from mating and laying eggs to the development of spiderlings and molting. Gibbons explains and shows the various types of webs—tangled, sheet, funnel, triangle, and orb—that are woven by various spiders. Other methods used by the wolf spider, water spider, trapdoor spider, and crab spider to capture food are explained and illustrated. Information about dangerous spiders, enemies of spiders, spiders' life span, helpful spiders, and 10 bits of trivia about spiders complete the book.

Connections: Other Creepy Crawlers

Gail LaBonte's 59-page book, *The Tarantula* (Dillon, 1991), gives a fascinating life history of the tarantula and information, including common misconceptions, about this very large spider. A very basic book about insects is Angela Royston's *What's Inside? Insects* (Dorling, 1992). Royston's 17-page book is filled with outstanding color photographs and diagrams that show basic insect anatomy. Jerry Pallotta introduces several creepy, buglike creatures in *The Icky Bug Alphabet Book* (Charlesbridge, 1989) and *The Icky Bug Counting Book* (Charlesbridge, 1991). Pallotta's books give brief bits of information, but more complete information must be researched in other books.

One book that gives much information about wasps is *Wasps at Home* by Bianca Lavies (Dutton, 1991). Exquisite photographs show how a social wasp queen establishes a large and industrious colony of wasps. The author also shows the stages of growth of a worker wasp. Lavies presents similar information about a praying mantis in *Backyard Hunter: The Praying Mantis* (Dutton, 1990). This photo-essay shows the life cycle of the praying mantis.

A selection of excellent resources about insects, spiders, or other crawly things include *Monarch Butterfly* by Gail Gibbons (Holiday, 1989); *Where Butterflies Grow* by Joanne Ryder (Lodestar, 1989); *Eight Legs* by D. M. Souza (Carolrhoda, 1991); *Insects Around the House* by D. M. Souza (Carolrhoda, 1991); *Insects in the Garden* by D. M. Souza (Carolrhoda, 1991); *What Bit Me?* by D. M. Souza (Carolrhoda, 1991); *Amazing Butterflies and Moths* by John Still (Knopf, 1991); *The*

Ladybug and Other Insects by Pascale de Bourgoing (Scholastic, 1991); and *Fireflies in the Night* by Judy Hawes (HarperCollins, 1991).

Tainos

Jacobs, Francine. **The Tainos: The People Who Welcomed Columbus.** Illustrated by Patrick Collins. Putnam, 1992. 108 pp. ISBN 0-399-22116-6. (972.9 Jac). (Photograph of the jacket is courtesy of the publisher and is reprinted with the permission of Putnam & Grosset Group.)
Target Audience: Grades 4-6; Ages 9-11

A powerful tale that will shock those who have read (and believed) the romantic accounts of Columbus and his "discovery" of America. When the three ships under his command landed on an island in the Bahamas, the men on the ship were greeted by Tainos, a peaceful farming people whose ancestors had come from South America to islands in the Caribbean hundreds of years earlier. The Tainos were a friendly and generous people. They welcomed Columbus and his men, helped them find food, showed them how to get around on the island, and helped them as much as they could. The Spaniards noticed the gold ornaments the Tainos wore and were eager to find the gold for themselves. The Spaniards exploited the Tainos, enslaved them, and forced some Tainos to return to Spain, where they were exhibited like objects. The Tainos (also called Arawaks) were the first Americans to welcome Columbus in 1492, but there are no Tainos in the Caribbean today. This book tells the story of how the population of nearly one million was reduced to one-third by the year 1496 and to fewer than 500 by 1548. Today the West Indies population is overwhelmingly of African and European origins. Jacob's story is compelling; it is one that all children should be acquainted with.

130 / Seeking Information

⚛ Connections: Stories of Columbus's Coming

Jacobs's book presents a gentle and sympathetic picture of the Taino people before the arrival of Columbus and then unfolds the story of their abuse and the demise of their idyllic life, as a result of Columbus's arrival in the new world. This story must be told to complete the historical picture of the coming of Columbus to America. Jacobs's book balances the highly romanticized story of Columbus that is presented in standard accounts. Books that tell the standard story of Columbus's arrival include *A Picture Book of Christopher Columbus* by David A. Adler, illustrated by John Wallner and Alexandra Wallner (Holiday, 1991); *Westward with Columbus* by John Dyson, photographs by Peter Christopher (Scholastic, 1991); *Where Do You Think You're Going, Christopher Columbus?* by Jean Fritz, illustrated by Margot Tomes (Putnam, 1981); *The Great Adventure of Christopher Columbus*, a pop-up book by Jean Fritz with illustrations by Tomie dePaola (Putnam, 1992); *I, Columbus: My Journal—1492-3*, edited by Peter Roop and Connie Roop with illustrations by Peter E. Hanson (Walker, 1990); *Follow the Dream* by Peter Sis (Knopf, 1991); *The High Voyage: The Final Crossing of Christopher Columbus* by Olga Litowinsky (Delacorte, 1991); and *Christopher Columbus: From Vision to Voyage* by Joan Anderson, illustrated with photographs by George Ancona (Dial, 1991). Anderson's book presents information about the six-and-a-half years of negotiations with Queen Isabelle of Spain; negotiations that resulted in the financial arrangements that allowed Columbus's voyages.

Milton Meltzer has written a book for older intermediate readers that deals with Columbus's exploitation of the people of the Caribbean and his desire to carry the riches of the new land back to Spain. Meltzer shows Columbus to be a product of his society. The book, *Columbus and the World Around Him* by Milton Meltzer (Watts, 1990), will supplement the information in Jacobs's book and will help to balance the representations in the standard books written by Fritz, Roop, Litowinsky, and others cited.

Thanksgiving

George, Jean Craighead. **The First Thanksgiving.** Illustrated by Thomas Locker. Philomel, 1993. n.p. ISBN 0-399-21991-9. (394.2 Geo).
Target Audience: Grades 4-6; Ages 9-11

Although the length and information in this book make it appropriate for primary readers, the time period makes the book more appropriate for slightly older readers. George's carefully researched text presents a careful blending of information about the Pilgrims and about Squanto, a Pawtuxet Indian, and the Wampanoag community. One hundred and two Pilgrims arrived on the shores of North America in 1620. They endured a severe winter by staying aboard the Mayflower after the captain agreed to delay sailing back to England. By April 1621 the Mayflower was headed back to England, leaving behind the 57 Pilgrims (17 of which were children) who survived the winter. Before long Samoset came to welcome the Pilgrims. A week later he returned with the chief, Massasoit, and Squanto, an Indian that would become the Pilgrims' mentor. Squanto immediately set about showing the Pilgrims how to plant crops and where and how to fish and hunt. He taught some of them to trap lobsters and others to dig up artichokes and to gather cranberries, gooseberries, and nuts. When the harvest of 1621 was larger than the Pilgrims had hoped, they decided to share the bounty with Squanto, Massasoit, and a *few* friends. When the day arrived Massasoit showed up with five deer and many turkeys—and instead of the few guests that the Pilgrims expected, Massasoit brought 90 guests. The Pilgrims were not prepared for so many guests, but they quickly prepared more food, and the celebration stretched for three days. To the Pilgrims, the celebration was a Harvest Feast; to the Native Americans it was a Green Corn Dance. Now it is recognized as the first Thanksgiving.

Connections: Thanksgiving Stories

President George Washington was the first to issue a Thanksgiving proclamation, but it wasn't until President Abraham Lincoln was in office that a day of thanksgiving and praise was proclaimed for the last Thursday in November. Later the day was moved to the third Thursday in November. Many families in the United States celebrate the holiday each year. Thanksgiving is the focus of many stories for young readers. A traditional Thanksgiving song has been illustrated by Iris Van Rynbach in *Over the River and Through the Wood* (Little, 1989). Watercolors bring life to the song, which is included (in the key of C).

A Thanksgiving story first published in 1881 has been reissued with illustrations by Michael McCurdy. *An Old-Fashioned Thanksgiving* by Louisa May Alcott (Holiday, 1989) tells the story of a family of seven active children who find themselves alone while their parents are away. The children prepare a traditional holiday feast with several exciting episodes.

A picture book depicting a traditional Thanksgiving holiday is Wendy Watson's *Thanksgiving at Our House* (Clarion, 1991). The village people in Watson's book are charming, and the illustrations are filled with fall colors and verses that narrate the gathering of the friendly group enjoying an elaborate feast.

Less traditional is a humorous Thanksgiving story written by Eileen Spinelli *Thanksgiving at the Tappletons'* (HarperCollins,

1992). The Tappletons come together for a huge potluck feast each year on Thanksgiving. This year members of the family find that they are unable to contribute their usual part of the meal: pet rabbits eat the salad makings, and the turkey accidently falls in the pond. The family discovers that being together is cause enough for being thankful, and together they eat liverwurst and cheese sandwiches. *Happy Thanksgiving Rebus* by David A. Adler (Viking, 1991) presents a tale featuring Thanksgiving traditions and contemporary customs. A translation of the rebus is included.

Trains

Ammon, Richard. **Trains at Work.** Illustrated with photographs by Darrell Peterson and Richard Ammon. Atheneum, 1993. n.p. ISBN 0-689-31740-9. (625.1 Amm).
Target Audience: Grades K-3; Ages 5-8

Box cars, hopper cars, and powerful engines are just three of the components that are featured in Ammon's description of trains. The author depicts what rail workers do and how trains carry products all over the country. Cocoa beans are brought from Latin America to warehouses, where sacks of the beans are loaded onto a boxcar. From this point readers follow the boxcar through switching stations and to its hook-up to a train. The author explains the demise of the caboose, now seen only on local trains, as we follow the cocoa beans on their way to the chocolate plant. After the beans arrive at the factory they are unloaded and stored in tall silos. Meanwhile another train is bringing raw sugar from the Caribbean to a sugar plant, where it is refined into pure sugar. Sugar is transported in covered hopper cars. The sugar and cocoa beans and other ingredients are combined to make chocolate bars, which are loaded into truck trailers. The trailers are loaded onto flat cars. The trailers travel across the continent by train; when they are near their final destination, the trailers are lifted off the flat cars and hooked up to trucks (this type of truck is called a semi) that haul the trailers to their final destination.

Connections: Trains

Various types of train cars are shown and discussed in Ammon's book about working trains. A simple picture book that focuses on freight trains and the types of cars used on them is Donald Crews's *Freight Train* (Greenwillow, 1978). The inspiration for that book came from Crews's many childhood memories of visits to Cottondale, Florida, where trains thundered by his grandparents' home. Other memories involving trains are recounted in tales of the Crews family's visit to Florida: *Bigmama's* (Greenwillow, 1991) and *Shortcut* (Greenwillow, 1992). Other books about trains include Gail Gibbons's *Trains* (Holiday, 1987) and *Train Song* by Diane Siebert, illustrated by Mike Wimmer (Crowell, 1990).

Turtles

Berger, Melvin. **Look Out for Turtles!** Illustrated by Megan Lloyd. Let's-Read-and-Find-Out Science Book series. HarperCollins, 1992. 32 pp. ISBN 0-06-022539-4. (597.92 Ber).
Target Audience: Grades K-3; Ages 5-8

A fascinating look at the remarkable turtle, an animal that can live in many environments, eat almost anything, and range in size from very small to gigantic. Turtles live longer than any other animal. While some land turtles move very slowly, other turtles can swim a mile in less than three minutes. Turtles are thought to have existed for more than 200 million years. The physical characteristics of turtles, especially the hard shell, have contributed to the turtle's ability to survive. Habitats, hibernation, nesting habits, and hatching activities are described in this book, along with information on predators. One turtle is known to have lived 170 years before it was accidentally killed. Among the smallest turtles are the mud turtles, which are 3-6 inches long; the largest turtle is four feet long and weighs an average of 600 pounds. Common characteristics are described, along with information about pollution and its effects on many types of turtles. Factors endangering turtles are also discussed.

Connections: Watching for Turtles

The differences and similarities of turtles and tortoises are explained in Q. L. Pearce's *Why Is a Frog Not a Toad? Discovering the Differences Between Animal Look-Alikes* (Lowell House, 1992). A tortoise is a variety of turtle. In general, a tortoise lives on land, and a turtle spends much of its time in the water. But there are exceptions. Information about the largest tortoises, those on the Galápagos Islands, is the subject of *The Galápagos Tortoise* by Susan Schafer (Dillon, 1992). The Galápagos tortoise, the largest living tortoise, is an endangered species with a protected environment. Schafer focuses on the Galápagos tortoise but also includes general information about turtles and tortoises, their habitats, and lifestyles. Color photographs supplement the text. The Cousteau Society focuses on the life cycle of the green sea turtle in *Turtles* (Simon, 1992). The simply written text is accompanied by clear color photographs. Another photo-filled book about turtles is George Ancona's *Turtle Watch* (Macmillan, 1987).

United States, History

Fisher, Leonard Everett. **Stars and Stripes: Our National Flag.** Illustrated by Leonard Everett Fisher. Holiday, 1993. n.p. ISBN 0-8234-1053-6. (973.7 Fis).

Target Audience: Grades K-3; Ages 5-8

Fifteen American flags that have been used since 1775 are depicted with text that explains the origin and history of each flag. In 1777 the Continental Congress decided that the flag should have 13 stripes, alternating white and red, and 13 white stars on a field of blue. Later the number of 13 stars and stripes was changed to 15. Eventually the pattern was changed to the pattern used today. The 13 stripes would remain constant but the number of white stars increased to match the number of states; with each state admitted to the union another star would be added. The final page of the book shows the current version of Old Glory, with 13 stripes and 50 stars. The format of the book is a series of double-page spreads. On the left page is the illustration of a historic flag. On the right page, the text appears in two parts. At the bottom of the page is the explanation of the origin of the flag in the accompanying illustration; at the top of the text page is a phrase from the 31-word "Pledge of Allegiance." When the book is read from front to back the entire pledge will be read. This book offers an introduction to one of the long-standing traditions observed by citizens of the United States.

Connections: Traditions from History

The tradition of pledging allegiance has been observed and challenged throughout our nation's history. The pledge is just one controversial element of our national heritage. Another is the set of freedoms guaranteed by the Constitution and Bill of Rights. Two of the most readable books about the writing of the Constitution are Betsy Maestro's and Giulio Maestro's *A More Perfect Union: The Story of Our Constitution* (Lothrop, 1987) and Jean Fritz's *Shh! We're Writing the Constitution,* illustrated by Tomie dePaola (Putnam, 1987). Both books give an illustrated view of the events that surrounded the writing of this important document.

The Statue of Liberty evokes feelings of patriotism. The statue has become a symbol of immigrants and immigration to a country of freedom. The origin of the statue is the focus of Eleanor Coerr's *Lady with a Torch*

(HarperCollins, 1986). Coerr tells how the French sculptor Frédéric Auguste Bartholdi planned and built the Statue of Liberty.

Veterinarians

Gibbons, Gail. **Say Woof! The Day of a Country Veterinarian.** Illustrated by Gail Gibbons. Macmillan, 1992. n.p. ISBN 0-02-736781-0. (636.089 Gib).
Target Audience: Grades K-3; Ages 5-8

Taking care of animals' medical needs is the job of a veterinarian. A veterinarian goes to college to learn how to take care of pets and farm animals. Gibbons explains the job of assistants and office workers in a veterinarian's office. The author describes the doctor's work in fixing a parakeet's broken wing; giving a dog a yearly checkup and rabies and distemper shots; and taking care of various other animals, including a kitten, a goat, and a baby groundhog that has an eye infection. Later in the morning the veterinarian must operate on a dog's infected tooth and remove a tumor on a cat's leg. A country veterinarian often spends part of the day making "house calls" to take care of animals too large or ill to bring to the office. The veterinarian takes blood samples to test cows for diseases that would make milk unsafe, checks a horse's lame leg, and gives iron shots to a litter of new pigs. He takes care of a herd of sheep and quickly goes to the aid of a dog hit by a car. This account of a day in the life of a veterinarian is followed by nine suggestions for caring for a pet.

Connections: Careers with Animals

Jennifer Bryant also tells about the life of a veterinarian in *Jane Sayler: Veterinarian* (Childrens Press, 1991). If available, *A Day in the Life of a Veterinarian* by William Jaspersohn (Little, Brown, 1978), can help provide a perspective of how the life of a veterinarian has changed over the years from 1978 to the 1990s. More information about what a veterinarian does can be found in two titles by Susan Kuklin: *Taking My Cat to the Vet* (Bradbury, 1988) and *Taking My Dog to the Vet* (Bradbury, 1988). A field trip to a small animal hospital and a visit to the classroom by a veterinarian will provide additional information to the reader wishing to have more information about this career. Careers associated with animals are part of Sylvia Root Tester's *A Visit to the Zoo* (Childrens Press, 1987) and other more unusual careers involving animals are surveyed in Laurence Pringle's *Batman: Exploring the World of Bats* (Scribner's, 1991), *Bearman: Exploring the World of Black Bears* (Scribner's, 1991), and *Jackal Woman: Exploring the World of Jackals* (Scribner's, 1993). Pringle's books capitalize on photographs to weave descriptions of the respective animal's life cycle and facts about contemporary working scientists who work to study and photograph each of these animals. Readers get much information about the animals themselves, in addition to information about how scientists work and about the methods used to study the animals.

Warthogs

Leslie-Melville, Betty. **Walter Warthog.** Doubleday, 1989. 48 pp. ISBN 0-385-26378-3. (599.73 Les).
Target Audience: Grades 4-6; Ages 9-11
   Leslie-Melville is best known for her efforts to protect the endangered Rothschild giraffes. For 30 years she has lived in Africa, where she and her late husband Jock established the African Fund for Endangered Wildlife. That organization has saved the Rothschild giraffe from extinction. Because of her work with the Rothschild giraffe, her home in Nairobi, Kenya, is known as Giraffe Manor. Giraffes roam on the grounds and sometimes stick their heads in the second floor windows. Walter Warthog came into their lives one day when Leslie-Melville was caring for a baby giraffe. The first warthog that wandered onto the grounds was enormous. He had eight-inch tusks and weighed close to 200 pounds. Warthogs are known as fierce fighters, so at first Leslie-Melville ran away into the house. But eventually she made friends with the warthog, and he became a regular guest at the manor. The Leslie-Melvilles named the warthog Walter after Leslie-Melville's friend Walter Cronkite. The story of the warthog and the author's family is told in an interesting account of the evolution of the relationship developed between the author's family and Walter Warthog.

Connections: Animals in Africa

Before writing the account of Walter the Warthog, Leslie-Melville wrote about her experiences with the Rothschild giraffe. The Rothschild giraffe is the largest of three species of giraffe in Kenya. It is the only species with pure white legs. Leslie-Melville and her late husband Jock were dedicated to saving the Rothschild giraffe from extinction. Read the account of their efforts in *Daisy Rothschild: The Giraffe That Lives with Me* by Betty Leslie-Melville (Doubleday, 1987). Additional information about other giraffes can be found in *Giraffes: The Sentinels of the Savannas* by Helen Roney Sattler (Lothrop, 1989).

In the conclusion to *Walter Warthog,* Leslie-Melville discusses the African Fund for Endangered Wildlife and speaks about her own efforts to save the Rothschild giraffe, the elephant, and the black rhinoceros. She describes the black rhino as the most endangered animal in Africa today. An educational nature center has been opened so that African children can see wildlife. Each month more than 2,500 children visit the center free of charge. Leslie-Melville also discusses the efforts of many people to save Africa's endangered animals. The address for the African Fund for Endangered Animals is 1512 Bolton St., Baltimore, MD 21217.

Those wishing to read more about the fight to save the African elephant will find information in *African Elephants: Giants of the Land* by Dorothy Hinshaw Patent (Holiday, 1991). The photographs by Oria Douglas-Hamilton add much to the text, particularly in the discussion of the differences between African and Asian elephants. The focus of the book is on African elephants: where they live, their family units, and the threats to their existence. In the final chapter Patent pleads with readers to do everything "we can to help these magnificent animals survive." A photograph of a pile of ivory is captioned with a reminder that "Each pair of tusks means a dead elephant." Patent's book has a good index, which makes it an excellent addition to research materials.

Washington, D.C.

Hilton, Suzanne. **A Capital Capital City, 1790-1814.** Atheneum, 1992. 156 pp. ISBN 0-689-31641-0. (975.3 Hil). (Photograph of the jacket is courtesy of the publisher and is reprinted with the permission of Macmillan Children's Book Group.)

Target Audience: Grades 4-6; Ages 9-11

Pierre L'Enfant, a French architect, was hired to design the "Federal City." Because his ideas were not accepted by all those involved, he was fired, and he returned to France. Other designers, including Benjamin Banneker, adapted L'Enfant's plans and completed the city's design. However, there were many problems in getting the city built. President Washington died and other presidents followed. Workers were hard to find, and many would not come to the new city, where the comforts of life were definitely lacking. Hilton's account chronicles the city's development through Thomas Jefferson's presidency (he did not live for very long in the president's house in Washington, D.C. but had couriers bring his messages to his residence, Monticello). The city began to develop and was eventually administered by a mayor. The city became the home of President James Madison and his wife, Dolley Madison. During Madison's presidency, the city was attacked by the British and partially destroyed by fire. The burning of Washington, D.C., caused Americans to band together to defend their country.

Connections: The Presidents and the Building Years

The original site of the nation's capital city was 10 acres of swampland among thick forests and corn fields. It was years before the city became a viable part of the nation. Hilton's title gives a perspective of the city during the nation's early years, focusing on the building of the city. Many presidents' biographies chronicle the same events in relation to the lives of the presidents.

Two of the most important contributors to the building of the city of Washington were presidents George Washington and James Madison. Stories of their lives provide interesting collaborative readings for Hilton's title. Jean Fritz's *The Great Little Madison* (Putnam, 1989) presents the events surrounding the British attack on the city of Washington and the subsequent events during Madison's presidency.

James Madison and Dolley Madison and Their Times (Pippin, 1992), a shorter and somewhat less comprehensive biography by Robert Quackenbush, details the major events in the lives of James and Dolley Madison. Patricia Ryon Quiri focuses on Dolley Madison's role as first lady in *Dolley Madison* (Watts, 1993).

James Cross Giblin's *George Washington: A Picture Book Biography* (Scholastic, 1992) includes the important dates in Washington's life, from youth to death, but focuses on his life as a politician. Not much is told about Washington's personal life or the people around him. Other biographies about Washington include *Washington* by William Jay Jacobs (Scribner's, 1991) and *George Washington: Leader of a New Nation* by Mary Pope Osborne (Dial, 1991).

Whales, Endangered

Kraus, Scott, and Kenneth Mallory. **The Search for the Right Whale.** Illustrated with photographs. Face to Face with Science series. Crown, 1993. 36 pp. ISBN 0-517-57844-1. (599.5 Kra).
Target Audience: Grades 4-6; Ages 9-11

This book recounts the history of whaling and the demise of the right whale. The earliest whaling crews hunted the right whale almost to extinction. They were so scarce that alternative species of whales were hunted in the 1700s. In the 1980s a team of scientists from the New England Aquarium in Boston began surveying and studying a small group of North American right whales, one of the rarest species. By 1991 the scientists had followed some of the whales for more than 10 years. The researchers assembled a right whale catalog. The catalog includes photographs of the whales with dates of sightings as well as drawings and statistics. This log will enable other researchers to identify the whales and to note sightings. Scientists were not the only ones to contribute to the catalog; sailors on commercial ships, fishermen, and people in sailboats also sent photographs of right whales to the research team at the New England Aquarium. Film contributed by the Georgia Department of Natural Resources contributed evidence that verified migration patterns. Private airplane pilots also have assisted in air surveys almost every winter since 1984. The work of more than 100 volunteers and staff members has contributed to the research since 1980.

Connections: Where Are the Sea Animals? Are They Endangered?

Joanne Ryder's *Winter Whale* (Morrow, 1991) takes readers on an imaginative journey to the tropical seas where humpback whales go for the winter. The life of whales in southern waters is not always tranquil. A fictional account of a girl and her parents who spot a humpback whale in distress is told in *Whale* by Judy Allen (Candlewick, 1992).

In Allen's book the general plight of whales is discussed. A note from the author suggests that letters requesting more information about efforts to save whales be sent to Save the Whales, P.O. Box 3650, Washington, DC 20007. Greenpeace USA and the World Wildlife Federation are two other organizations that work to save whales. Greenpeace distributes a newsletter, *Peace Three.* The address for Greenpeace USA, Inc., is 1436 U St., NW, Washington, DC 20009. The address for the World Wildlife Federation, U.S., is 1250 24th St., NW, Washington, DC 20037. The WWF sends children fact sheets about animals; it also sells newsletters, atlases, books, and other educational materials through a catalog.

Whales are not the only sea creatures that need protection. Seals are among the sea creatures whose existence is threatened. At the center of *Seals* by Eric S. Grace (Sierra, 1991) is a world map that shows the locations of true seals, eared seals, fur seals, sea lions, and walruses. Charts and illustrations team with the 64 pages of text to give much information about the various types of seals, the life of seals in cold regions, and the life of seals underwater. Seals' adaptation to their environment is discussed, as are what seals hunt and what they eat, how they keep warm, and the animals who hunt them. Efforts to protect the seal are discussed.

Read about other sea creatures in *Whales and Other Creatures of the Sea* by Joyce Milton (Random, 1993); *Sharks and Other Creatures of the Deep* by Philip Steele (Dorling, 1991); *Dolphins* by Sharon Bokoske and Margaret Davidson (Random, 1993), a book in the Step into Reading series; *Seals, Sea Lions and Walruses* by Dorothy Hinshaw Patent (Holiday, 1990); and *Where Are My Puffins, Whales, and Seals?* by Ron Hirschi (Bantam, 1992).

Whales, History

Carrick, Carol. **Whaling Days.** Illustrated with woodcuts by David Frampton. Clarion, 1993. 40 pp. ISBN 0-395-50948-3. (639.2 Car).
Target Audience: Grades 4-6; Ages 9-11

Frampton's woodcuts give an old-time feeling to this survey of the whaling industry. In the early 1600s the New England settlers learned to hunt whales from Native Americans, who harpooned whales from their canoes. From whales they obtained food, oil that was produced when the blubber was cooked, and whalebone that was used for fishing rods, hoops, and ladies' corsets. As settlers moved down the coast, so did whaling. A type of whale known as the "right whale" became scarce, and by the 1700s the Atlantic right whales had almost disappeared. In 1712 sperm whales became valued for spermaceti, pure, clear oil contained in a hollow area in the whales' enormous heads. When the oil was exposed to air, the oil hardened into a waxy substance that was valued for making candles. Whaling became a new world industry. Oil and whalebone were exported to England. Whaling was an important part of life in early New England. By 1859 petroleum had become a more important source of oil in the United States, and it was much cheaper than whale oil. The importance of whaling in this country declined. However, other countries continued to hunt whales, and many species almost vanished from the northern oceans. So many whales were killed by 1946 that 17 nations formed the International Whaling Commission to regulate the killing of whales. Now whaling is prohibited in the United States, and other materials are used to make soap, paint, varnish, cosmetics, margarine, and lubricants for fine machinery. However, other countries still use whale meat for food and use the meat and bone in animal food and fertilizer. Many people are becoming more and more concerned about the endangered whales. A glossary of whaling terms, a selected bibliography, and an index are included.

Connections: Whales, Whales, Whales

A very simple, lyrical book about whales by Tony Johnston, *Whale Song* (Putnam, 1987), could introduce the topic of whales and the beauty of their existence. Another poetic look at whales includes poems collected by Myra Cohn Livingston in *If You Ever Meet a Whale* (Holiday, 1992). The ultimate in information books about whales might be *Whale* by Vassili Papastavrou (Knopf, 1993). Papastavrou's book, a volume in the Eyewitness series, also includes information about other ocean animals, including seals, sea lions, dolphins, porpoises, and walruses.

Books that give additional information about whales, whaling, and other sea animals include Dorothy Hinshaw Patent's *Killer Whales,* illustrated by John K. B. Ford (Holiday, 1993); Joyce Milton's *Whales and Other Creatures of the Sea,* illustrated by Jim Deal (Random, 1993); and Scott Kraus's and Kenneth Mallory's *The Search for the Right Whale* (Crown, 1993). An account of a humpback whale that swam through the San Francisco Bay and upstream to dangerously low waters is told in Toni Knapp's *The Six Bridges of Humphrey the Whale,* illustrated by Craig Brown (Roberts Rinehart, 1989). The story of the same whale is told in *Humphrey the Wrong-Way Whale* by Kathryn A. Goldner and Carole G. Vogel (Dillon, 1987) and *Humphrey, the Lost Whale* by Wendy Tokuda (Heine, 1988). Tokuda's book is featured in a segment of Reading Rainbow, a public television series that promotes books and reading. As part of the Reading Rainbow segment, the book is read aloud and the host is shown accompanying a crew on a whale watch expedition. The whales they are attempting to spot are humpback whales, but the trip takes place off the Atlantic coast rather than the Pacific coast, where Humphrey swam.

Bruce McMillan uses diagrams, color photographs, and well-written text to document a whale watch. McMillan's photo-essay, *Going on a Whale Watch* (Scholastic, 1992), focuses on humpback whales and fin whales. McMillan's skillfully drawn diagrams and photographs follow the whale under the water—a view most whale watchers never see.

Windows

Giblin, James Cross. **Let There Be Light: A Book About Windows.**
Illustrated with photographs and prints. Crowell, 1988. 162 pp.
ISBN 0-690-04693-6. (690 Gib).
Target Audience: Grades 4-6; Ages 9-11

Before there were windows, uncovered holes in walls admitted light and fresh air into buildings. Windows that block out the elements and admit sunshine came later. Theories about how ancient Greeks and Romans provided for light in their magnificent structures are examined. Some early windows were made of clear, freshwater ice; others were made of the translucent gut of a seal or walrus. The Japanese created light-filled rooms with the use of translucent *shoji* paper that covered windows and doors. And then there were magnificent pieces of painted glass, enameled and fired in a kiln.

Windows became so prestigious that the British taxed them in 1697. America established its own glass-making industry in 1739.

Often when log cabins were built the builders did not cut out the windows. When coverings for the windows could be obtained, the openings were cut. Some of the first windows were covered with oil paper. Wood shutters protected the oil paper coverings from wind, rain, and snow. More prosperous builders made larger openings and inserted glazed windows. Some modern structures, such as the R. J. Reynolds Industries building in Winston-Salem, North Carolina, and the Garden Grove Community Church in Garden Grove, California, are completely covered with reflective glass. The Garden Grove church is known as the "Crystal Cathedral."

This book contains much information about lights, windows, and houses made of glass. Few will wish to read the entire text aloud, but sections will stimulate much interest. Chapter 1, "To See the World Outside" is particularly interesting; it recounts the beginnings of a modern world filled with windows. Chapter 8, "The Crystal Palaces," is also quite interesting; it recounts the development of buildings with windows in the United States, beginning with dwellings built by settlers in 1620 at Plymouth, Massachusetts. From tarpaper-covered openings to a magnificent crystal palace in New York, this chapter covers some of the most interesting developments in the history of glass, particularly in the United States. Photographs and prints illustrate the text.

Connections: James Cross Giblin's Histories of Everyday Objects

James Cross Giblin has researched the history of several everyday objects and subjects from chimney sweeps to Santa Claus. Chimney sweeps are examined in *Chimney Sweeps: Yesterday and Today,* illustrated by Margot Tomes (Harper, 1982). Building skyscrapers is the subject of *The Skyscraper Book* (Harper, 1981), and the history of Santa Claus is examined in *The Truth About Santa Claus* (Harper, 1986). Information about milk and the history of the pasteurized, packaged milk industry is told in *Milk: The Fight for Purity* (Harper, 1986). In *From Hand to Mouth: Or, How We Invented Knives, Forks, Spoons, and Chopsticks & the Table Manners to Go with Them* (Crowell, 1987), the history of eating utensils and many other utensils used to serve and eat food are described. Giblin's books are rather detailed, but each chapter stands alone with interesting information. Many of the individual chapters provide excellent read-alouds.

Wolves

Simon, Seymour. **Wolves.** HarperCollins, 1993. n.p. ISBN 0-06-022531-9. (599.7 Sim).
Target Audience: Grades 4-6; Ages 9-11

Portrayed as villains in many folk and fairy tales wolves and the mystic that surrounds them are examined in this explanation of what wolves eat, what their big eyes and noses are for, and how wolves use their senses, natural instincts, and sophisticated social structure to survive in nature. Wolves are compared to dogs and lions in terms of their attributes. Wolves can be almost any color and eat almost anything they can catch—from moose to mouse. Various types of wolves are discussed from the red wolf (*Canis rufus*) to the hybrids (wolf-dogs or wolf-coyotes). Every aspect of the wolf's existence is included in Simon's narrative: color, attributes, size, howl, social behavior, the role of male as hunter and female as nurturer. The final page portrays the wolf as an endangered species with only a few hundred still living in the northern hemisphere compared with the thousands of wolves that roamed the same area over 200 years ago.

Connections: Wolves and Their Image in Books

R. D. Lawrence attempts to dispel some of the mysteries and common misperceptions that surround wolves in his *Wolves* (Little, Brown/Sierra, 1990). The early chapters examine the family relationships among wolves and others in the pack. The history of wolves is discussed, and maps show their distribution throughout Europe, Asia, and North America. Interesting questions are answered in regard to wolves: Why do wolves howl? Who leads the wolf pack? How do wolves avoid fights? Answers to those questions and many other interesting bits of information are included by Lawrence, including information about Native Americans' respect for the wolf. The Pawnee of Kansas and Nebraska named stars after the wolf and the

Cree of Canada believed that heavenly wolves visited Earth when the northern lights shone in winter. Many Native Americans named themselves after the wolf in part because they were impressed by the animal's strength but also because of its courage and its ability to hunt. In Paul Goble's retelling of a literary Native American folktale, *Dream Wolf* (Dial, 1991) the reverence the Native Americans have for the wolf is a central element of the tale. Thomas Locker's book, *The Land of Gray Wolf* (Dial, 1991) presents a majestic portrait of the wolf, as does Dorothy Hinshaw Patent's *Gray Wolf, Red Wolf* (Clarion, 1990).

Three other authors give information about the wolf in a format that will appeal especially to primary-aged readers. Mary Ling's *Amazing Wolves, Dogs & Foxes*, illustrated by Jerry Young (Knopf, 1991), is part of the Eyewitness Junior series; Joyce Milton's *Wild, Wild Wolves*, illustrated by Larry Schwinger (Random, 1992), is in Random's Step into Reading series; and Gail Gibbons's *Wolves* (Holiday, 1994) includes information on gray wolves (timber wolves)—their lives in a pack and their territories that sometimes are as large as 500 square miles. Information about the red wolf and the endangered status of all wolves is included along with four myths and legends about wolves and a list of curious facts.

Compare the portrayal of the wolf in the titles cited above and the many fairy tales that often portray the wolf as a sly and evil creature. In *Little Red Riding Hood*, the wolf preys on a grandmother and a young girl. In *The Three Little Pigs*, the wolf eats two of the pigs and terrorizes the third. Read versions of *The Wolf and the Seven Little Kids* and other folk tales in which the wolf is a major character.

Worms

Glaser, Linda. **Wonderful Worms.** Illustrated by Loretta Krupinski. Millbrook, 1992. n.p. ISBN 1-56294-703-6. (595.1 Gla).
Target Audience: Grades K-3; Ages 5-8

A simple text accompanies gloriously executed illustrations showing worms in their underground habitat. Readers find out where worms live, what they do (dig), how they move through the earth, and how they help the ecological balance. The final two pages elaborate with "Facts About Wonderful Worms." Several pictures in the book are sure to appeal to readers who like "yucky" topics.

Connections: Worms and Other Hard-to-Love Creatures

More information about how worms help the environment is given in *Squirmy Wormy Composters* by Bobbie Kalman and Janine Schaub (Crabtree, 1992). From this book readers will learn more about how worms eat, how they help plants grow, how to start a vermi-composter using worms, harvesting the vermi-compost, and growing more worms. After reading these worm books, share poems about worms. Favorites include "Willie Ate a Worm," in *Rolling Harvey Down the Hill* by Jack Prelutsky, illustrated by Victoria Chess (Greenwillow, 1980); and "The Worm" by Ralph Bergengren, in *The Random House Book of Poetry for Children*, edited by Jack Prelutsky, illustrated by Arnold Lobel (Random, 1983). There are many other creatures that some of us find hard to love; information about several of them are included in the National Wildlife Federation's *The Unhuggables: The Truth About Snakes, Slugs, Skunks, Spiders, and Other Animals That Are Hard to Love* (National Wildlife, 1988).

Wounds and Injuries

Berger, Melvin. **Ouch! A Book About Cuts, Scratches, and Scrapes.** Illustrated by Pat Stewart. Lodestar, 1991. n.p. ISBN 0-525-67323-7. (617.1 Ber).
Target Audience: Grades K-3; Ages 5-8
Realistic drawings illustrate the healing process as a cut bleeds, platelets help the blood to clot, the scab forms, white blood cells clean up the wound, and the new skin forms and forces the scab to loosen and fall off. This book offers a straightforward introduction to the properties of blood and the purpose of red blood cells, white blood cells, and platelets. Even the make-up of "pus" is discussed and explained.

Connections: Blood System

In 1989, Crowell released a new edition of the 1967 title by Paul Showers, *A Drop of Blood* (Crowell, 1989). With Steve Parker's *The Heart and Blood* (Watts, 1989), it will serve as an introduction to the blood system. Other information about the circulatory system can be found in general books about the human body.

FOCUS BOOKS ARRANGED BY AUTHOR

Each focus book is listed alphabetically by author. The subject heading under which the title may be found follows the title in parentheses.

Aaseng, Nathan. *Better Mousetraps: Product Improvements That Led to Success.* (Inventions and Inventors)

———. *Close Calls: From the Brink of Ruin to Business Success.* (Business)

Alexander, Sally Hobart. *Mom Can't See Me.* (Blindness)

Aliki. *Dinosaur Bones.* (Dinosaurs)

———. *Fossils Tell of Long Ago.* (Fossils)

Ammon, Richard. *Growing Up Amish.* (Amish)

———. *Trains at Work.* (Trains)

Ancona, George. *Man and Mustang.* (Horses)

Ashabranner, Brent. *People Who Make a Difference.* (Helping Others)

Bailey, Jill. *Frogs in Three Dimensions.* (Frogs)

Banish, Roslyn, with Jennifer Jordan-Wong. *A Forever Family.* (Adoption)

Bare, Colleen Stanley. *This Is a House.* (Houses)

———. *Who Comes to the Water Hole?* (Animals, African)

Bash, Barbara. *Urban Roosts: Where Birds Nest in the City.* (Birds)

Bauer, Marion Dane. *What's Your Story? A Young Person's Guide to Writing Fiction.* (Authorship)

Behrens, June. *Dolphins.* (Dolphins)

Berger, Melvin. *Look Out for Turtles.* (Turtles)

———. *Ouch! A Book About Cuts, Scratches, and Scrapes.* (Wounds and Injuries)

Bernhard, Emery. *Dragonfly.* (Insects)

Branley, Franklyn M. *Shooting Stars.* (Meteors)

Brown, Don. *Ruth Law Thrills a Nation.* (Flight)

Burleigh, Robert. *Flight: The Journey of Charles Lindbergh.* (Flight, Aviators)

Carrick, Carol. *Whaling Days.* (Whales, History)

Cerullo, Mary M. *Sharks: Challengers of the Deep.* (Sharks)

Cohen, Daniel, and Susan Cohen. *Where to Find Dinosaurs Today.* (Dinosaurs)

Cole, Joanna. *The Magic School Bus on the Ocean Floor.* (Ocean)

Focus Books Arranged by Author / 147

Cone, Molly. *Come Back, Salmon.* (Pollution)

Cummings, Pat, compiler and editor. *Talking with Artists: Conversations with Victoria Chess, Pat Cummings, Leo Dillon and Diane Dillon, Richard Egielski, Lois Ehlert, Lisa Campbell Ernst, Tom Feelings, Steven Kellogg, Jerry Pinkney, Amy Schwartz, Lane Smith, Chris Van Allsburg, and David Wiesner.* (Artists)

Ehrlich, Amy. *The Story of Hanukkah.* (Hanukkah)

Fisher, Leonard Everett. *Stars and Stripes: Our National Flag.* (United States, History)

Fritz, Jean. *Just a Few Words, Mr. Lincoln: The Story of the Gettysburg Address.* (Gettysburg Address)

George, Jean Craighead. *One Day in the Tropical Rain Forest.* (Rain Forest)

———. *The First Thanksgiving.* (Thanksgiving)

Gibbons, Gail. *Beacons of Light: Lighthouses.* (Lighthouses)

———. *Catch the Wind! All About Kites.* (Kites)

———. *Dinosaurs, Dragonflies & Diamonds: All About Natural History Museums.* (Museums)

———. *Easter.* (Easter)

———. *Great St. Lawrence Seaway.* (Saint Lawrence Seaway)

———. *Pirates: Robbers of the High Seas.* (Pirates)

———. *Recycle! A Handbook for Kids.* (Recycling)

———. *Say Woof! The Day of a Country Veterinarian.* (Veterinarians)

———. *Spiders.* (Spiders)

———. *Surrounded by Sea: Life on a New England Fishing Island.* (Fishing)

Giblin, James Cross. *Let There Be Light: A Book About Windows.* (Windows)

Gilks, Helen. *Bears.* (Bears)

Glaser, Linda. *Wonderful Worms.* (Worms)

Goble, Paul, and Dorothy Goble. *Brave Eagle's Account of the Fetterman Fight: 21 December 1866.* (Native Americans, History)

Goedecke, Christopher J. *The Wind Warrior: The Training of a Karate Champion.* (Karate)

Greenberg, Keith Elliot. *Erik Is Homeless.* (Homeless)

Grosshandler, Janet. *Winning Ways in Soccer.* (Soccer)

Hackwell, W. John. *Diving to the Past: Recovering Ancient Wrecks.* (Shipwrecks)

Hariton, Anca. *Egg Story.* (Chickens)

Harrison, Ted. *O Canada.* (Canada)

Haskins, James. *Amazing Grace: The Story Behind the Song.* (Music, Origin of Hymns)

Haskins, Jim. *One More River to Cross: The Stories of Twelve Black Americans.* (African Americans)

Hewett, Joan. *Hector Lives in the United States Now: The Story of a Mexican-American Child.* (Mexican Americans)

Hilton, Suzanne. *A Capital Capital City, 1790-1814.* (Washington, D.C.)

Horvatic, Anne. *Simple Machines.* (Machines)

Hoyt-Goldsmith, Diane. *Pueblo Storyteller.* (Pueblos)

Irvine, Georgeanne. *The Visit of Two Giant Pandas at the San Diego Zoo.* (Pandas)

Jacobs, Francine. *The Tainos: The People Who Welcomed Columbus.* (Tainos)

Jacobs, William Jay. *Ellis Island: New Hope in a New Land.* (Ellis Island)

Jakobsen, Kathy. *My New York.* (New York City)

Janeczko, Paul B., selector. *The Place My Words Are Looking For: What Poets Say About and Through Their Work.* (Poets)

Johnson, Neil. *All in a Day's Work: Twelve Americans Talk About Their Jobs.* (Careers)

———. *Fire & Silk: Flying in a Hot Air Balloon.* (Ballooning)

Jones, Charlotte Foltz. *Mistakes That Worked.* (Inventions, Accidental)

Jordan, Sandra. *Christmas Tree Farm.* (Farming, Trees)

Kahney, Regina. *The Glow-in-the-Dark Book of Animal Skeletons.* (Skeleton)

Keegan, Marcia. *Pueblo Boy: Growing Up in Two Worlds.* (Pueblos)

Kitchen, Bert. *And So They Build.* (Animal Shelters)

Kraus, Scott, and Kenneth Mallory. *The Search for the Right Whale.* (Whales)

Kuklin, Susan. *Fighting Fires.* (Firefighters)

Lang, Aubrey. *Eagles.* (Birds)

Lankford, Mary D. *Hopscotch Around the World.* (Hopscotch)

Lasky, Kathryn. *Monarchs.* (Butterflies)

Leedy, Loreen. *Blast Off to Earth! A Look at Geography.* (Geography)

———. *Messages in the Mailbox: How to Write a Letter.* (Letter Writing)

———. *Postcards from Pluto: A Tour of the Solar System.* (Solar System)

Lemmon, Tess. *Apes.* (Apes)

Leslie-Melville, Betty. *Walter Warthog.* (Warthog)

Littlewood, Valerie. *Scarecrow!* (Scarecrows)

MacCarthy, Patricia. *Herds of Words.* (Animal Words)

Maestro, Betsy, and Giulio Maestro. *A More Perfect Union: The Story of Our Constitution.* (Constitutional Convention)

McFarland, Cynthia. *Cows in the Parlor: A Visit to a Dairy Farm.* (Farming, Dairy)

McGovern, Ann. *Swimming with Sea Lions and Other Adventures in the Galápagos Islands.* (Galápagos Islands)

Milton, Joyce. *Bats: Creatures of the Night.* (Bats)

Morey, Janet Nomura, and Wendy Dunn. *Famous Asian Americans.* (Asian Americans)

———. *Famous Mexican Americans.* (Mexican Americans)

Moser, Barry. *Fly! A Brief History of Flight Illustrated.* (Flight, History)

Munro, Roxie. *Blimps.* (Airships)

O'Connor, Karen. *Dan Thuy's New Life in America.* (Immigrants)

Paladino, Catherine. *Our Vanishing Farm Animals: Saving America's Rare Breeds.* (Animals, Endangered)

Pallotta, Jerry. *The Extinct Alphabet Book.* (Animals, Extinct)

Patent, Dorothy Hinshaw. *Feathers.* (Birds)

Pearce, Q. L. *Why Is a Frog Not a Toad? Discovering the Differences Between Animal Look-Alikes.* (Animals, Differences Among)

Peeples, H. I. *Where Does This Come From? Ice Cream.* (Ice Cream)

Pinkney, Andrea Davis. *Seven Candles for Kwanzaa.* (Kwanzaa)

Rochelle, Belinda. *Witnesses to Freedom: Young People Who Fought for Civil Rights.* (Civil Rights)

Ryden, Hope. *Your Cat's Wild Cousins.* (Cats)

Schwartz, David M. *If You Made a Million.* (Money)

Sewall, Marcia. *People of the Breaking Day.* (Native Americans, History)

Simon, Seymour. *Autumn Across America.* (Seasons)

———. *Wolves.* (Wolves)

Skurzynski, Gloria. *Here Comes the Mail.* (Postal Service)

Sneve, Virginia Driving Hawk. *The Navajos: A First Americans Book.* (Navajos)

Sullivan, George. *Racing Indy Cars.* (Automobile Racing)

Taylor, Barbara. *Pond Life.* (Ponds)

150 / Seeking Information

Taylor, David. *Animal Magicians: Mystery and Magic of the Animal World.* (Animal World, Mysteries)

Wexler, Jerome. *Wonderful Pussy Willows.* (Pussy Willow)

FOCUS BOOKS ARRANGED BY TITLE

Each focus book is listed alphabetically by title in this list. The subject under which the title is entered in the main section of this chapter is in the parentheses immediately following the title and author's name.

All in a Day's Work: Twelve Americans Talk About Their Jobs by Neil Johnson. (Careers)

Amazing Grace: The Story Behind the Song by James Haskins. (Music, Origins of Hymns)

And So They Build by Bert Kitchen. (Animal Shelters)

Animal Magicians: Mystery and Magic of the Animal World by David Taylor. (Animal World, Mysteries)

Apes by Tess Lemmon. (Apes)

Autumn Across America by Seymour Simon. (Seasons)

Bats: Creatures of the Night by Joyce Milton. (Bats)

Beacons of Light: Lighthouses by Gail Gibbons. (Lighthouses)

Bears by Helen Gilks. (Bears)

Better Mousetraps: Product Improvements That Led to Success by Nathan Aaseng. (Inventions and Inventors)

Blast Off to Earth! A Look at Geography by Loreen Leedy. (Geography)

Blimps by Roxie Munro. (Airships)

Brave Eagle's Account of the Fetterman Fight: 21 December 1866 by Paul Goble and Dorothy Goble. (Native Americans, History)

A Capital Capital City, 1790-1814 by Suzanne Hilton. (Washington, D.C.)

Catch the Wind! All About Kites by Gail Gibbons. (Kites)

Christmas Tree Farm by Sandra Jordan. (Farming, Trees)

Close Calls: From the Brink of Ruin to Business Success by Nathan Aaseng. (Business)

Come Back, Salmon by Molly Cone. (Pollution)

Focus Books Arranged by Title / 151

Cows in the Parlor: A Visit to a Dairy Farm by Cynthia McFarland. (Farming, Dairy)

Dan Thuy's New Life in America by Karen O'Connor. (Immigrants)

Dinosaur Bones by Aliki. (Dinosaurs)

Dinosaurs, Dragonflies & Diamonds: All About Natural History Museums by Gail Gibbons. (Museums)

Diving to the Past: Recovering Ancient Wrecks by W. John Hackwell. (Shipwrecks)

Dolphins by June Behrens. (Dolphins)

Dragonfly by Emery Bernhard. (Insects)

Eagles by Aubrey Lang. (Birds)

Easter by Gail Gibbons. (Easter)

Egg Story by Anca Hariton. (Chickens)

Ellis Island: New Hope in a New Land by William Jay Jacobs. (Ellis Island)

Erik Is Homeless by Keith Elliot Greenberg. (Homeless)

Extinct Alphabet Book by Jerry Pallotta. (Animals, Extinct)

Famous Asian Americans by Janet Nomura Morey and Wendy Dunn. (Asian Americans)

Famous Mexican Americans by Janet Morey and Wendy Dunn. (Mexican Americans)

Feathers by Dorothy Hinshaw Patent. (Birds)

Fighting Fires by Susan Kuklin. (Firefighters)

Fire & Silk: Flying in a Hot Air Balloon by Neil Johnson. (Ballooning)

First Thanksgiving by Jean Craighead George. (Thanksgiving)

Flight: The Journey of Charles Lindbergh by Robert Burleigh. (Flight, Aviators)

Fly! A Brief History of Flight Illustrated by Barry Moser. (Flight, History)

Forever Family by Roslyn Banish with Jennifer Jordan-Wong. (Adoption)

Fossils Tell of Long Ago by Aliki. (Fossils)

Frogs in Three Dimensions by Jill Bailey. (Frogs)

Glow-in-the-Dark Book of Animal Skeletons by Regina Kahney. (Skeleton)

Great St. Lawrence Seaway by Gail Gibbons. (Saint Lawrence Seaway)

Growing Up Amish by Richard Ammon. (Amish)

Hector Lives in the United States Now: The Story of a Mexican-American Child by Joan Hewett. (Mexican Americans)

Herds of Words by Patricia MacCarthy. (Animal Words)

152 / Seeking Information

Here Comes the Mail by Gloria Skurzynski. (Postal Service)

Hopscotch Around the World by Mary D. Lankford. (Hopscotch)

If You Made a Million by David M. Schwartz. (Money)

Just a Few Words, Mr. Lincoln: The Story of the Gettysburg Address by Jean Fritz. (Gettysburg Address)

Kwanzaa by Deborah M. Newton Chocolate. (Kwanzaa)

Let There Be Light: A Book About Windows by James Cross Giblin. (Windows)

Look Out for Turtles by Melvin Berger. (Turtles)

Magic School Bus on the Ocean Floor by Joanna Cole. (Ocean)

Man and Mustang by George Ancona. (Horses)

Messages in the Mailbox: How to Write a Letter by Loreen Leedy. (Letter Writing)

Mistakes That Worked by Charlotte Foltz Jones. (Inventions, Accidental)

Mom Can't See Me by Sally Hobart Alexander. (Blindness)

Monarchs by Kathryn Lasky. (Butterflies)

More Perfect Union: The Story of Our Constitution by Betsy Maestro and Giulio Maestro. (Constitutional Convention, United States)

My New York by Kathy Jakobsen. (New York City)

Navajos: A First Americans Book by Virginia Driving Hawk Sneve. (Navajos)

O Canada by Ted Harrison. (Canada)

One Day in the Tropical Rain Forest by Jean Craighead George. (Rain Forest)

One More River to Cross: The Stories of Twelve Black Americans by Jim Haskins. (African Americans)

Ouch! A Book About Cuts, Scratches, and Scrapes by Melvin Berger. (Wounds and Injuries)

Our Vanishing Farm Animals: Saving America's Rare Breeds by Catherine Paladino. (Animals, Endangered)

People of the Breaking Day by Marcia Sewall. (Native Americans, History)

People Who Make a Difference by Brent Ashabranner. (Helping Others)

Pirates: Robbers of the High Seas by Gail Gibbons. (Pirates)

Place My Words Are Looking For: What Poets Say About and Through Their Work by Paul B. Janeczko, selector. (Poets)

Pond Life by Barbara Taylor. (Ponds)

Postcards from Pluto: A Tour of the Solar System by Loreen Leedy. (Solar System)

Pueblo Boy: Growing Up in Two Worlds by Marcia Keegan. (Pueblos)

Pueblo Storyteller by Diane Hoyt-Goldsmith. (Pueblos)

Racing Indy Cars by George Sullivan. (Automobile Racing)

Recycle! A Handbook for Kids by Gail Gibbons. (Recycling)

Ruth Law Thrills a Nation by Don Brown. (Flight)

Say Woof! The Day of a Country Veterinarian by Gail Gibbons. (Veterinarians)

Scarecrow! by Valerie Littlewood. (Scarecrows)

Search for the Right Whale by Scott Kraus and Kenneth Mallory. (Whales)

Seven Candles for Kwanzaa by Andrea Davis Pinkney. (Kwanzaa)

Sharks: Challengers of the Deep by Mary M. Cerullo. (Sharks)

Shooting Stars by Franklyn M. Branley. (Meteors)

Simple Machines by Anne Horvatic. (Machines)

Spiders by Gail Gibbons. (Spiders)

Stars and Stripes: Our National Flag by Leonard Everett Fisher. (United States, History)

Story of Hanukkah by Amy Ehrlich. (Hanukkah)

Surrounded by Sea: Life on a New England Fishing Island by Gail Gibbons. (Fishing)

Swimming with Sea Lions and Other Adventures in the Galápagos Islands by Ann McGovern. (Galápagos Islands)

Tainos: The People Who Welcomed Columbus by Francine Jacobs. (Tainos)

Talking with Artists: Conversations with Victoria Chesso, Pat Cummings, Leo Dillon and Diane Dillon, Richard Egielski, Lois Ehlert, Lisa Campbell Ernst, Tom Feelings, Steven Kellogg, Jerry Pinkney, Amy Schwartz, Lane Smith, Chris Van Allsburg, and David Wiesner by Pat Cummings, compiler and editor. (Artists)

This Is a House by Colleen Stanley Bare. (Houses)

Trains at Work by Richard Ammon. (Trains)

Urban Roosts: Where Birds Nest in the City by Barbara Bash. (Birds)

Visit of Two Giant Pandas at the San Diego Zoo by Georgeanne Irvine. (Pandas)

Walter Warthog by Betty Leslie-Melville. (Warthog)

Whaling Days by Carol Carrick. (Whales, History)

What's Your Story? A Young Person's Guide to Writing Fiction by Marion Dane Bauer. (Authorship)

Where Does This Come From? Ice Cream by H. I. Peeples. (Ice Cream)

Where to Find Dinosaurs Today by Daniel Cohen and Susan Cohen. (Dinosaurs)

Who Comes to the Water Hole? by Colleen Stanley Bare. (Animals, African)

Why Is a Frog Not a Toad? Discovering the Differences Between Animal Look-Alikes by Q. L. Pearce. (Animals, Differences Among)

Wind Warrior: The Training of a Karate Champion by Christopher J. Goedecke. (Karate)

Winning Ways in Soccer by Janet Grosshandler. (Soccer)

Witnesses to Freedom: Young People Who Fought for Civil Rights by Belinda Rochelle. (Civil Rights)

Wolves by Seymour Simon. (Wolves)

Wonderful Pussy Willows by Jerome Wexler. (Pussy Willow)

Wonderful Worms by Linda Glaser. (Worms)

Your Cat's Wild Cousins by Hope Ryden. (Cats)

THREE
Biographies

Biographies tell us about people from the past and the present. They are filled with lively dialogue, joys of discovery, triumphs of the human spirit, new ideas, and reflections on the times and societies in which the subjects lived. The momentous events in each subject's life present opportunities for creative dramatics, such as "You Are There" segments or imaginary conversations between contemporaries. Collaborative reading of biographies about people who were contemporaries, such as the artist Goya and President James Madison, can give meaningful insight into world events during the time in which they lived and can help readers construct conversations between them.

A similar conversation could be written for figures from two different time periods. Theories about what two historical figures might have discussed could lead to a mock conversation. During President Bill Clinton's campaign, his wife, Hillary Rodham Clinton, said she had conversations (in her mind) with the late Eleanor Roosevelt, the wife of President Franklin D. Roosevelt. What would they have said to one another? What other conversations could be constructed? For example, what would Sojourner Truth say to your U.S. senator about the state of civil rights in the United States today? What would Astrid Lindgren, an author and advocate of animal rights, say to Jane Goodall, an anthropologist studying chimpanzees in the depths of Africa?

Most biographies focus on well-known figures from the worlds of entertainment, politics, or history. But biographies are not limited to those individuals. A good biography needs only a subject who is of interest or who has been involved in an incident that is interesting or who has made a significant contribution to the world. Sometimes the person is not well known, and the event becomes the focus. That is true of *Kate Shelley and the Midnight Express* by Margaret K. Wetterer, illustrated by Karen Ritz (Carolrhoda, 1990) and *Keep the Lights Burning, Abbie* by Peter Roop and Connie Roop, illustrated by Peter E. Hanson (Carolrhoda, 1985). Each of these books tells the story of a young woman who exhibited extraordinary courage. Kate Shelley crawled across a washed out railroad bridge in the dark during a storm to warn an oncoming passenger train of the washout. Her courage saved dozens of lives. Abbie Burgess kept the light in a lighthouse burning for several stormy days when her father was away from home and her mother was seriously ill. Her perseverance saved countless ships. Each of these girls would have been forgotten but for her courageous act. It is the act that is the focus of their biographies.

Other biographies focus on people who became famous for what they accomplished: inventors, politicians, presidents, civil rights leaders, and so forth. Biographies about notable people generally fall into two categories: (1) biographies that recount major events from birth to death (or birth to the present) or (2) biographies that focus on accomplishments, saying little about the subject's youth or private life. For example, a biography of President John F. Kennedy might focus on his youth, his college and military careers, his presidency, and his assassination. Another biography might only focus on his accomplishments as president.

In the following list 22 biographies are featured. They have been chosen because they are interesting and because they present opportunities for further reading and exploration. For example, the biography of Sojourner Truth is a natural for sharing during any discussion of slavery, civil rights, or perseverance. Information about Faith Ringgold might spark an interest in quilts, storytelling, growing up in Harlem, or the work of artists. The other biographies listed present similar opportunities for making connections between the subject and other events or areas of interest.

THE BIOGRAPHY BOOKSHELF

Abolitionist:
Truth, Sojourner (1797-1883)

McKissack, Patricia C., and Fredrick McKissack. **Sojourner Truth: Ain't I a Woman?** Illustrated with photographs. Scholastic, 1992. 186 pp. ISBN 0-590-44690-8. (305.5 McK) (B Tru). (Photograph of the jacket is courtesy of the publisher and is reprinted with the permission of Scholastic.)

Target Audience: Grades 4-6; Ages 9-11

Sojourner Truth was born Isabella Van Wagener, a slave, in 1797. Her experiences as a northern slave were somewhat different than those of a southern slave but no less painful or difficult. Her early childhood years were spent under a master who spoke low Dutch. Although he could speak English, he spoke only Dutch around his slaves because if they heard only Dutch they would be unable to communicate with other slaves and therefore be easier to control. Her sisters and brothers were sold to other families. Isabella "Belle" was sold to another family, which abused her, beat her, and gave her little to eat. After more than a year of this abuse, another family bought her; this family treated her much better. It was during her years with this family that her parents, both slaves, died. Belle began to learn about abolitionists.

As with many other topics, Belle always wanted to know more. She was very interested in the idea of freedom.

Over a period of years she was sent from one family to another, but in 1799 a New York state law was passed that said all northern slaves born after July 4, 1799, were to be set free. Women were to be freed at the age of 25; men at the age of 28. By the year 1827, Belle was freed, and in 1850 she dictated her autobiography (she could neither read or write). In that book she shed her slave name and took the name Sojourner Truth. She successfully sued to get back her son, whom she said had been illegally sold into slavery in the South. She sought to protect her children and to keep them as a family, but years of slavery had separated them, and it was difficult for a slave with no schooling to get a job that would pay enough to allow her to keep her children with her.

She began to travel and lecture throughout the country. She spoke about the evils of slavery. One of her most famous speeches—a speech that fused the efforts of women's rights groups with those of the abolitionists—is now called the "Ain't I a Woman?" speech. The circumstances surrounding the delivery of that speech and the text of the speech are contained on pages 112-115 of *Sojourner Truth: Ain't I a Woman?*

Connections: Equal Rights for All

The struggle for freedom and equal rights has spanned decades, from the nineteenth century to today. Books about those whose activities contributed to the civil rights movement include *John Brown and the Fight Against Slavery* by James L. Collins (Millbrook, 1991); *Malcolm X and Black Pride* by Robert Cwiklik (Millbrook, 1991); *Sojourner Truth and the Voice of Freedom* by Jane Shumate (Millbrook, 1991); *Sojourner Truth* by Norman L. Macht (Chelsea, 1992); *W. E. B. DuBois: Crusader for Peace* by Kathryn T. Cryan-Hicks (Discovery, 1991); and *Frederick Douglass: Leader Against Slavery* by Patricia McKissack and Fredrick McKissack (Enslow, 1991). Those who are continuing the fight for equal rights today are the focus of *Jesse Jackson and Political Power* by Teresa Celsi (Millbrook, 1991); *I Am Somebody! A Biography of Jesse Jackson* by James Haskins (Enslow, 1992); *Coretta Scott King: Keeper of the Dream* by Sondra Henry and Emily Taitz (Enslow, 1992); *Nelson Mandela: The Fight Against Apartheid* by Steven Otfinoski (Millbrook, 1992); *Nelson*

Mandela: Voice of Freedom by Libby Hughes (Dillon, 1992); and *Thurgood Marshall: A Life for Justice* by James Haskins (Holt, 1992).

Animal Researcher: Goodall, Jane (1934-)

Lucas, Eileen. **Jane Goodall, Friend of the Chimps.** Illustrated with photographs. Millbrook, 1992. 48 pp. Gateway Biography series. ISBN 1-56294-135-6. (599.8 Luc) (B Goo). (Photograph of the jacket is courtesy of the publisher and is reprinted with the permission of The Millbrook Press.)
Target Audience: Grades 4-6; Ages 9-11

As a one-year-old child, Jane Goodall was given a stuffed toy chimpanzee to celebrate the birth of Jubilee the chimp at the London Zoo. Jane grew up dreaming of seeing the real animals in the jungles and plains of Africa. After she graduated from high school, there was no money for college, so Jane went to secretarial school. She wanted to go to Africa very badly, but she did not know how to arrange it. One day she received a letter from a school friend whose parents lived in Kenya. She saved her money, and by 1957 she had enough to make the three-week trip to Kenya. Once in Africa she traveled to Nairobi to the National Museum of Natural History, where she met Dr. Louis Leakey. She convinced him of her desire to learn about animals, and he gave her a secretarial position. Months later Jane Goodall traveled with Dr. Leakey and his wife to Tanzania, where they intended to find and study fossils. Dr. Leakey introduced Jane to some areas in the jungle of Tanzania where chimpanzees lived. Dr. Leakey asked Jane if she would conduct a study of the chimpanzees. Jane was flattered and was pleased to be able to take the challenge. The officials in the area wanted Jane to have a companion, so her mother joined her for several months. The research took place in the Gombe Stream Chimpanzee Reserve. The Goodalls lived in two tents for six months. Jane's mother stayed in the camp while Jane went each day in search of a vantage point to observe the chimpanzees. For a long while the chimps stayed away and then, just before the study ended, there was a breakthrough. Goodall had been able to observe the chimps in their family units but two observations were most exciting. She had observed chimps eating meat (when they had previously been thought to be vegetarians), and she had observed a chimp using a tool to obtain termites to eat. The study funding was renewed and extended. This was the beginning of a lifetime of work with chimpanzees.

Jane Goodall met a photographer, Hugo Van Lawick, and they soon married. Their child, Hugo Eric Louis "Grub" Van Lawick, was reared in the rain forest. To protect him, Jane and Hugo built a cage for him to play in. Grub often went with his parents on trips to photograph or study animals. Jane continued to study the chimps, and Hugo continued to travel all over Africa to photograph animals for *National Geographic*. They began to grow apart, and they divorced in 1974. Jane married an Englishman, Derek Bryceson, who had spent years protecting the rain forest and its wildlife. Jane was happy to have the companionship, but Derek died in 1980. Jane continued to study the chimps and continues to speak throughout the world on behalf of wildlife preservation. She founded the Jane Goodall Institute for Wildlife Research Education and Conservation in 1975. She is also concerned about how animals are treated in captivity. Her project to promote better treatment of chimps in zoos is called ChimpanZoo.

Connections: More About Chimps

Excellent books about apes and chimps include Tess Lemmon's *Apes* (Ticknor, 1993) and three books by Jane Goodall: *My Life with the Chimpanzees* (Pocket, 1988); *The Chimpanzee Family Book* (Picture Book Studio, 1989); and *Jane Goodall's Animal World: Chimps* (Atheneum/Byron Preiss, 1989). Jane Goodall has devoted her life to the study of wildlife. Another researcher who has devoted her life to the study of animals in Africa is Betty Leslie-Melville. Her first project was to protect the Rothschild giraffe, an endangered species. The book that describes some of Leslie-Melville's experiences is *Daisy Rothschild: The Giraffe That Lives with Me* (Doubleday, 1987). During her work to protect the giraffe, a warthog wandered onto the grounds of the Leslie-Melville home. Eventually the warthog became a welcome and regular sight. Leslie-Melville tells about the warthog and other warthogs who followed it in *Walter Warthog* (Doubleday, 1989).

Artist:
Cassatt, Mary (1844-1926)

Turner, Robyn Montana. **Mary Cassatt**. Portraits of Women Artists for Children series. Little, Brown, 1992. 32 pp. ISBN 0-316-85650-9. (759.13 Tur) (B Cas). (Photograph of the jacket is courtesy of the publisher and is reprinted with the permission of Little, Brown and Company.)
Target Audience: Grades 4-6; Ages 9-11

Mary Cassatt was born into a prestigious family in the area now known as Pittsburgh. Later her family settled in Philadelphia but was not accepted into the upper social circles. Mary's father decided to take the family to Europe so that the children would become well educated and cultured. As a young girl in Paris Cassatt developed her love of art. She visited the Louvre and other art museums. By the time she was nine the family had moved to Germany so that her older brother could study engineering at a university there, and a younger brother could be treated for bone disease. The family stayed in Germany for several months: her brother died of the bone disease. Her older brother Aleck stayed in Germany to continue his studies when the family returned to Philadelphia.

At the age of 15 Mary decided she wanted to be an artist, but opportunities were limited. She studied at the Pennsylvania Academy of Fine Arts in Philadelphia, one of the few art schools that would admit female students. She learned a great deal during her four years of study, but at the age of 22 she decided to take a bold step and traveled to France to study. However, she found that the formal opportunities in France were even more limited than those in America. Being resourceful she created her own plan of study. She practiced by copying paintings and drawings at the Louvre. She studied the work of major artists, and she attended informal schools open to women. Later, she visited art colonies in rural France and created scenes of everyday life. Her paintings soon attracted the attention of teachers in Paris, and one of her paintings was selected for an exhibit in the Paris Salon of 1868.

War was raging in Europe. Prussia invaded France in 1870, and Mary's family implored her to return to the United States. Her paintings did not attract as much attention in the United States as they did in Paris, and paintings she created for an exhibit in Chicago were destroyed in the Chicago fire of 1871. When she was offered a commission for a painting to be created in Italy, she quickly accepted and returned to Europe, where she studied the work of Correggio, Velázquez, Goya, and Murillo. By 1873 she returned to France which had, despite the war, become the art capital of the world. During this time her work began to capture the interest of collectors in America. She met French artist Edgar Degas, who remained her lifelong friend and mentor.

Cassatt's painting began to emerge as part of the impressionistic movement. She sought to capture instant impressions of what she saw. Her family joined her in France, and she used them as models for many paintings. The theme of mother and child dominates her work. Cassatt felt a compulsion to create. In 1880 she created 29 paintings and pastels. Her paintings increasingly portrayed subjects in informal settings, with the subjects at play or enjoying a quiet moment of interaction, tenderness, and contentment. Inspired by Japanese wood-block prints, she experimented in creating prints, which were featured in an exhibit in 1890. In 1894 she created an oil painting *The Boating Party* that depicted a couple and a young child on a boat. Still, her work did not enjoy the popularity in the United States that she wished for. By 1895 all of her family members, as well as her friend Degas, had died. Because of World War I she had to leave her home. Her eyesight failed. She continued to advise collectors about European works of art. By the early 1900s she had received many awards, and her work finally became popular in the United States. In 1913 a book-length study of her work was published, and in 1914 the Pennsylvania Academy of Fine Arts awarded her the Gold Medal of Honor. Cassatt died 12 years later.

Connections: *Women of Achievement*

The author of this book, Robyn Montana Turner, became interested in the lives of women achievers when, as a fourth grader, she uncovered a biography of Jane Addams. That biography made a difference in the direction of her life. As an adult she found that most biographies about women artists were written for adults. She set out to create a series of books about women and their art. In addition to the biography of Mary Cassatt, Turner has written *Rosa Bonheur* (Little, Brown, 1991); *Georgia O'Keeffe* (Little, Brown, 1991); and *Faith Ringgold*

(Little, Brown, 1993). Faith Ringgold is an artist and children's book illustrator.

Another biography of Cassatt is *Mary Cassatt* by Susan E. Meyer (Abrams, 1990), which is in the First Impressions series.

Artist:
Goya, Francisco (1746-1828)

Waldron, Ann. **Francisco Goya.** First Impressions series. Abrams, 1992. 91 pp. ISBN 0-8109-3368-3. (760 Wal) (B Goy). (Photograph of the jacket is courtesy of the publisher and is reprinted with the permission of Harry N. Abrams, Inc.)
Target Audience: Grades 4-6; Ages 9-11

Goya is a well-known Spanish painter who rose through the ranks to become the First Painter to the King, a financially lucrative position of power and prestige. Goya grew up far from the royal court in a poor family in the farming region of Spain. He developed a fierce desire to draw and paint. He practiced and learned his craft as an apprentice to many respected painters. His first paintings were of religious subjects, but gradually his range extended to portraits of the royal court and nobility. At the royal court he was sought as an official portrait painter. In addition to portraits he painted bullfighting scenes, political events, and informal scenes in noble households. He also created pictures of an imaginary world, a world filled with witches, giants, devils, and ghoulish characters. Later in life he learned to make lithographs; this technique, he felt, gave him more artistic freedom. In his older days he was a widower, deaf, and often ill. It was during this period that his Black paintings were created. He died with his grandson, his grandson's wife, and his son's wife at his side. His own wife had died years before, and his son arrived four days too late. After Goya's death, King Ferdinand VII ordered Vincente López, the artist who replaced Goya as First Painter to the King, to pay homage to Goya by painting a portrait of him. The portrait, *Francisco Goya y Lucientes,* is a magnificent study of a man with his ever-ready palette. It is one of 51 paintings reproduced as illustrative matter in this biography.

Connections: Life in Spain

Goya's biography gives readers a sense of the events that occurred during Goya's lifetime. From the year of his birth in 1746 to his death in 1828 several rulers ruled Spain. Napoleon Bonaparte was building his empire, and France and Spain were on hostile terms. Eventually Napoleon Bonaparte forced both Carlos IV and his oldest son, Ferdinand, to give up the throne of Spain. Napoleon made his brother Joseph ruler of Spain. All Spanish citizens, including Goya, were required to swear allegiance to Joseph Bonaparte in 1808. Joseph ended the Inquisition.

During Goya's lifetime the American Revolution took place. Read biographies of revolutionary war heroes, particularly those written by Jean Fritz, and compare the events that occurred in America to events that occurred in Spain. Of particular interest is *The Great Little Madison* by Jean Fritz (Putnam, 1989). Create a time line that shows which revolutionary heroes could have, had they traveled to Spain, met Goya.

Artist:
Ringgold, Faith (1930-)

Turner, Robyn Montana. **Faith Ringgold.** Portraits of Women Artists for Children series. Little, Brown, 1993. 32 pp. ISBN 0-316-85652-5. (709 Tur) (B Rin).
Target Audience: Grades 4-6; Ages 9-11

The well-known illustrator and creator of several award-winning books for children was first and foremost an artist of story quilts, or quilts that tell a story. When some of her quilts captured the attention of children's book publishers, she was asked to tell her stories in books for children. Her *Tar Beach* is a Caldecott honor book, and it won the Coretta Scott King Award for illustration.

Faith developed her interest in both art and reading at a very early age. Her family was very supportive and encouraged all of her endeavors. Her mother taught her to sew, and Faith created many items with fabric. As a very young student she was plagued with asthma and missed many days of school. Her mother took good care of her and taught her at home on the days that she could not go to school.

Faith dreamed of becoming an artist. However, most of her art training was classic, and she became dissatisfied. She wanted a form, palette, and style that reflected her African-American heritage. She looked to the women in her family, and generations past, for inspiration. Eventually she developed a technique using the rich tradition of storytelling with vibrant paintings on quilted canvas. Her story quilts have become legendary. Her work has been exhibited in art museums across the nation. When her quilt *Tar Beach* was exhibited at a New York City museum, it attracted the attention of a children's book editor, who asked Faith to retell the story in a children's book. Faith did, basing the book's illustrations on her story quilts. Her work continues to attract attention. Faith Ringgold and her family now live in Englewood, New Jersey, which is across the Hudson River from Harlem where she grew up.

Connections: Faith Ringgold's Works

Faith Ringgold's story quilts have become the basis for several books. *Tar Beach* (Crown, 1991) tells about the dream adventures of eight-year-old Cassie, who recalls events that took place in Harlem in 1939. Cassie's memories include events that took place on tar beach, the tar roof of her family's apartment building. Faith Ringgold linked the history of the Underground Railroad and Harriet Tubman with fantasy in her picture book *Aunt Harriet's Underground Railroad in the Sky* (Crown, 1992). *Dinner at Aunt Connie's House* (Hyperion, 1993) was based on a quilt titled *The Dinner Quilt*. In this story a young African-American girl, Melody, goes with her family to have dinner with her Aunt Connie and Uncle Bate. Aunt Connie is an artist who always unveils her new works at the family's annual dinner. With her aunt's newly adopted son, Lonnie, Melody discovers Aunt Connie's latest creations in the attic: 12 beautiful portraits of the most influential and inspiring African-American women of all time. The women are Rosa Parks, Fannie Lou Hamer, Mary McLeod Bethune, Augusta Savage, Dorothy Dandridge, Zora Neale Hurston, Maria W. Stewart, Bessie Smith, Harriet Tubman, Sojourner Truth, Marian Anderson, and Madame C. J. Walker. One by one the women in the paintings share their stories with Melody and Lonnie. Ringgold's illustrations are lush and brilliant oil paintings, each inspired by her story quilts. Turner's biography of Faith Ringgold includes information about the quilts that inspired the three books.

Author:
Hopkins, Lee Bennett (1938-)

Hopkins, Lee Bennett. **The Writing Bug.** Illustrated with photographs by Diane Rubinger. Meet the Author series. Owen, 1993. 32 pp. ISBN 1-878450-38-7. (183 Hop) (B Hop). (Photograph of the jacket is courtesy of the publisher and is reprinted with the permission of Richard C. Owens Publishers, Inc.)
Target Audience: Grades K-3; Ages 5-8

Author, poet, anthologist, teacher, and friend—Lee Bennett Hopkins describes himself as all of these things. He grew up in Newark, New Jersey, and attended college. For a time he taught school, and then he began to write articles for teachers and librarians. Soon he found himself collecting poetry for anthologies and then writing his own poems. He still writes his first drafts in longhand in pencil; later he types the second draft on a typewriter. Twenty years ago he moved to Kemey's Cove, New York, where he enjoys the change of seasons, the quiet countryside, the cool streams, and the plants and animals. Many photographs are used to illustrate the text.

Connections: Poetry, Poetry, Poetry

Lee Bennett Hopkins's poetry and his anthologies are among the most popular collections in many libraries serving children. Among his most popular titles are *Beat the Drum: Independence Day Has Come* (Harcourt, 1977); *Best Friends* (HarperCollins/Zolotow, 1986); *Rainbows Are Made: Poems by Carl Sandburg* (Harcourt, 1982); *Voyages: Poems by Walt Whitman* (Harcourt, 1988); *Ring Out, Wild Bells: Poems About Holidays and Seasons* (Harcourt, 1992); *Good Books, Good Times!* (HarperCollins, 1990); *Happy Birthday* (Simon, 1991); and *Side by Side: Poems to Read Together* (Simon, 1988).

Author:
Lindgren, Astrid (1907-)

Hurwitz, Johanna. **Astrid Lindgren: Storyteller to the World.** Illustrated by Michael Dooling. Women of Our Time series. Viking, 1989. 54 pp. ISBN 0-670-82207-8. (839.7 Hur) (B Lin).

Target Audience: Grades 4-6; Ages 9-11

Astrid Anna Emilia Ericsson was born November 14, 1907, in Sweden. She was the oldest daughter of four children. Astrid had two sisters and an older brother, Gunnar. Astrid Ericsson grew up in a time without television or radio; her family did not have a car or a telephone. Astrid learned to love animals, and she often explored the fields of her parents' farm. Books for young readers were not available in bookstores, and there were no public libraries. One of her teachers found a catalog of children's books and allowed each child in the class to choose one book to receive as a gift. Astrid Ericsson's first book was *Snow White.* She treasured that book for years. As she grew older she read *Robinson Crusoe, Tom Sawyer,* and *Huckleberry Finn.* Her friends thought that she would grow up to become a writer, but she knew that she would not. She thought it was much better not to write a book than to write a bad one.

Astrid Ericsson married Sture Lindgren on April 4, 1931. Soon they had a son, Lars, and in 1934 they had a daughter, Karin. One day when Karin was ill, she asked her mother to tell her a story. That was the first time Astrid Lindgren told the story of Pippi Longstocking. The story of Pippi became very popular and was translated into dozens of languages, including English. *Pippi Longstocking* came to the United States in the 1950s. At first it did not seem that the book would be as popular as it was in Sweden, but before long it became one of the most popular titles in the country. Lindgren became famous for her stories about Pippi, but she also wrote other stories—stories about the Noisy Village; about Ronia, the Robber's daughter; and about other interesting characters. She also translated many books written in the United States for her Swedish publishing house, Raben and Sjogren. As a translator she used two pseudonyms, Anna Ericsson and Emilia Ericsson, which were formed using her middle names and her birth name.

Astrid Lindgren worked as an editor at Raben and Sjogren for 24 years. By the time she retired in 1970 she had helped the company become the biggest publisher of children's books in Sweden. She has received many awards for her writing and translating. Her other interests involve animal rights, crusades for better treatment of animals, and protests against the high tax rate in Sweden. Many of the streets in Vimmerby, Sweden, are named after books by her. Now in her late eighties, Astrid Lindgren owns the farm where she and her brothers and sisters were raised. That is the place where her grandchildren and great-grandchildren regularly come together to celebrate being a family.

Connections: Pippi Longstocking

Astrid Lindgren is perhaps best known for her stories about Pippi Longstocking. Reading the stories will give readers insight into some of the things that Astrid Lindgren did as a child, although the incidents are certainly exaggerated. Her first book about Pippi was *Pippi Longstocking* (Viking, 1950). That book aptly describes Pippi as an unorthodox young girl who is able to take care of herself, even in the absence of both of her parents. Later two other stories were published, *Pippi Goes on Board* (Viking, 1957) and *Pippi in the South Seas* (Viking, 1959). The stories have continued to be popular with each new generation of intermediate readers.

Author:
Rylant, Cynthia (1954-)

Rylant, Cynthia. **Best Wishes.** Illustrated with photographs by Carlo Ontal. Meet the Author series. Owen, 1992. 32 pp. ISBN 1-878450-20-4. (813 Ryl) (B Ryl).
Target Audience: Grades K-3; Ages 5-8

From her early life in Virginia, where she lived with her grandparents, to her years in Beaver, West Virginia, as a young teen, Cynthia Rylant describes her growing up years and how she drew upon them in writing her books. Now she lives in Kent, Ohio, with her son, Nate. She helps him fold newspapers for his paper route; enjoys walks in the woods; and writes, often as she sits on a porch bench. She saves her thoughts for many days and weeks, and then the words pour out. She enjoys going to West Virginia to visit her grandmother and her mother.

Connections: Cynthia Rylant's Works

Several of Rylant's books, although fiction, are autobiographical in nature. *When I Was Young in the Mountains* (Dutton, 1982) tells of the years she spent between the ages of four and eight living with her grandparents in the Appalachian Mountains. *The Relatives Came* (Bradbury, 1985) comes from the same years, when aunts and uncles and cousins came from Virginia to visit her and her grandparents. *Waiting to Waltz: A Childhood* (Bradbury, 1984), a collection of poems, brings out memories of her preteen years in Beaver, where she lived with her mother. One of the poems speaks simply of her deep sense of loss when she found out her father had died. *Miss Maggie* (Dutton, 1983) is the story of a person she knew in the mountains. Other books come from her imagination, such as *All That I See* (Orchard, 1988). Still others are based on the actions of people or animals; the Henry and Mudge series (Bradbury) is based on ideas she got watching her son Nate play with a dog they once had.

Author and Environmentalist: Carson, Rachel (1907-1964)

Accorsi, William. **Rachel Carson.** Illustrated by William Accorsi. Holiday, 1993. n.p. ISBN 0-8234-0994-5. (574 Acc) (B Car).
Target Audience: Grades 4-6; Ages 9-11

Rachel Carson was born in Springdale, Pennsylvania, in 1907. Accorsi chronicles Rachel's early life, her budding interest in writing, her college years in Pittsburgh, her interest in famous authors, and her emerging interest in plants and animals. Her devotion to her parents continued throughout her life; her parents moved to Baltimore to be near her as she studied for her master's degree. After she earned that degree, she began to work for the U.S. Bureau of Fisheries. During this time she sent many articles to magazines, and when she was 31 years old she wrote a book about the sea and sea creatures entitled *Under the Sea-Wind: A Naturalist's Picture of Ocean Life* (Oxford, 1941; 1952). The book was not successful because World War II had begun and people were preoccupied. After the war she wrote a very popular book, *The Sea Around Us* (1941; revised Oxford, 1961). Another book, *Silent Spring* (Houghton, 1962) was read by President John F. Kennedy, who agreed with Carson. They decided that they must find alternatives to the many poisons used to control insects and grow food.

Connections: For the Love of Nature

Ginger Wadsworth has written a much longer (128-page) biography of Rachel Carson. In *Rachel Carson: Voice for the Earth* (Lerner, 1992), Wadsworth tells of Rachel's dedication to her family, her struggles to be financially solvent, and her efforts to establish credibility and to open the study of nature to women. Another writer, Eve Stwertka, focuses on Carson's childhood, her decision to study marine biology, and her writing in *Rachel Carson* (Watts, 1991). Stwertka also discusses Carson's writing and the inspiration she provides those who work for environmental concerns. Rachel Carson's books focused on the wonder of nature and the importance of conserving and protecting our environment.

Several years before her death from cancer, Carson wrote a sensitive essay, *The Sense of Wonder* (Harper, 1956; 1965), for her grand-nephew, Roger. The book focuses on the joy, excitement and mystery of the world. After Carson died at the age of 56, she was honored with the establishment of the Rachel Carson Wildlife Refuge. The refuge was established on 4,700 acres of marshland from Kittery, Maine, to Cape Elizabeth, Maine. Her interest in the wildlife in her environment was similar to that of Betty Leslie-Melville and Jane Goodall. See the index for references to books about Goodall, Leslie-Melville, and John Muir, who worked to preserve natural environments in the West.

Bullfighter:
El Chino (Bong Way Wong)

Say, Allen. **El Chino.** Houghton, 1990. 32 pp. ISBN 0-395-52023-1. (791.8 Say) (B Won). (Photograph of the jacket is courtesy of the publisher and is reprinted with the permission of Houghton Mifflin Children's Book.)
Target Audience: Grades 4-6; Ages 9-11

This is a biography of the first Chinese American to become a famous bullfighter in Spain. Bong Way Wong was called Billy Wong by his brothers and sisters as they grew up in Nogales, Arizona. The parents of the six Wong children had come to the United States from Canton, China. The father was a grocer, and their home was attached to the store. Some of the children wanted to be a teacher, librarian, engineer, or doctor; Billy wanted to play basketball. Their father had taught them that they could be whatever they wanted to be, and although his brothers and sisters sometimes laughed at his aspirations, Billy became a great high-school basketball player. He was fast and quick but was too short to play basketball in college, so Billy abandoned his dream and studied engineering.

After college Billy got a job, saved money, and took his first vacation in Europe. He saw many interesting castles, museums, and other attractions. He liked Spain the best. It was in Spain that he saw his first bullfight. He stayed in Spain to train as a matador. Although he was a good athlete and had courage and grace, the others at the school doubted if he would ever become a matador because he was not Spanish. When he finished school he attempted to work as a Spanish bullfighter. He did not succeed. Eventually he realized that what he should seek was a position as a Chinese bullfighter. He exchanged his Spanish clothing for a Chinese costume and became an instant spectacle. He got his first chance to fight a real bull the same day; later, a bullfighter manager helped him become a real matador. His first fight made him a sensation. He was fitted out in a "suit of lights" and was victorious before a sold-out plaza. When the fight was over El Chino was carried from the arena on the shoulders of the Spaniards. He had become a famous athlete.

Connections: Triumph over Challenges

Bong Way Wong worked hard to become a basketball player, but his height was something that he could not overcome, and it prevented him from becoming a professional ball player. In Spain he found another path to athletic fame. Others who have overcome social obstacles, physical disabilities, and other challenges to become renowned athletes include Ben Hogan, golfer; Carol Heiss Jenkins, Olympic gold medalist figure skater; Jerry Kramer, football player; and Althea Gibson, tennis player. Their stories are told in *Glorious Triumphs: Athletes Who Conquered Adversity* by Vernon Pizer (Dodd, 1980). Maria Tallchief is a Native American who overcame the tribal customs of the Osage to become a world-famous ballerina. Her story is told in *Maria Tallchief* by Tobi Tobias (Crowell, 1970). Toyomi Igus, Veronica Freeman Ellis, and Diane Patrick have collected short biographical sketches of African American women achievers in *Great Women in the Struggle: An Introduction for Young Readers* (Just Us, 1992). Janet Nomura Morey and Wendy Dunn have collected stories of 14 Asian Americans who have achieved success in *Famous Asian Americans* (Cobblehill, 1992). African Americans whose inventions have made lasting contributions are profiled in Jim Haskins's *Outward Dreams: Black Inventors and Their Inventions* (Walker, 1991). Nathan Aaseng has profiled several business people who overcame financial failure, poverty-filled childhoods, prejudice, and other challenges. Among Aaseng's titles are: *From Rags to Riches: People Who Started Businesses from Scratch* (Lerner, 1990); *The Fortunate Fortunes: Business Successes That Began with a Lucky Break* (Lerner, 1989); and *Close Calls: From the Brink of Ruin to Business Success* (Lerner, 1990).

Civil Rights Activist:
Parks, Rosa (1913-)

Adler, David A. **A Picture Book of Rosa Parks.** Illustrated by Robert Casilla. Picture Book Biography series. Holiday, 1993. ISBN 0-8234-1041-2. (323 Adl) (B Par).
Target Audience: Grades 4-6; Ages 9-11

Martin Luther King, Jr., is often remembered for his work for civil rights, but it was Rosa Parks who served as a catalyst for the Montgomery, Alabama, bus boycott, a boycott that brought the fight for civil rights into the consciousness of mainstream America. Parks was born in Alabama in 1913 and was confronted with discrimination throughout her childhood. African Americans were separated from whites on trains and buses and in restaurants, churches, and schools. When Parks refused to give her seat on a bus to a white passenger, she was arrested. The protest resulted in a boycott of the city's buses by African Americans. That boycott is said to mark the real beginning of the modern civil rights movement in America. Even after the Supreme Court desegregated public transportation, Rosa Parks continued to work for African-Americans' civil rights. She received many awards for her work, including the Presidential Medal of Freedom.

Connections: Mother of Civil Rights

Rosa Parks has often been referred to as the Mother of Civil Rights. Since 1957 she has lived in Detroit, Michigan. A book about the life and work of Rosa Parks is *The Year They Walked: Rosa Parks and the Montgomery Bus Boycott* by Beatrice Siegel (Four Winds, 1992). Siegel's book is a survey of the boycott. The people involved in the boycott, including Rosa Parks, are depicted as ordinary but courageous people who did not back down in the face of adversity.

More able readers will be able to glean details and information about the people involved in the boycott from *Rosa Parks: My Story* by Rosa Parks and Jim Haskins (Dial, 1992). Through almost 200 pages, Rosa Parks describes her early years in Alabama, her family, her involvement with the National Association for the Advancement of Colored People, and finally the day in December 1955 when she refused to give up her seat on the bus. Through her actions as well as her views on the events that followed, the reader will gain an understanding of many events that occurred in the name of civil rights from the 1940s to the 1960s. One of the titles in the Burdett History of the Civil Rights Movement series focuses on Rosa Parks and the movement. That book, *Rosa Parks: The Movement Organizes* (Burdett, 1990) by Kai Friese, focuses on the strengths and weaknesses of the activists and of the civil rights organizations.

Dancer:
Ailey, Alvin (1931-1989)

Pinkney, Andrea Davis. **Alvin Ailey.** Illustrated by Brian Pinkney. n.p. Hyperion, 1993. ISBN 1-56282-413-9. (792.8 Pin) (B Ail).
Target Audience: Grades 4-6; Ages 9-11

The author has invented some dialogue (based on extensive research) to weave facts into a readable tale that depicts the life of an incredible dancer and choreographer, Alvin Ailey. Alvin was 11 years old when he and his mother moved from Texas to Los Angeles, California. In the middle 1940s, Alvin and his mother, Lula, lived in Los Angeles. While his mother worked Alvin strolled downtown, where he became interested in the action that was taking place behind the blinking marquees in the theater district. One day he spotted a billboard that announced the appearance of Katherine Dunham and her dancers. Curious, he and a new found friend found an open stage door and watched the dancers' performance. The dancers swirled to the rhythms of West Indian drums. It was one of the first times that Alvin Ailey saw black dancers moving in such fluid dance movements.

He wanted to study dance. Few studios accepted African American students, but the Lester Horton Dance Theater School did accept students of all races. He danced and moved to a beat only he could explain. He began to teach other students how he moved. Soon Alvin was choreographing and performing his own dances. His dances often told stories; his inspiration was his African-American heritage. By the late 1950s Alvin Ailey had moved on to New York City, where he took classes and eventually founded his own dance theater. He incorporated gospel harmonies into his dance music. Members of the audience often swayed in their seats. His theater's performance of *Revelations* honored African-American people and brought Alvin Ailey one of his greatest triumphs. Brian Pinkney's masterful scratchboard illustrations help the reader understand the power of movement in Alvin Ailey's dances.

⁌ Connections: Ailey's Inspiration

Katherine Dunham, Alvin Ailey's inspiration, was an anthropologist who shared her vision through dance. Ailey first saw Dunham in her Tropical Revue, a dance about the people of the Caribbean. Ailey was spellbound by the costumes, the make-up, and the movement. That inspiration led Ailey to begin his career in dance in 1958 and led to his involvement in 28 world tours. He was responsible for creating 79 dances, two thriving dance companies, and establishing a dance school. These facts and more are included in Kathilyn Solomon

Probosz's *Alvin Ailey, Jr.* (Bantam, 1991). Probosz's book gives more details concerning Dunham's influence on Ailey.

Carol Greene has written a simple-to-read biography of Katherine Dunham. *Katherine Dunham: Black Dancer* (Childrens, 1992) tells the story of Dunham's development as a dancer. She left home at age 18 and studied dance. Eventually she established her own dance theater and toured Europe, Mexico, and Latin America. For a time Dunham lived in retirement in Haiti, but she returned to Illinois, where she established a dance school in East St. Louis. The school is more than 20 years old. In the early 1990s Katherine Dunham focused her efforts on working on behalf of Haitians who were refused entry to the United States.

Entrepreneur:
Strauss, Levi (1829-1902)

Weidt, Maryann N. **Mr. Blue Jeans: A Story About Levi Strauss.** Illustrated by Lydia M. Anderson. Creative Minds Biographies series. Carolrhoda, 1990. 64 pp. ISBN 0-87614-421-0. (338.7 Wei) (B Str). (Photograph of the jacket is courtesy of the publisher and is reprinted with the permission of Lerner Publications/Carolrhoda Books.)

Target Audience: Grades 4-6; Ages 9-11

Löb Strauss was born in a tiny Bavarian village, Buttenheim, near the German/Austrian border. When his father died, Löb tried to support his mother and two sisters by peddling goods door-to-door. Times were difficult and the government made life more difficult with restrictions against Jews. Löb's stepbrothers, Louis and Jonas, had already gone to the United States, and they encouraged Löb, his mother and two sisters to join them. Eventually the entire family traveled to the United States. Upon their arrival in the New York harbor, the passenger list had to be confirmed by calling out each family member's name. When Löb's name was called, it sounded like "Levi," so Levi is what he was called in his new country.

The brothers continued to peddle goods in the United States, and their peddling business led Louis and Jonas to establish a retail business. Levi continued to peddle his wares in the countryside and eventually decided to try his luck in the western part of the United States, where gold had been discovered. In 1853 he traveled around Cape Horn, at the tip of South America, on his way to California. The trip took four months. When he arrived he was greeted by his sister Fanny and her husband, David Stern, who had already settled in San Francisco and had established a dry goods store. Levi began to help David in the store, and it was not long before Stern and Levi Strauss became a major business.

Levi expanded the store's business to selling wholesale to more remote trading posts and stores nearer mining towns. One day on a selling trip a customer expressed a need for sturdy overalls. Levi had some canvas, and he asked a tailor to make a pair of canvas pants for the man. Levi had other pants made in a variety of sizes. Soon many miners were wearing "those pants of Levi's." David Stern and Levi Strauss teamed up with Levi's brothers back in New York to have more material—this time denim—sent to them. Over a period of years, David and Levi's partnership was expanded to include Levi's brothers and his brother-in-law, William Sahlein, who had married Levi's oldest sister, Mary. Sahlein, Stern, and Levi Strauss worked in the San Francisco office, while Jonas and Louis supervised the manufacturing and importing of fabric in New York. Their business became known as Levi Strauss & Co., and they continued to prosper. A tailor in Reno, Nevada, suggested that rivets be used to reinforce some of the seams of the pants. Levi and his partners liked the idea and began to incorporate the idea into their manufacturing. They invited the tailor, Jacob Davis, to join them as production foreman.

Levi Strauss was the youngest of the partners but he seemed to be the driving force in the business expansion. As the company's success grew, so did Levi's reputation as a generous and thoughtful businessman. Levi never married; throughout his years in San Francisco he lived with his sister Fanny and her family. When David Stern died at the age of 51, his son Jacob took his place in the business. Fanny was left with seven children but soon married her widowed brother-in-law, William Sahlein. Mary, Fanny and Levi's sister, had died a few years earlier. Levi moved with Fanny and William Sahlein into a house large enough to hold the 13 members of the two families. Levi taught his nephews the business and eventually he made Fanny's sons partners in the firm. Levi prospered personally and shared his good fortune with many others. He gave much money and time to charitable organizations. He helped to support Jewish, Catholic, and Protestant orphanages, established scholarships to Hebrew schools, and established more than 28 scholarships to the University of California. He became especially interested in the California School for the Deaf and gave the school large donations of time and money. Levi Strauss died September 26, 1902, at the age of 73. Almost every store in San Francisco closed on the day of his funeral. The company is still known for its sturdy jeans, which are now sold in more than 70 countries.

Connections: Pioneers in Action

Levi Strauss was a pioneer in the clothing business. Everyone has worn or knows someone who has worn Levis. Other pioneers brought about changes in how we live. Movies are also a part of everyone's life. The story of one of the people who was involved in the early filmmaking industry is told in *Samuel Goldwyn: Movie Mogul* by Jeremy Barnes (Burdett, 1989). Many of the items that we use today are the result of the inventive genius of people like Charles Goodyear who helped create the rubber tire used on automobiles (and other vehicles). Information about Goodyear is included in *Dreamers and Doers* by Norman Richards (Atheneum, 1984) along with information about other inventors: Robert Goddard, Thomas Edison, and George Eastman. Nathan Aaseng has written a book profiling the lives of 10 significant inventors, including the Wright brothers and the inventor of the laser, Gordon Gould. Intermediate readers will enjoy reading Aaseng's book *Twentieth-Century Inventors* (Facts on File, 1991). Selections from the book could be read aloud to children in earlier grades. While inventors that are commonly known: Thomas Edison, Robert Goddard, Wright brothers, and others, are often profiled in books for young readers, more difficult to find is information about minority inventors who contributed to our everyday life. For example, Granville T. Woods is an African American whose work is thought by many to precede Edison's work with electric motors, the telephone, and air brakes. Lewis Howard Latimer invented the incandescent lamp (making the use of electricity practical) and created a method for telegraphing messages from moving trains. Jan Matzeliger is perhaps the one inventor who affects the lives of most of the people in developed countries. Matzeliger invented the shoe-lasting machine that revolutionized the shoe industry, created thousands of jobs, cut shoe prices in half, and made possible the shoe sizing that we have today. Information about some of these lesser-known, but no less important inventors can be found in Jim Haskins's *Outward Dreams: Black Inventors and Their Inventions* (Walker, 1991) and *Extraordinary Black Americans from Colonial to Contemporary Times* by Susan Altman (Children's Press, 1988).

King:
Keita, Sundiata (d. 1255)

Wisniewski, David. **Sundiata: Lion King of Mali.** Illustrated by David Wisniewski. Clarion, 1992. n.p. ISBN 0-395-61302-7. (966.23 Wie) (B Sun). (Photograph of the jacket is courtesy of the publisher and is reprinted with the permission of Clarion Books.)
Target Audience: Grades K-3; Ages 5-8

In Africa around the year 300 A.D., several chiefdoms between the Niger and Senegal rivers merged and formed the first great empire of West Africa. The Ghana empire became a thriving trade center for gold, salt, and slaves for the next 700 years. In 1076 Ghana was invaded by Islamic Berbers who wanted the riches of the people of Ghana. The invaders were driven away, but the empire was weakened. The small kingdom of Sosso rebelled, and by 1200 the kingdom of Sosso controlled Ghana. When Sumanguru came to power in Sosso, he attempted to control the Malinke kingdom of Mali. Some say Sumanguru killed 11 royal princes of the Keita family. Sumanguru thought Sundiata, the crippled son of the dead king, was relatively harmless, so he allowed Sundiata and his mother to flee into exile. For seven years Sundiata lived in exile. During that time the king of Mema became his mentor. Eventually the time was right for Sundiata to return to his homeland and claim his father's throne. It was time to deliver his country from the rule of the sorcerer king Sumanguru. The king of Mema gave Sundiata half of his army, and along the way Sundiata gathered troops from the many kingdoms that had aided him during his exile. The clash between Sundiata's armies and those of Sumanguru lasted all day. During the battle Sundiata's old friend Balla Fasséké appeared. For seven years he had pretended to be loyal to Sumanguru, but he had used that time to discover Sumanguru's weakness. Now he told that secret information to his friend Sundiata, who used the information to help him defeat Sumanguru and his army. When Sundiata returned to Mali he was greeted by crowds of people. The 12 kings who had aided him in exile and in battle waited at his throne. Each pledged his allegiance and Sundiata, the Lion King, ruled the country for many years. Sundiata died in 1255.

Connections: Life in Medieval Africa

The history of Africa did not begin with slave ships. The continent of Africa had thriving trade centers. Between 500 A.D. and 1600 A.D., three medieval kingdoms of West Africa flourished. The kingdoms of

Ghana, Mali, and Songhay were those flourishing kingdoms. From the oral histories of the Malinke and the Soninke *griots,* archeological reports, and Arabic texts, Fredrick McKissack and Patricia McKissack have put together a rich and fascinating history of the three kingdoms. These kingdoms acquired such vast wealth that their great cities—Gao, Timbuktu, and Jenné—were centers of learning, medicine, and religion for centuries. The McKissacks' historical account of these countries is told in a 128-page book, *The Royal Kingdoms of Ghana, Mali, and Songhay: Life in Medieval Africa* (Holt, 1993). The book is aimed at intermediate and middle grades (ages 10-15), but much of its information can be used selectively with audiences at other levels and ages.

King: Louis XIV of France (1638-1715)

Aliki. **The King's Day: Louis XIV of France.** Illustrated by Aliki. Crowell, 1989. n.p. ISBN 0-690-04588-3. (944 Ali) (B Lou).
Target Audience: Grades K-3; Ages 5-8

In seventeenth century France, Louis XIV was a magnificent king. He wore rich robes, jewels, and fancy shoes. He had a courtier to help him get dressed in the morning and a courtier to assist him in getting ready to go to bed. Everything Louis XIV did was an event. His afternoon walks were grand events that attracted many subjects, who came to catch a glimpse of the royal king. His family included his wife, their son, two mistresses, and his eight children by his mistresses. Louis XIV enjoyed the countryside and often went hunting and riding. Sometimes he walked through his vast gardens at Versailles. His gardens were filled with four million tulips and 2,000 orange trees. Aliki describes the elaborate routines that were repeated throughout the 77 years of Louis XIV's life. His son died four years before Louis XIV, so the heir to the throne was Louis XV, the king's five-year-old grandson.

Connections: Living in Splendor

The king lived a life of splendor. In the Middle Ages a European king who visited a lord's manor was feted with a splendid feast that took days to prepare. The lord and lady of the manor supervised the preparations, but hundreds of servants helped. Aliki discusses the preparations of such a feast in *A Medieval Feast* (Crowell, 1983).

The lives of specific members of royalty are told in other books. A king who emerged as a powerful influence in the history of Africa is told in *Sundiata: Lion King of Mali* by David Wisniewski (Clarion, 1992). Sundiata was a Mandingo king who died in 1255. He was the son of the king of Mali in the time of the great trading empires of Africa, more than 800 years ago. Another title that tells the story of an African king is *Shaka: King of the Zulus* by Diane Stanley and Peter Vennema, illustrated by Diane Stanley (Morrow, 1988). Shaka was a powerful nineteenth century military genius and Zulu chief. In 1787, Shaka Zulu and his mother were banished from their small Zulu clan in southern Africa. During the course of his life he overcame his status as an outcast and rose to lead a mighty nation. When Europeans came to Zululand in hopes of colonizing it, they were told that the land belonged to the powerful Shaka, a ruler whose power was immeasurable.

The story of a royal chieftain who conquered and ruled China and Persia is retold by Demi in *Chingis Khan* (Holt, 1992). The life of Grace Kelly, a movie star who became a member of the royal family of Monaco, is told in *Grace Kelly: American Princess* by Elizabeth Gillen Surcouf (Lerner, 1992). Today Prince Charles is heir to the throne of England. His wife, Princess Diana, married him and became a princess. Patricia Reilly Giff tells the story of Diana's efforts to become a popular princess in *Diana: Twentieth-Century Princess* (Viking, 1991).

Naturalist:
Muir, John (1838-1914)

Naden, Corinne J., and Rose Blue. **John Muir: Saving the Wilderness.** Illustrated with photographs. Gateway Biography series. Millbrook, 1992. 48 pp. ISBN 1-56294-110-0. (333.7 Nad) (B Mui). (Photograph of the jacket is courtesy of the publisher and is reprinted with the permission of The Millbrook Press.)
Target Audience: Grades 4-6; Ages 9-11

John Muir was a native of Scotland, but at the age of 11 he traveled to the United States with his father, a brother, and a sister. Later his mother and six other brothers and sisters joined them in Wisconsin. John's home life was harsh, and he often took walks in the woods and along streams. He was a tinkerer and invented devices to make work easier. He also invented what he called an "early rising machine." When it was time to get up, the machine tilted the bed so that the sleeper stood right up. John displayed many of his clocks at the 1860 state fair in Madison, Wisconsin. He fell in love with the town and decided to stay. For a time he attended classes at the University of Wisconsin, but in 1863 he left the university to travel to Canada. That began his journeys all over the United States and into Cuba. After a trek to the Gulf of Mexico, John Muir took a boat to New York and then sailed to the west coast to California. He spent years tramping through the countryside. He was enamored of the Yosemite Valley, now known as Yosemite National Park. In time Muir traveled all over the valley and viewed what he considered the grandest of all waterfalls—The Yosemite Falls. The water fell from a height of more than 2,400 feet over rock cliffs to the stream below. Muir lived in the valley for two years and later wrote many pieces about the area and its beauty. He, over a period of years, explored more of the valley, traveled to Mount Shasta in California, explored Alaska, and climbed Mount Whitney. When he traveled to the Amazon River region of South America he was given a hero's welcome. When John Muir was 42, in 1880, he married Louie Wanda Strentzel and settled down as much as he could. He still traveled and tramped through wilderness areas, but he spent much time at home in Martinez, a town just north of San Francisco, California, where he was a devoted father to his two daughters, Anna Wanda and Helen. That home is now a national historic site. It was in the den of this home that Muir wrote many of his books and penned articles about conservation and the need to preserve our natural sites. It was some of these writings that contributed to the creation of Yosemite National Park in 1890. He established the Sierra Club, in 1892, and became its first president. He became an adviser to the U.S. government. All his life he worked to establish nature sanctuaries. Many sites bear his name: Muir Park in California; Muir Woods National Monument, an area filled with giant trees in Northern California; the town of Muir, California; Muir Lake in Australia; and Muir Glacier in Alaska. John Muir, known as the "father of our national parks," died December 24, 1914.

Connections: About John Muir

Several authors have written about John Muir's life and work. Eden Force tells the story of John Muir's life and his influence in *John Muir* (Burdett, 1990). Force mentions important people who lived during Muir's time and includes some important events. Ginger Wadsworth includes many photographs in her biography of Muir, *John Muir: Wilderness Protector* (Lerner, 1992). She focuses on Muir's love of Yosemite and speaks of his life, journeys, and values.

Physician:
Picotte, Susan LaFlesche (1865-1915)

Ferris, Jeri. **Native American Doctor: The Story of Susan LaFlesche Picotte.** Trailblazers series. Carolrhoda, 1991. 88 pp. ISBN 0-87614-443-1. (610 Fer) (B Pic). (Photograph of the jacket is courtesy of the publisher and is reprinted with the permission of Lerner Publications/Carolrhoda Books.)
Target Audience: Grades 4-6; Ages 9-11

Susan LaFlesche Picotte was one of the most persistent, determined, and compassionate people of her time. She saw a need of her fellow Omaha Indians and set out to fill that need. She became one of the first Native Americans to earn a medical degree when women doctors were very few and when Native Americans doctors were even fewer. Susan LaFlesche was born June 17, 1865, on the Omaha Indian Reservation. She was the fourth child of Joseph LaFlesche (Iron Eye), chief of the Omaha, and Mary Gale (The One Woman). Susan's three older sisters were Susette (Bright Eyes), Rosalie, and Marguerite. Their father believed that the Omaha would have to learn to survive in a world populated by whites. LaFlesche encouraged his people to build frame houses, to engage in farming, and to move toward the ways of the dominant culture. He sent his daughters to boarding school to give them the best education possible. In 1879 Susan and Marguerite were sent to a New Jersey boarding school, the Elizabeth Institute for Young Ladies.

When Susan was a child, she had observed the reservation doctor, and when she attended the Hampton Institution in Virginia, she met the school doctor, Martha M. Waldron. Susan became more interested in a medical career. By May 1886 Susan had graduated from Hampton and had been accepted for admission to the Women's Medical College in Philadelphia. In March 1889 she graduated in the top half of her class. At the age of 24 Dr. Susan LaFlesche returned to her home in Nebraska. She became a doctor and treated both Indian and white. Wherever there was a sick person she went. After five years of intense work, Susan LaFlesche lost her own strength. For the rest of her life she was plagued with earaches, headaches, and backaches, but she continued to work. She was not only doctor but advisor and friend to the many people she met. One of the patient problems she continually fought was alcoholism. With less and less meaningful work on the reservation, lost traditions, and loss of their land and their way of life, many Omaha turned to alcohol. Susan

LaFlesche's own illness forced her to resign as reservation doctor, but after a few month's rest she began again to help her people.

Susan LaFlesche married Henry Picotte, a Sioux who helped her when she wanted to return to her medical career. When their first son was born, her husband took care of the new baby. In 1897 Susan became ill and almost died. Eventually the Picottes had two sons, Caryl and Pierre. Susan worked tirelessly for her people, but she could not conquer the one problem that plagued her people and her own family. Her husband died of alcoholism in 1905. Their sons were just seven and nine. Susan lived out the rest of her life on the reservation. She doctored, interpreted, explained legal papers, settled arguments, wrote letters, collected rents, and kept financial records. She wrote articles for local newspapers about tribal customs, Native-American farming practices, and legends about corn.

For years Dr. Susan LaFlesche Picotte had worked to have a hospital built on the reservation. In the last years of her life she finally won that battle. The whole community raised $10,000 to build and equip the hospital. The hospital was built on a hilltop in Walthill, Nebraska. That hospital is now called the Dr. Susan Picotte Memorial Hospital. In 1989 it was placed on the National Register of Historic Places. Dr. Susan LaFlesche Picotte died in September 1915. Much information about the Omaha and the treatment of Native Americans is incorporated into the story of Dr. Susan LaFlesche Picotte's life. Explanatory notes, a bibliography of sources used and an index are included.

Connections: Women Who Inspire

Carolrhoda has included several women in its Trailblazer series and in its Creative Minds Biographies. Women who are in the Trailblazer series and their titles are: Jane Addams, a social worker in Chicago, *Peace and Bread: The Story of Jane Addams* by Stephanie Sammartino McPherson (Carolrhoda, 1993); and Zora Neale Hurston, an African-American writer, *Jump at de Sun: The Story of Zora Neale Hurston* by A. P. Porter (Carolrhoda, 1992). Women in the Creative Minds Biographies series and their titles are: Lucy Stone, who fought for women's rights and the abolition of slavery, *I Speak for the Women: A Story About Lucy Stone* by Stephanie Sammartino McPherson (Carolrhoda, 1993); Alice Hamilton, a doctor and social worker in the Chicago slums, *The Workers' Detective: A Story About Alice Hamilton* by Stephanie Sammartino McPherson (Carolrhoda, 1992); Ellen Richards, the Massachusetts Institute of Technology's first female student and the first woman to teach on its faculty, *Adventurous Spirit: A Story About Ellen Richards* by Ethlie Ann Vare (Carolrhoda, 1992); and Eleanor Roosevelt, a humanitarian and President Franklin D. Roosevelt's wife, *Stateswoman to the World: A Story About Eleanor Roosevelt* by Maryann N. Weidt (Carolrhoda, 1991).

Politician and Social Activist: Jackson, Jesse (1941-)

McKissack, Patricia C. **Jesse Jackson: A Biography.** Illustrated with photographs. Scholastic, 1989. 108 pp. ISBN 0-590-43181-1. (970 McK) (B Jac). (Photograph of the jacket is courtesy of the publisher and is reprinted with the permission of Scholastic.)
Target Audience: Grades 4-6; Ages 9-11

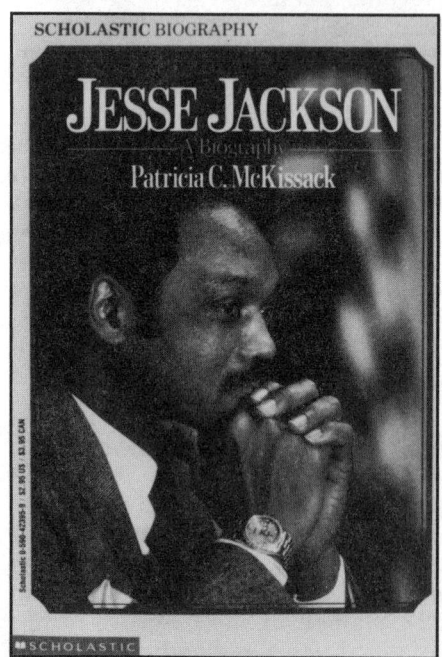

From his childhood in Greenville, South Carolina, to his present role as a politician and social activist, McKissack recounts each phase of Jackson's rise to national prominence. His early years were marred by incidents of segregation. When he was offered a major league baseball contract—tens of thousands of dollars lower than a comparable white player's contract—he turned it down. Instead he went to the North to attend college on a football scholarship. He quickly discovered that an African American would not be allowed to quarterback a team. He left his scholarship behind and enrolled in a college in the South, where he became a student leader and excelled on the football team. He became a friend of Dr. Martin Luther King, Jr., and other leaders. He became involved in sit-ins to obtain food service at segregated lunch counters and instigated boycotts against companies that sold goods in African-American communities but refused to hire African-American workers. He motivated others to join the boycotts and eventually gained many jobs for African Americans in organizations that had not previously hired them. In 1988 Jesse Jackson showed the people of the United States that an African-American man could be a viable candidate for the presidency. That year is sometimes referred to as the year of Jackson. Jesse Jackson is still very politically active and continues to focus on activities to raise social consciousness.

Connections: Working Together for Equality

Jesse Jackson's political life is the focus of another biography, *Jesse Jackson: Still Fighting for the Dream* (Burdett, 1990). The author, Brenda Wilkinson, follows the history of the civil rights movement and Jackson's involvement in it, discussing the strengths and weaknesses of Jackson's activism and political aspirations. More adept readers may want to read more about Jesse Jackson in James Haskins's *I Am Somebody! A Biography of Jesse Jackson* (Enslow, 1992).

Many others came before Jesse Jackson in the long struggle for civil rights and equality. Chelsea House's Junior World Biographies series focuses on several people who worked over three centuries for freedom and equality. *Harriet Tubman* by Bree Burns (Chelsea, 1992); *Martin Luther King, Jr.* by Kathy Kristensen Lambert (Chelsea, 1992); and *Sojourner Truth* by Norman Macht (Chelsea, 1992) are three of those titles. Thurgood Marshall was heralded as a civil rights lawyer before he became the first African American to sit on the U.S. Supreme Court. Jim Haskins's *Thurgood Marshall: A Life for Justice* (Holt, 1992) is a revealing portrait of the man from his childhood to his work on the bench.

After the assassination of Martin Luther King, Jr., his widow, Coretta Scott King, took up the banner and continued much of her husband's work. Her work is the subject of Sondra Henry's and Emily Taitz's *Coretta Scott King: Keeper of the Dream* (Enslow, 1992).

President of the United States: Madison, James (1751-1836)

Fritz, Jean. **The Great Little Madison.** Putnam, 1989. 159 pp. ISBN 0-399-21768-1. (973.5 Fri) (B Mad). (Photograph of the jacket is courtesy of the publisher and is reprinted with the permission of Putnam & Grosset Group.)
Target Audience: Grades 4-6; Ages 9-11

James Madison was a sickly child with a weak voice who became the fourth president of the United States. He was a good friend of Thomas Jefferson and played a pivotal role in the Constitutional Convention. His notes from the convention have provided much of the information about what actually happened there. His relationships with other well-known figures give some insight into the history of the United

States. He was a college classmate of Aaron Burr. He disliked Patrick Henry, admired George Washington, and was a close friend of Jefferson. He often corresponded with Jefferson. Their letters were usually written in code and discussed such topics as politics or the business of their respective estates.

Madison's family home was called Montpelier. James Madison did not marry until he was in his forties, when Aaron Burr introduced him to a widow, Dolley Todd. Her husband and one son had died of fever during an epidemic that swept Philadelphia in 1793. Dolley was left to raise a one-year-old son, Payne. Shortly after her husband's death James Madison met Dolley Todd. She was just 25 years old and still mourning her husband's death. Dolley Todd was a Quaker and James Madison was not, but that did not seem to interfere with their relationship. They married, and Dolley Madison turned to helping her husband's political career. They did not have children of their own. Her son Payne was troublesome throughout his life. Eventually James Madison was elected president of the United States, and he and Dolley Madison moved into the White House.

Dolley Madison was known for her social events and her courage. When the British marched on Washington, D.C., and set fire to the White House, Dolley Madison would not leave without taking some of the valuable paintings. One painting of George Washington was in a frame so heavy that it had been bolted to the wall. To rescue it, the painting had to be cut from the frame. The nation owes Dolley Madison a debt of gratitude for her persistence in saving some national treasures.

In 1836, after a lifetime devoted to making the U.S. Constitution work, James Madison died at Montpelier. He was buried in the family plot a short distance from the house. Dolley Madison lived for 13 years—during which her son mismanaged her affairs so badly that she had to sell Montpelier and move to Washington, D.C. She loved the social activity and was known for her open houses on New Year's

Day and the Fourth of July. When she died at the age of 81, she was buried in Washington, D.C. Ten years later funds were raised to move her remains to Montpelier, beside her husband. Fritz's account is lively and interesting. Several photographs of historical buildings and objects along with black and white reproductions of period portraits of the Madisons and other people and places mentioned in the text help to establish the historical setting.

Connections: More About the Madisons

Jean Fritz tells about researching the life of James Madison and taking notes at his home in her autobiography *Surprising Myself* (Owen, 1992). Her book gives some insight into the research biographers do. Undoubtedly others who have written about Madison have done similar research. Robert Quackenbush has written a 37-page biography that details the major events in the lives of James Madison and Dolley Madison. The book, *James Madison and Dolley Madison and Their Times* (Pippin, 1992) is illustrated with two-color, cartoonlike drawings. It serves as an introduction to other, lengthier and more detailed works about the Madisons. General reference books about presidents yield additional information about James Madison.

Patricia Ryon Quiri focused on Dolley Madison's role as first lady in *Dolley Madison* (Watts, 1993). Quiri followed Dolley Madison from her childhood in the Quaker community of Scotchtown, Virginia, to the inner circle of Washington, D.C., as the wife of the fourth President of the United States. Quiri shows Dolley Madison as defining the role of the first lady of the United States.

President of the United States: Washington, George (1732-1799)

Giblin, James Cross. **George Washington: A Picture Book Biography.** Illustrated by Michael Dooling. Scholastic, 1992. 48 pp. ISBN 0-590-42550-1. (973.4 Gib) (B Was). (Photograph of the jacket is courtesy of the publisher and is reprinted with the permission of Scholastic.)
Target Audience: Grades K-3; Ages 5-8

The life of our nation's first president is chronicled from childhood to his final days. He was the third of seven children. The two older children were his half-brothers; one of them, Lawrence, became George Washington's mentor, but he died when George Washington was 20. At this time the French and Indian War was being fought, and George Washington joined the militia. He fought with the British to claim the western frontier. After the war George Washington returned to Virginia and took up residence

George Washington: A Picture Book Biography

in Mount Vernon, the estate once owned by Lawrence Washington, and became a farmer. With the help of his slaves George Washington became a successful farmer, and he soon courted and married a widow, Martha Custis. Martha Custis had two small children when she married George Washington. George and Martha Washington did not have any children together.

When George Washington was in his early forties, the American Revolution began. George Washington was asked to serve as commander-in-chief of the colonies' militia. Although he did not wish to leave Mount Vernon, he felt that he must serve for the good of his country. Before the war ended both of George Washington's stepchildren died. Both were buried at Mount Vernon. After the war George Washington returned to Mount Vernon. Two of Martha Washington's grandchildren lived with them. It was not long before George Washington was asked to leave once again, this time to join the Constitutional Convention in Philadelphia, Pennsylvania. After the Constitution was written, many people promoted George Washington as the first president of the United States of America. He served as president for two terms. Near the end of his second term more states joined the union and a new capital city was established. The city would be named for him.

George Washington spent his final days at Mount Vernon. His years away from the South had given him a new perspective on slavery. He decided that slavery should not have a place in a free country, and he changed his will so that, after he and Martha Washington died, all the slaves would be freed. George Washington died in December 1799.

Realistic oil paintings illustrate the text. The final pages of the book include a time line of important dates in George Washington's life, a map of the United States in 1797, a discussion about the authenticity of the tale of George Washington and the cherry tree, information about Martha Washington and the fate of Mount Vernon after George Washington's death, and other miscellaneous information. An index adds to the book's usefulness.

Connections: Other Views of Washington's Life

Each biographer, especially in a noncomprehensive biography, tends to focus on specific aspects of the subject's life. Giblin's treatment of George Washington is fairly straightforward and focuses on his life as a politician. Not much is told about his personal life or about the people around him. Reading other biographies exposes readers to additional information about George Washington and allows them to gain new insight into his life. Biographies that will be of interest include *Washington* by William Jay Jacobs (Scribner's, 1991), a 42-page biography that uses scholarly research and direct quotes to help tell the story; *George Washington: Leader of a New Nation* by Mary Pope Osborne (Dial, 1991), which helps to establish a feeling for the time during which Washington lived; and *George Washington Wasn't Always Old* by Alice Fleming (Simon, 1991), a lively recounting of Washington's childhood. Jean Fritz conveys additional information about Washington's childhood in *George Washington's Mother* (Grosset, 1992). Fritz's characteristic style offers revealing details and glimpses of the relationship between the stubborn and eccentric Mary Ball and her famous son, George Washington.

Printer:
Gutenberg, Johann (1397?-1468)

Fisher, Leonard Everett. **Gutenberg.** Illustrated by Leonard Everett Fisher. Macmillan, 1993. n.p. ISBN 0-02-735238-2. (686.2 Fis) (B Gut).
Target Audience: Grades 4-6; Ages 9-11

Johann Gutenberg was born in Mainz, Germany, but little is known about his early life. His parents' names were Friele and Else Gensfleisch. The house they lived in was called Gutenberg Hof (Good Mountain House). Some speculate that Johann might have been called Johann von Gutenberg (Johann of Gutenberg), especially if he had relatives also named Johann. But that is only speculation.

Fisher recounts early attempts by the Chinese, Japanese, and Koreans to print individual characters using wood, tin, and porcelain. But not until Johann Gutenberg experimented with metal letters did the process become popular. Its popularity was not instant. Many of Johann Gutenberg's contemporaries could not read or write.

There was unrest in Europe, and Johann Gutenberg's family fled to Strasbourg. There Johann Gutenberg began to prosper as a gem cutter, but he was more interested in printing words mechanically and in making multiple copies. In 1436 Johann Gutenberg began to experiment with metal type. For the next 15 years he attempted to earn a profit as a printer. He had limited success and often came close to bankruptcy. Johann Gutenberg's financial instability allowed a financial backer, Johann Fust, to seize Johann Gutenberg's printing press and all of the materials and equipment in the printing shop. Fust took Johann Gutenberg's associate as his partner. They took over a Bible printing project and made a substantial profit. Meanwhile Johann Gutenberg found another backer, Konrad Humery, and began again. This time Gutenberg's backer supported Johann Gutenberg's efforts. Before his death in 1468 Johann Gutenberg printed several landmark books: a huge Latin dictionary, a Bible, and an encyclopedia. He trained many young apprentices and helped to expand the printing trade.

Connections: Gutenberg and Printing

Gutenberg's struggle to perfect his printing process is depicted in another look at his life. Joann Johansen Burch tells the history of Gutenberg's efforts in *Fine Print: A Story About Johann Gutenberg* (Carolrhoda, 1991). Kent Alan Aldrich contributes to the mood of Burch's book with black-and-white woodblock illustrations.

Social Activist:
Keller, Helen (1880-1968)

St. George, Judith. **Dear Dr. Bell ... Your Friend, Helen Keller.** Illustrated with photographs. Putnam, 1992. 96 pp. ISBN 0-399-22337-1. (362.4 St. G) (B Kel). (Photograph of the jacket is courtesy of the publisher and is reprinted with the permission of Putnam & Grosset Group.)
Target Audience: Grades 4-6; Ages 9-11

By the age of six months Helen Keller was speaking a couple of words, but at the age of 19 months illness left her deaf and blind. Because of her deafness and blindness, her parents let her behave any way she wanted to, with little guidance. She was very ill-behaved. One day she locked her mother in the pantry and sat for three hours, enjoying the vibrations of her mother pounding on the door. Helen Keller's mother did not get out until a household worker happened by and unlocked the pantry door. That incident convinced her parents that they must get help for her.

Helen Keller's father soon took her to see a world-famous eye doctor, hoping that he might be able to restore some of her sight. The doctor did not hold out any hope for the restoration of her eyesight, but he did recommend that she be taken to see Alexander Graham Bell. The Kellers did. It was through Alexander Graham Bell's advice and interest that Anne Sullivan joined the Keller household on March 3, 1887. Coincidentally, that date marked Alexander Graham Bell's fortieth birthday. Throughout her life, Helen Keller was befriended by Bell. He was her advisor and helped her financially. He encouraged her to speak out on political issues and supported her through good times and bad. This account of Helen Keller's life focuses on the relationship and remarkable friendship between two extraordinary people.

Connections: Challenging the Limits

Much of the work done with Helen Keller was based on the work done 50 years earlier with Laura Bridgman, the first deaf-blind child taught to communicate. Laura Bridgman's story is told in Edith Fisher Hunter's *Child of the Silent Night* (Houghton, 1963). Many biographies have been written about both Helen Keller and Alexander Graham Bell. Two successful titles are *Alexander Graham Bell* by Patricia Ryon Quiri (Watts, 1991) and *Helen Keller* by Lois Markham (Watts, 1993).

FOCUS BOOKS ARRANGED BY BIOGRAPHEE

Entries are arranged alphabetically by the last name of the biographee. The topic under which the biographee may be found follows the title in parentheses.

Ailey, Alvin.
    Pinkney, Andrea Davis. *Alvin Ailey.* (Dancer)

Carson, Rachel.
    Accorsi, William. *Rachel Carson.* (Author and Environmentalist)

Cassatt, Mary.
    Turner, Robyn Montana. *Mary Cassatt.* (Artist)

El Chino (Bong Way Wong).
    Say, Allen. *El Chino.* (Bullfighter)

Goodall, Jane.
    Lucas, Eileen. *Jane Goodall, Friend of the Chimps.* (Animal Researcher)

Goya, Francisco.
    Waldron, Ann. *Francisco Goya.* (Artist)

Gutenberg, Johann
    Fisher, Leonard Everett. *Gutenberg.* (Printer)

Hopkins, Lee Bennett.
    Hopkins, Lee Bennett. *The Writing Bug.* (Author)

Jackson, Jesse.
    McKissack, Patricia C. *Jesse Jackson: A Biography.* (Politician and Social Activist)

Keller, Helen.
    St. George, Judith. *Dear Dr. Bell ... Your Friend, Helen Keller.* (Social Activist)

Keita, Sundiata.
    Wisniewski, David. *Sundiata: Lion King of Mali.* (King)

Lindgren, Astrid.
    Hurwitz, Johanna. *Astrid Lindgren: Storyteller to the World.* (Author)

Louis XIV of France.
    Aliki. *The King's Day: Louis XIV of France.* (King)

Madison, James.
    Fritz, Jean. *The Great Little Madison.* (President of the United States)

Muir, John.
 Naden, Corinne J., and Rose Blue. *John Muir: Saving the Wilderness.* (Naturalist)

Parks, Rosa.
 Adler, David A. *A Picture Book of Rosa Parks.* (Civil Rights Activist)

Picotte, Susan LaFlesche.
 Ferris, Jeri. *Native American Doctor: The Story of Susan LaFlesche Picotte.* (Physician)

Ringgold, Faith.
 Turner, Robyn Montana. *Faith Ringgold.* (Artist)

Rylant, Cynthia.
 Rylant, Cynthia. *Best Wishes.* (Author)

Strauss, Levi.
 Weidt, Maryann N. *Mr. Blue Jeans: A Story About Levi Strauss.* (Entrepreneur)

Truth, Sojourner.
 McKissack, Patricia C., and Fredrick McKissack. *Sojourner Truth: Ain't I a Woman?* (Abolitionist)

Washington, George.
 Giblin, James Cross. *George Washington: A Picture Book Biography.* (President of the United States)

FOCUS BOOKS ARRANGED BY AUTHOR

Entries are arranged alphabetically by the author's last name. The topic under which the main entry for the title may be found follows the title in parentheses.

Accorsi, William. *Rachel Carson.* (Author and Environmentalist)

Adler, David A. *A Picture Book of Rosa Parks.* (Civil Rights Activist)

Aliki. *The King's Day: Louis XIV of France.* (King)

Ferris, Jeri. *Native American Doctor: The Story of Susan LaFlesche Picotte.* (Physician)

Fisher, Leonard Everett. *Gutenberg.* (Printer)

Fritz, Jean. *The Great Little Madison.* (President of the United States)

Giblin, James Cross. *George Washington: A Picture Book Biography.* (President of the United States)

Hopkins, Lee Bennett. *The Writing Bug.* (Author)

192 / Biographies

Hurwitz, Johanna. *Astrid Lindgren: Storyteller to the World.* (Author)

Lucas, Eileen. *Jane Goodall, Friend of the Chimps.* (Animal Researcher)

McKissack, Patricia C., and Fredrick McKissack. *Sojourner Truth: Ain't I a Woman?* (Abolitionist)

McKissack, Patricia. *Jesse Jackson: A Biography.* (Politician and Social Activist)

Naden, Corinne J., and Rose Blue. *John Muir: Saving the Wilderness.* (Naturalist)

Pinkney, Andrea Davis. *Alvin Ailey.* (Dancer)

Rylant, Cynthia. *Best Wishes.* (Author)

Say, Allen. *El Chino.* (Bullfighter)

St. George, Judith. *Dear Dr. Bell ... Your Friend, Helen Keller.* (Social Activist)

Turner, Robyn Montana. *Faith Ringgold.* (Artist)

Turner, Robyn Montana. *Mary Cassatt.* (Artist)

Waldron, Ann. *Francisco Goya.* (Artist)

Weidt, Maryann N. *Mr. Blue Jeans: A Story About Levi Strauss.* (Entrepreneur)

Wisniewski, David. *Sundiata: Lion King of Mali.* (King)

FOCUS BOOKS ARRANGED BY TITLE

Entries are arranged alphabetically by the title. The topic under which the main entry for the title may be found follows the author's name in parentheses.

Alvin Ailey by Andrea Davis Pinkney. (Dancer)

Astrid Lindgren: Storyteller to the World by Johanna Hurwitz. (Author)

Best Wishes by Cynthia Rylant. (Author)

Dear Dr. Bell ... Your Friend, Helen Keller by Judith St. George. (Social Activist)

El Chino by Allen Say. (Bullfighter)

Faith Ringgold by Robyn Montana Turner. (Artist)

Francisco Goya by Ann Waldron. (Artist)

George Washington: A Picture Book Biography by James Cross Giblin. (President of the United States)

Great Little Madison by Jean Fritz. (President of the United States)

Gutenberg by Leonard Everett Fisher. (Printer)

Focus Books Arranged by Title / 193

Jane Goodall, Friend of the Chimps by Eileen Lucas. (Animal Researcher)

Jesse Jackson: A Biography by Patricia C. McKissack. (Politician and Social Activist)

John Muir: Saving the Wilderness by Corinne J. Naden and Rose Blue. (Naturalist)

King's Day: Louis XIV of France by Aliki. (King)

Mary Cassatt by Robyn Montana Turner. (Artist)

Mr. Blue Jeans: A Story About Levi Strauss by Maryann N. Weidt. (Entrepreneur)

Native American Doctor: The Story of Susan LaFlesche Picotte by Jeri Ferris. (Physician)

Picture Book of Rosa Parks by David A. Adler. (Civil Rights Activist)

Rachel Carson by William Accorsi. (Author and Environmentalist)

Sojourner Truth: Ain't I a Woman? by Patricia C. McKissack and Fredrick McKissack. (Abolitionist)

Sundiata: Lion King of Mali by David Wisniewski. (King)

The Writing Bug by Lee Bennett Hopkins. (Author)

Author/Title/Illustrator Index

Featured entries for authors, titles, and illustrators are indicated by the use of bold-faced type for the page numbers of that entry.

Aardema, Verna, 35
Aaseng, Nathan, **47**, 48, 70, **86**, 170, 175
About Birds: A Guide for Children, 44
Abraham Lincoln, 74
Accorsi, William, **168**
Ackerman, Karen, 78
Adler, David A., 22, 55, 75, 130, 132, **171**
Adoff, Arnold, 36, 122
Adventurous Spirit: A Story About Ellen Richards, 181
Africa's Animal Giants, 25
African Elephants: Giants of the Land, 137
Aida, 35
Airplanes and Flying Machines, 69
Alcott, Louisa May, 131
Aldrich, Kent Alan, 188
Alexander Graham Bell, 189
Alexander, Sally Hobart, **46**
Alexander Who Used to Be Rich Last Sunday, 98
Aliki, 40, 57, 58, 64, **70**, 81, 125, **177**
All in a Day's Work, **51**
All That I See, 168
All the Small Poems, 112
Allen, Judy, 139
Allergies: What They Are, What They Do, 125
Altman, Susan, 22, 175
Alvin Ailey, 22, **172**, 173
Amazing Animal Facts, 30
Amazing Bats, 42
Amazing Bears, 43
Amazing Butterflies and Moths, 49, 128
Amazing Flying Machines, 69
Amazing Frogs and Toads, 71
Amazing Grace: The Story Behind the Song, **99**
Amazing Spiders, 85
Amazing Tropical Birds, 29

Amazing Wolves, Dogs & Foxes, 30, 144
Amelia Earhart: Flying for Adventure, 67, 68
American Family Farm, The, 64
Amish Family, An, 24
Amish People: Plain Living in a Complex World, 24
Ammon, Richard, **24**, **132**
Amphibian, 45
Ancona, George, 64, **79**, 130, 134
Anderson, Joan, 64, 130
And So They Build, **25**
And Then There Was One: The Mysteries of Extinction, 28
And Then What Happened, Paul Revere?, 56
Andretti, Michael, 41
Angel and Me and the Bayside Bombers, 126
Angelou, Maya, 36
Animal Camouflage: A Closer Look, 28
Animal Homes and Societies, 25
Animal Magicians: Mystery and Magic of the Animal World, **27**
Animals Galore!, 26
Antelope, 29
Apes, 31, **33**, 159
Apple a Day: From Orchard to You, An, 65
Arbuthnot Anthology of Children's Literature, The, 112
Archambault, John, 36
Archbold, Rick, 123
Arctic Hunter, 106
Ardley, Neil, 93
Arndt, Ursula, 61
Arnold, Caroline, 29, 32, 33, 44, 71, 99, 110
Arnosky, Jim, 44
As Dead As a Dodo, 32, 33
As the Crow Flies: A First Book of Maps, 73
Ashabranner, Brent, 39, 75, **76**

195

196 / AUTHOR/TITLE/ILLUSTRATOR INDEX

Ashanti to Zulu: African Traditions, 35
Asher, Sandy, 40
Astrid Lindgren: Storyteller to the World, **166**
Astronaut Training Book, The, 52
At Christmastime, 112
At Home in the Rain Forest, 29
At the Controls: Women in Aviation, 67
Auch, Mary Jane, 126
Aunt Harriet's Underground Railroad in the Sky, 164
Aust, Siegfried, 69
Auto Mechanic, An, 52
Autumn Across America, **121**
Ayres, Carter M., 69

Baboons, 29
Bach, Alice, 35
Backup Goalie, 126
Backyard Hunter: The Praying Mantis, 128
Baer, Gene, 36
Bahti, Mark, 106
Bailey, Jill, 44, **71**
Baker, Keith, 117
Balian, Lorna, 116
Ballard, Robert D., 123
Banish, Roslyn, **20**
Bannatyne-Cugnet, Jo, 50
Barbara Jordan: Congresswoman, 22
Bare, Colleen Stanley, **28**, 31, **80**
Barn Owls, 44
Barnes, Jeremy, 175
Barrett, Joyce Durham, 35
Barrett, Norman, 110
Barth, Edna, 61
Baseball in April and Other Stories, 97
Bash, Barbara, 44
Bat, Ball, Glove, 52
Bat Time, 42
Bathtubs, Slides, Roller Coaster Rails, 93
Batman: Exploring the World of Bats, 135
Bats, 42
Bats: Creatures of the Night, **42**
Bats, Butterflies, and Bugs: A Book of Action Toys, 43
Bauer, Caroline Feller, 122
Bauer, Marion Dane, **39**
Beacons of Light: Lighthouses, **91**
Bear Family, The, 44
Bearman: Exploring the World of Black Bears, 135
Bears (Gilks), **43**
Bears (Jeunesse), 44

Beat the Drum: Independence Day Has Come, 165
Bees Dance and Whales Sing, 28
Beetle, The, 85
Before the Wright Brothers, 69
Behrens, June, **59**
Belov, Ruth, 75
Benjamin, Carol Lea, 40
Berger, Gilda, 95
Berger, Melvin, 31, 95, **133**, **145**
Bergman, Thomas, 47
Berliner, Don, 69
Bernhard, Emery, **83**, 84
Beryl Epstein, 65
Best Friends, 165
Best Wishes, **167**
Better Mousetraps, **86**
Betz, Dieter, 44
Bial, Raymond, 65
Big Cats, 53
Big Pets, The, 36
Bigmama's, 133
Binch, Caroline, 100
Bird, 45
Bird Alphabet Book, The, 72
Bird Atlas, The, 72
Birds, 44, 54
Blackberry Ink, 112
Blacks in America, 1754-1979, 56
Blast Off to Earth! A Look at Geography, **73**
Blimps, **22**
Blow Me a Kiss, Miss Lilly, 36
Blue, Rose, **178**
Boating Party, The, 161
Bokoske, Sharon, 59, 140
Bour, Laura, 44
Brain and Nervous System, The, 125
Branley, Franklyn M., **94**, 127
Brave Eagle's Account of the Fetterman Fight, **102**
Breaking the Sound Barrier, 70
Brenner, Richard J., 126
Brian Wildsmith's Birds, 26
Brian Wildsmith's Wild Animals, 26
Brickyard Summer, 113
Briggs, Carole S., 42, 67
Brisson, Pat, 36
Brother Eagle, Sister Sky, 113
Brown, Craig, 141
Brown, Don, 23, **67**, 68
Brown, Laurie Krasny, 118, 125
Brown, Marc, 118, 125
Bryan, Ashley, 100
Bryant, Jennifer, 135
Bugs, 28
Bundle of Sticks, A, 88
Bunting, Eve, 78

Author/Title/Illustrator Index / 197

Burch, Joann Johansen, 188
Burleigh, Robert, 23, **67**, 70
Burnett, Frances Hodgson, 116
Burnie, David, 44, 45, 54
Burningham, John, 32, 110
Burns, Bree, 183
Burns, Diane, 64
Butterfield, Moira, 49
Butterfly, 49, 84
Byard, Carole, 89
Byars, Betsy, 20

Cache of Jewels and Other Collective Nouns, A, 26
Caines, Jeannette, 35
Caldecott, Barrie, 88
Calmenson, Stephanie, 79
Cambodia, 39
Camper of the Week, 36
Canesso, Claudia, 39
Canyons, 41
Capital Capital City, 1790-1814, A, **137**
Careers for Animal Lovers, 52
Careers for People Who Like People, 52
Careers for People Who Like to Perform, 52
Careers in Banking and Finance, 52, 98
Careers in Computer Sales, 52
Careers in Fashion Retailing, 52
Careers in Law Enforcement and Security, 51
Carle, Eric, 84
Carlstrom, Nancy White, 35, 36
Carmi, Giora, 76
Carpenter, A, 52
Carrick, Carol, **140**
Carroll, Pamela, 59, 114
Carrot Seed, The, 116
Carver, Douglas, 41
Carver, Robert, 41
Carver, 46
Cassedy, Sylvia, 40
Cat, 53
Catch the Wind! All About Kites, **88**
Celebrating Kwanzaa, 89
Celsi, Teresa, 157
Cerullo, Mary M., **122**
Cesar Chavez: Man of Courage, 95, 96
Cha, Dia, 83
Chaikin, Miriam, 76
Chair for My Mother, A, 21
Chandler, David P., 39
Chanukkah Guest, The, 76
Cheetahs, 29
Cherokee Summer, 106
Cherry, Lynne, 117

Chess, Victoria, 35, 145
Chicka Chicka Boom Boom, 36
Chicken Sunday, 61
Chico Mendes: Fight for the Forest, 117
Child of the Silent Night, 189
Child's Book of Wildflowers, A, 116
Chimney Sweeps: Yesterday and Today, 142
Chimpanzee Family Book, The, 159
Chingis Khan, 178
Chocolate, Deborah M., 89
Christmas in July, 35
Christmas Tree Farm, **64**
Christopher, Peter, 130
Christopher Columbus: From Vision to Voyage, 130
Circle of Seasons, A, 112
Circus, 35
Civil Rights Movement in America from 1865 to the Present, The, 56
Clark, Barry, 45, 71
Clean Your Room, Harvey Moon, 35
Clear the Cow Pasture, I'm Coming in for a Landing!, 23, 67
Clementine, 100
Climbing Jacob's Ladder, 100
Close Calls: From the Brink of Ruin to Business Success, **47**, 170
C.L.O.U.D.S., 35
Clouse, Nancy L., 73
Clutton-Brock, Juliet, 53
Coerr, Eleanor, 134
Cohen, Daniel, **57**, 99
Cohen, Paul, 51
Cohen, Shari, 51
Cohen, Susan, **57**, 99
Cole, Joanna, 71, 79, **108**, 109, 122, 127
Colin Powell, 22
Collins, James L., 157
Collins, Larry R., 110
Color Farm, 35
Columbus and the World Around Him, 130
Come Back, Salmon, **113**
Coming Out Right: The Story of Jacqueline Cochran..., 23
Complete Frog: A Guide for the Very Young Naturalist, The, 71
Complete Story of the Three Blind Mice, The, 35
Cone, Molly, **113**
Conrad, Pam, 35
Cookcamp, The, 41
Cooke, David, 86
Cooney, Barbara, 66
Cooper, Kay, 73
Cooper, Michael, 51
Corbett, Pie, 79

198 / AUTHOR/TITLE/ILLUSTRATOR INDEX

Coretta Scott King: Keeper of the Dream, 157, 183
Corn: What It Is, What It Does, 81
Corn Belt Harvest, 65
Cosman, Ann, 40
Cousteau Society, The, 133
Cowcher, Helen, 117
Cows in the Parlor: A Visit to a Dairy Farm, **63**
Cranberries, 65
Crews, Donald, 132
Crinkleroot's Guide to Knowing the Birds, 44
Crocodiles, 29
Cryan-Hicks, Kathryn T., 157
Cummings, Pat, **34**, 35
Cutchins, Judy, 27, 34
Cwiklik, Robert, 157
Czernecki, Stefan, 61

Daisy Rothschild: The Giraffe That Lives with Me, 29, 31, 33, 136, 159
Dan Thuy's New Life in America, **82**
d'Aulaire, Edgar Parin, 74
d'Aulaire, Ingri Mortenson, 74
Davidson, Margaret, 59, 140
Day in the Life of a Veterinarian, A, 135
Day Jimmy's Boa Ate the Wash, The, 108
Daydreamers, 36
de Bourgoing, Pascale, 128, 129
De Kay, James T., 55
Deal, Jim, 141
Dear Dr. Bell ... Your Friend, Helen Keller, **188**
Dear Rebecca, Winter Is Here, 107
December Stillness, 78
Deem, James M., 123
Defense!, 126
Demi, 178
Demuth, Patricia, 65
dePaola, Tomie, 56, 76, 130, 134
DeStefano, Susan, 117
Dewan, Ted, 27
Diana: Twentieth-Century Princess, 178
Digging to the Past, 124
Digging Up Dinosaurs, 58
Dillon, Diane, 35
Dillon, Jana, 120
Dillon, Leo, 35
Dinner at Aunt Connie's House, 164
Dinner Quilt, The, 164
Dinosaur Bones, **57**, 58
Dinosaur Dig, 58
Dinosaur Questions and Answer Book, The, 57

Dinosaurs Alive and Well! A Guide to Good Health, 125
Dinosaurs Down Under and Other Fossils from Australia, 99
Dinosaurs, Dragonflies & Diamonds, **98**
Dinosaurs to the Rescue! A Guide to Protecting Our Planet, 118
Distance Flights, 69
Diving to the Past: Recovering Ancient Wrecks, **123**
Dolin, Edward F., 70
Dolley Madison, 138, 185
Dolphins, **59**, 140
Dolphins and Me, The, 59
Dolphins and Porpoises, 59
Dorros, Arthur, 117
Douglas-Hamilton, Oria, 137
Dove Dove: Funny Homograph Riddles, The, 26
Downing, Julie, 115
Dragon Kite of the Autumn Moon, 88
Dragonfly, **83**, 84
Dream Planes, 70
Dream Wolf, 144
Dreamers and Doers, 86, 175
Drop of Blood, A, 145
Drysolong, 36
Dubrovin, Vivian, 40
Duel on the Diamond, 126
Dulcie Dando, Soccer Star, 126
Dunn, Wendy, **37**, **96**, 170
Dyson, John, 130

Eagles, **59**
Ears Are for Hearing, 125
Easter, **60**
Easter Story, The, 61
Easter: The King James Version, 61
Edgar Allan, 21
Egg Story, **54**
Egg Tree, The, 61
Eggert, John F., 114
Egielski, Richard, 35
Ehlert, Lois, 35, 36
Ehrlich, Amy, **75**
Eight Legs, 128
El Chino, **169**
Elephant Never Forgets Its Snorkel, An, 28
Ellis, Veronica Freeman, 48, 170
Ellis Island Christmas, An, 63
Ellis Island: New Hope in a New Land, **61**
Endangered Animals, 32, 110
Entrepreneurs: An American Adventure, The, 87

Entrepreneurs: The Men and Women Behind Famous Brand Names, 87
Epple, Wolfgang, 44
Epstein, Lawrence, 52
Epstein, Sam, 65
Erik Is Homeless, **77**
Ernst, Lisa Campbell, 36
Evans, I. O., 86
Evans, Lisa Gollin, 28
Everston, Jonathan, 22
Exploring the Bismark, 123
Exploring the Titanic, 123
Extinct Alphabet Book, The, **32**, 60
Extraordinary Black Americans from Colonial to Contemporary Times, 22, 175
Exum, J. Cheryl, 35

Facklam, Margery, 28
Faith Ringgold, 161, **163**
Fall, 121
Family Hanukkah, A, 76
Famous Asian Americans, **37**, 170
Famous Firsts in Space, 70
Famous Mexican Americans, **96**
Fancy Aunt Jess, 36
Featherly, Jay, 80
Feathers, **45**
Feathers for Lunch, 35
Feathertop, 121
Feelings, Muriel, 36
Feelings, Tom, 36
Ferris, Jeri, **180**
Few, Roger, 32, 60
Fighting Fires, **65**
Fine Print: A Story About Johann Gutenberg, 188
Finkler, Lillian Fluek, 61
Fire & Silk: Flying in a Hot Air Balloon, 23, **41**
Fire Fighters, 52
Fire! Fire!, 66
Fireflies in the Night, 128
First Class! The Postal System in Action, 115
First Look at Bats, A, 42
First Teddy Bear, The, 44
First Thanksgiving, **130**
First Thanksgiving, The, 101
Fischer-Nagel, Andreas, 85
Fischer-Nagel, Heiderose, 85
Fish, 45
Fish Do the Strangest Things, 114
Fish Eyes: A Book You Can Count On, 35
Fisher, Leonard Everett, **134**, **187**
Fisher, Mel, 123

Fleischman, Paul, 112, 121
Fleming, Alice, 187
Flight! Free As a Bird, 69
Flight: The Journey of Charles Lindbergh, 23, **67**, 70
Florian, Douglas, 52
Fluek, Toby Knobel, 61
Fly! A Brief History of Flight Illustrated, **68**
Fly Away, Home, 78
Folk Stories of the Hmong, 83
Follow the Dream, 130
Force, Eden, 179
Forces and Machines, 93
Ford, John K. B., 141
Forest Fires, 66
Forever Family, **20**
Forsyth, Adrian, 117
Fortunate Fortunes, 170
Fossil, 71
Fossils Tell of Long Ago, **70**
Foster, Sally, 79
Four and Twenty Dinosaurs, 57
4-Way Stop and Other Poems, 112
Fox, Paula, 78
Fradin, Dennis Brindell, 46
Francisco Goya, **162**
Frederick Douglass: Leader Against Slavery, 157
Free Fall, 37
Freedman, Russell, 69, 102, 122
Freight Train, 132
Friese, Kai, 171
Fritz, Jean, 56, **74**, 130, 134, 138, 163, **183**, 185
Frog's Body, A, 71
Frogs, 30
Frogs & Toads, 71
Frogs in Three Dimensions, **71**
Frogs, Toads, Lizards, and Salamanders, 28
From Anna, 47
From Hand to Mouth, 143
From Path to Highway, 119
From Rags to Riches, 48, 170
Fucini, J. J., 87
Fucini, S., 87
Full of Hot Air, 42
Funny You Should Ask, 26
Funston, Sylvia, 57

Gag, Wanda, 98
Gaitskell, Susan, 47
Galápagos Tortoise, The, 133
Garbage! Where It Comes From, Where It Goes, 118

200 / AUTHOR/TITLE/ILLUSTRATOR INDEX

Garden for Groundhog, A, 116
Garden in the City, The, 116
Gardner, Robert, 93
George, Jean Craighead, 107, **117, 130**
George Washington: A Picture Book Biography, 138, **185**
George Washington: Leader of a New Nation, 138, 187
George Washington Wasn't Always Old, 187
George Washington's Mother, 187
Georgia O'Keeffe, 161
Gerstenfeld, Sheldon L., 28
Get to Know Bernard Most, 57
Getting Elected: The Story of a Campaign, 95
Ghosts! Ghostly Tales from Folklore, 35
Giant Pandas, 110
Gibbons, Gail, 30, 31, 49, 51, **60**, 64, **66**, 81, 84, **88, 91, 98,** 110, 115, **118, 119,** 123, 127, **128,** 133, **135,** 144
Giblin, James Cross, 138, **142, 185**
Giff, Patricia Reilly, 178
Gilbert, Thomas W., 96
Gilks, Helen, **43**
Gilson, Jamie, 83
Ginger Jumps, 36
Giraffes: The Sentinels of the Savannas, 29, 136
Glaser, Linda, **144**
Glasses (Who Needs 'Em?), 36
Gliori, Debi, 126
Glorious Triumphs, 170
Glow-in-the-Dark Book of Animal Skeletons, The, 27, **124**
Go Fish, 35
Go Tell Aunt Rhody, 100
Goble, Dorothy, **102**
Goble, Paul, **102,** 144
Goedecke, Christopher J., **87**
Going on a Whale Watch, 141
Gold! The Klondike Adventure, 51
Goldner, Kathryn A., 141
Gonna Sing My Head Off!, 100
Good Books, Good Times!, 165
Good News, 35
Good, the Bad, and the Goofy, The, 36
Goodall, Jane, 159
Goodman, Billy, 25, 117
Goor, Nancy, 85
Goor, Ron, 85
Gorman, Carol, 111
Grace, Eric S., 140
Grace Kelly: American Princess, 178
Gray Wolf, Red Wolf, 30, 144
Great Adventure of Christopher Columbus, The, 130
Great Big Enormous Turnip, The, 116

Great Big Especially Beautiful Easter Egg, The, 61
Great Butterfly Hunt, The, 49, 84
Great Gilly Hopkins, The, 21
Great Kapok Tree, The, 117
Great Little Madison, The, 56, 138, 163, **183**
Great St. Lawrence Seaway, The, 51, **119**
Great Women in the Struggle, 48, 170
Green Grass and White Milk, 64
Greenaway, Frank, 42, 117
Greenaway, Theresa, 43
Greenberg, Keith Elliot, **77**
Greene, Carol, 22, 173
Greenfield, Eloise, 35, 36
Greening the City Streets, 116
Grosshandler, Janet, **125**
Grossman, Bill, 35
Grouchy Ladybug, The, 84
Grow It!, 116
Growing Up Amish, **24**
Guarino, Deborah, 36
Guess Again: More Weird and Wacky Inventions, 86
Gumshoe Goose, Private Eye, 36
Gunning, Thomas G., 70
Guppies in Tuxedos: Funny Eponyms, 26
Gutenberg, **187**

Hackwell, W. John, **123**, 124
Haddock, Patricia, 52, 98
Hadingham, Evan, 118
Hadingham, Janet, 118
Hahn, Mary Downing, 78
Hale, Lucretia, 36
Hall, Donald, 66
Hallowell, Tommy, 126
Halpen, Shari, 114
Hamilton, Virginia, 36
Hands-On Book of Big Machines, The, 93
Hannah, 46
Hannotte, Dean, 58
Hanson, Peter E., 130, 155
Hanukkah, 76
Hanukkah: The Festival of Lights, 76
Happy Birthday, 165
Happy Thanksgiving Rebus, 132
Hariton, Anca, **54**
Harriet Tubman, 183
Harrison, Ted, **49**
Harrison, Virginia, 85
Hartman, Gail, 73
Harvey and Rosie ... and Ralph, 126
Haseley, Dennis, 37
Haskins, James, 55, **99**, 157, 158
Haskins, Jim, **21**, 22, 48, 170, 171, 175, 183

Author/Title/Illustrator Index / 201

Hatchet, 41
Have a Happy..., 89
Hawes, Judy, 129
Heart and Blood, The, 145
Hector Lives in the United States Now, **94**, 96
Helen Keller, 189
Hellard, Susan, 40
Heller, Ruth, 26
Hello, My Name Is Scrambled Eggs, 83
Helprin, Mark, 37
Heltshe, Mary Ann, 42
Henry Cisneros, Mexican-American Mayor, 95
Henry, Marguerite, 80
Henry, Sondra, 157, 183
Herberman, Ethan, 49, 84
Herds of Words, **26**
Here Comes the Mail, **114**
Hershel and the Hanukkah Goblins, 76
Herzfeld, Carol, 76
Hess, Amy, 36
Hewett, Joan, **94**, 95
Hewett, Richard, 29, 99
Hey, Al!, 35
Hey! Get Off Our Train, 32, 110
Hey, Hay! A Wagonful of Funny Homonym Riddles, 26
High Voyage, The, 130
Hilton, Suzanne, **137**
Himler, Ronald, 103, 106
Hippo, 29
Hippopotamusn't And Other Animal Verses, A, 35
Hirschi, Ron, 34, 54, 59, 121, 140
Hirschland, Roger B., 25
Hispanic Americans, The, 95
Hoang Anh, 83, 96
Hoffman, Mary, 29, 100
Holl, Kristi, 21
Honeybee in the Meadow, The, 85
Hopkins, Lee Bennett, **165**
Hopscotch Around the World, **78**
Hornblow, Arthur, 114
Hornblow, Leonora, 114
Horowitz, Ruth, 42
Horvatic, Anne, **92**
House Sparrows Everywhere, 44
Housefly, The, 85
How a Book Is Made, 40
How a House Is Built, 81
How a Seed Grows, 116
How Animals Care for Their Babies, 25
How Much Is a Million?, 98
How Smart Are Animals?, 28
How to Hunt Buried Treasure, 123
How to Make Pop-Ups, 71, 85

How to Make Super Pop-Ups, 71, 85
How to Read and Write Poetry, 40
How You Talk, 125
Hoyt-Goldsmith, Diane, 83, 89, 96, **104**, 105, 106
Huff, Barbara A., 116
Huffman, Tom, 81
Hughes, Dean, 126
Hughes, Libby, 158
Humphrey, the Lost Whale, 141
Humphrey the Wrong-Way Whale, 141
Hundred Penny Box, The, 98
Hungry, Hungry Sharks, 122
Hunt, Joyce, 42
Hunter, Edith Fisher, 189
Hurricane, 37
Hurwitz, Johanna, **166**
Hyman, Trina Schart, 76

I Am Phoenix, 112
I Am Somebody!, 157, 183
I, Columbus: My Journal—1492-3, 130
I Need a Lunch Box, 35
I Speak for the Women, 181
Icky Bug Alphabet Book, The, 128
Icky Bug Counting Book, The, 128
If You Ever Meet a Whale, 141
If You Made a Million, **97**
If Your Name Was Changed at Ellis Island, 63
Igus, Toyomi, 48, 170
In for Winter, Out for Spring, 36, 122
In Your Own Words, A Beginner's Guide to Writing, 40
Indian Chiefs, 102
Ingersoll, Norm, 52
Insect, 85
Insect Metamorphosis, 85
Insects Around the House, 128
Insects in the Garden, 128
Inside China, 39
Inside the Whale and Other Animals, 27
Intrepid, 107
Inventions That Made History, 86
Inventors of the World, 86
Irvine, Georgeanne, **109**
Irvine, Joan, 71, 85
Is Your Mama a Llama?, 36
Island of the Skog, The, 36
It Doesn't Always Have to Rhyme, 112
Ivimey, John W., 35

Jackal Woman, 135
Jackson, Florence, 56
Jacobs, Francine, **129**
Jacobs, William Jay, **61**, 138, 187

202 / AUTHOR/TITLE/ILLUSTRATOR INDEX

Jakobsen, Kathy, **107**
Jambo Means Hello, 36
James, Ian, 39
James Madison and Dolley Madison and Their Times, 138, 185
Jane Goodall, Friend of the Chimps, 33, **158**
Jane Goodall's Animal World: Chimps, 159
Jane Goodall's Animal World: Hippos, 29
Jane Sayler: Veterinarian, 135
Janeczko, Paul B., **112**, 113
Japan, 39
Jaspersohn, William, 52, 65, 135
Jeb Scarecrow's Pumpkin Patch, 120
Jeffers, Susan, 113
Jenson, Cynthia L., 29
Jesse Jackson: A Biography, **182**
Jesse Jackson and Political Power, 157
Jesse Jackson: Still Fighting for the Dream, 183
Jester on the Backcourt, 126
Jeunesse, Gallimard, 44, 69
Jimmy's Boa and the Big Splash Birthday Bash, 36
Joel: Growing Up a Farm Man, 65
John Brown and the Fight Against Slavery, 157
John Muir: Saving the Wilderness, **178**
John Muir: Wilderness Protector, 179
Johnson, Crockett, 116
Johnson, Linda Carlson, 22
Johnson, Neil, 23, **41**, **51**
Johnston, Ginny, 27, 34
Johnston, Tony, 35, 141
Jones, Charlotte Foltz, **85**, 87
Jordan, Helene J., 116
Jordan, Sandra, **64**
Jordan-Wong, Jennifer, **20**
Jorge Luis Borges, 96
Journey Through a Tropical Jungle, 117
Journey to the Planets, 127
Joyful Noises, 112
Jump at de Sun, 181
June 29, 1999, 37
Jungle Animals, 29, 117
Junkyard Bandicoots and Other Tales of the World's Endangered Species, 60
Just a Dream, 37
Just a Few Words, Mr. Lincoln, **74**
Just Like a Real Family, 21
Just Plain Fancy, 24

Kahney, Regina, 27, **124**
Kalman, Bobbie, 145

Kasza, Keiko, 20
Kate Shelley and the Midnight Express, 92, 155
Katherine Dunham: Black Dancer, 22, 173
Katz, Bobbi, 76
Kay, Helen, 44
Keegan, Marcia, **105**
Keep the Lights Burning, Abbie, 92, 155
Kellogg, Cynthia, 81
Kellogg, Steven, 36, 108
Kelly, M. A., 116
Kerrod, Robin, 69
Kickoff Time, 126
Killer Bees, 85
Killer Fish, 122
Killer Whales, 141
Killing Fields, The, 38
Kimmel, Eric, 76
King, Elizabeth, 65
King's Day: Louis XIV of France, **177**
Kitchen, Bert, **25**
Kite Flier, 37
Kites, 88
Klondike Fever, 51
Knapp, Toni, 141
Koester, Pat, 52
Kohler, Keith, 123
Koralk, Jenny, 76
Kostyal, K. M., 25
Kozol, Jonathon, 78
Kraus, Ruth, 116
Kraus, Scott, **139**, 141
Krementz, Jill, 116
Kroll, Virginia, 89
Krull, Kathleen, 100
Kuklin, Susan, **65**, 135
Kwanzaa, **89**
Kwitz, Mary DeBall, 36

LaBonte, Gail, 128
Lacey, Elizabeth A., 71
Lady Who Put Salt in Her Coffee, The, 36
Lady with a Torch, 134
Ladybug, 84
Ladybug and Other Insects, The, 128
Lambert, Kathy Kristensen, 183
Lampton, Christopher, 66, 93
Land and People of Cambodia, The, 39
Land and People of China, The, 39
Land and People of Korea, The, 39
Land of Gray Wolf, The, 144
Land of Hope, 62
Land of Promise, 62
Land of Yesterday, Land of Tomorrow, 39
Landau, Elaine, 117

Author/Title/Illustrator Index / 203

Lang, Aubrey, **59**
Langstaff, John, 100
Lankford, Mary D., **78**
Lasky, Kathryn, **48**, 58
Last Chance Quarterback, 126
Lauber, Patricia, 54, 127
Launching, Floating High, and Landing If Your Pilot Light Doesn't Go Out, 41
Lavies, Bianca, 31, 49, 128
Lawrence, R. D., 30, 143
Leaves of October, The, 78
Lee Trevino, 96
Leedy, Loreen, **73**, **90**, 107, 115, **127**
Legg, Gerald, 29
Leighton, Maxinne Rhea, 63
Lemmon, Tess, 31, **33**, 159
Lennon, Adrian, 96
Lenssen, Ann, 42
Leonard Marcus, 36
Leontyne Price: Opera Superstar, 22
Lepthien, Emilie U., 29
Leslie-Melville, Betty, 29, 31, 33, **136**, 159
Let There Be Light: A Book About Windows, **142**
Let's Go to the Museum, 98
LeVert, Suzanne, 50
Levine, Ellen, 63
Levinson, Riki, 96
Lewis, J. Patrick, 35
Life and Death of Martin Luther King, Jr., The, 55
Life in a Tidal Pool, 114
Lili, a Giant Panda of Sichuan, 110
Lilies, Rabbits, and Painted Eggs, 61
Lincoln, 75
Lindgren, Astrid, 167
Lindsay, Mary, 124
Ling-Ling and Hsing Hsing, 110
Ling, Mary, 30, 44, 49, 84, 144
Lion and the Savannah, The, 29
Listen for the Singing, 47
Litowinsky, Olga, 130
Little by Little: A Writer's Education, 47
Little, Jean, 47
Little Old Lady Who Was Not Afraid of Anything, The, 120
Little Red Riding Hood, 144
Littlest Dinosaur, The, 57
Littlewood, Valerie, **120**
Livingston, Myra Cohn, 112, 141
Livo, Norma J., 83
Lloyd, Megan, 120
Lobel, Arnold, 145
Locker, Thomas, 144
Long, Kim, 52
Look Out for Turtles, 31, **133**

Lost Soldier, The, 35
Lost Wreck of the Isis, The, 123
Lucas, Eileen, 33, **158**

Macaulay, David, 93
MacCarthy, Patricia, **26**
MacFarlane, Ruth B., 71, 99
Macht, Norman L., 157, 183
MacLachlan, Patricia, 21, 47
Macmillan Children's Guide to Dinosaurs and Other Prehistoric Animals, 57
Macmillan Children's Guide to Endangered Animals, 32, 60
Macmillan First Atlas, 73
MacQuitty, Miranda, 122
Mad As a Wet Hen! And Other Funny Idioms, 26
Madame C. J. Walker: Self-Made Millionaire, 48
Madden, Don, 127
Maestro, Betsy, **56**, 134
Maestro, Giulio, **56**, 134
Magic Carpet, 36
Magic School Bus at the Waterworks, The, 108
Magic School Bus Inside the Earth, The, 109
Magic School Bus Inside the Human Body, The, 109
Magic School Bus Lost in the Solar System, The, 109, 127
Magic School Bus on the Ocean Floor, The, **108**, 109
Major, John S., 39
Making Your Own Nature Museum, 71, 99
Malcolm X and Black Pride, 157
Mallory, Kenneth, **139**, 141
Mama One, Mama Two, 21
Man and Mustang, **79**
Man on the Flying Trapeze, The, 100
Marbles, Roller Skates, Doorknobs, 93
Maria Tallchief, 170
Markham, Lois, 189
Markle, Sandra, 124
Markmann, Erica, 116
Marston, Hope Irvin, 52
Martin, Bill, 36
Martin, Claire, 35
Martin, Jacqueline Briggs, 116
Martin Luther King, Jr., 183
Martin Luther King, Jr.: Free at Last, 55
Mary Cassatt, **160**, 162
Mathis, Sharon Bell, 98
Mayer, Marianna, 37
Mayle, Peter, 32, 33

204 / AUTHOR/TITLE/ILLUSTRATOR INDEX

Maynard, Christopher, 30
McCarthy, Colin, 45, 54
McCauley, Jane R., 25
McClung, Robert M., 110
McCurdy, Michael, 131
McFarland, Cynthia, **63**
McGovern, Ann, **72**
McKissack, Fredrick, 48, 56, **156**, 157, 177
McKissack, Patricia, 48, 56, **156**, 157, 177, **182**
McMillan, Bruce, 141
McPherson, Stephanie Sammartino, 181
McWilliams, Karen, 111
Medieval Feast, A, 177
Meet Martin Luther King, Jr., 55
Meltzer, Milton, 82, 95, 130
Melvin Berger, 31
Memorial for Mr. Lincoln, A, 75
Mendoza, George, 120
Menorahs, Mezuzas, and Other Jewish Symbols, 76
Mercury, 127
Merriam, Eve, 113
Messages in the Mailbox, **90**, 115
Meteor!, 94
Mexico: Giant of the South, 95
Meyer, Carolyn, 24
Meyer, Susan E., 162
Michael Andretti at Indianapolis, 41
Midstream Changes, 48
Migdale, Lawrence, 89
Miles, Betty, 113
Milhous, Katherine, 61
Milk from Cow to Carton, 64, 81
Milk Makers, The, 64
Milk: The Fight for Purity, 143
Miller, Margaret, 81
Millions of Cats, 98
Millionth Egg, The, 98
Milton, Joyce, 30, **42**, 59, 140, 141, 144
Miriam's Well: Stories About Women in the Bible, 35
Misadventures of Brer Rabbit, Brer Fox, Brer Wolf, the Doodang, and Other Creatures, The, 36
Miss Maggie, 168
Miss Mary Mack and Other Children's Street Rhymes, 79
Miss Penny and Mr. Grubbs, 36
Mistakes That Worked, **85**, 87
Mistral, 72
Moja Means One, 36
Mollel, Tololwa M., 43
Mom Can't See Me, **46**
Mom's Best Friend, 46
Monarch Butterflies: Mysterious Travelers, 49

Monarch Butterfly, 31, 49, 84, 128
Monarchs, **48**
Monkey Island, 78
Montgomery, Elizabeth, 86
Moon Rope: A Peruvian Folktale, 36
More Perfect Union, A, 134, **56**
Morey, Janet Nomura, **37**, **96**, 170
Morning Milking, 64
Morris, Linda Lowe, 64
Moser, Barry, **68**
Moser, Diane, 70
Moses's Ark: Stories from the Bible, 35
Most, Bernard, 57
Mother for Choco, A, 20
Mother Goose's Little Misfortunes, 36
Motorcycle: The Making of a Harley-Davidson, 52
Mound, Laurence, 85
Mr. Blue Jeans: A Story About Levi Strauss, **173**
Mr. Griggs' Work, 115
Mudd, Maria M., 85
Muller, Gerda, 116
Munro, Roxie, **22**
Murphy, Jim, 86
Musgrove, Margaret, 35
Music, Music for Everyone, 21
Mustang: Wild Spirit of the West, 80
Mustangs: Wild Horses of the American West, 80
Mutel, Cornelia, 117
My First Chanukah, 76
My Five Senses, 125
My Life with the Chimpanzees, 159
My Name Is San Ho, 83
My New York, **107**
My River, 114
Myers, Bernice, 98

Naden, Corinne J., **178**
National Wildlife Federation, 145
Native American Doctor, **180**
Navajos: A First Americans Book, The, **103**, 106
Naylor, Phyllis Reynolds, 24
Nelson Mandela: The Fight Against Apartheid, 157
Nelson Mandela: Voice of Freedom, 158
Neptune, 127
Neufeld, John, 21
Never Kiss an Alligator!, 31
New Questions and Answers About Dinosaurs, 57
Nez Perce: A First Americans Book, The, 104
Nina's Treasures, 61
Nixon, Jean Lowery, 62

Author/Title/Illustrator Index / 205

Noble, Trina Hakes, 36, 108
Northern Lullaby, 35
Northwest Territories, 50
Now Sheba Sings the Song, 36
Nutrition: What's in the Food We Eat, 82

O Canada, 49
O'Connor, Karen, **82**
O'Toole, Christopher, 85
Oceans & Seas, 109
Oh, Brother, 35
Old-Fashioned Thanksgiving, An, 131
Olney, Patricia J., 52
Olney, Ross R., 52
One Day in the Tropical Rain Forest, **117**
One More River to Cross, **21**, 48
Opening the Space Frontier, 70
Orr, Richard, 72
Osborne, Mary Pope, 138, 187
Ostriches, 29
Otfinoski, Steven, 158
Ouch! A Book About Cuts, Scratches, and Scrapes, **145**
Our Endangered Planet, 117
Our Fish Friends, 109
Our Vanishing Farm Animals, **31**
Our Yard Is Full of Birds, 44
Outside and Inside You, 124
Outward Dreams, 22, 170, 175
Over the River and Through the Wood, 131
Owl, 44
Ox-Cart Man, 66
Oxenbury, Helen, 116

Pacific Crossing, 88, 97
Page, James K., 110
Paladino, Catherine, **31**, 65
Pallotta, Jerry, **32**, 60, 72, 81, 128
Panda, 110
Pandas, 110
Papastavrou, Vassili, 141
Park, Margaret, 126
Parker, Nancy Winslow, 28
Parker, Steve, 27, 45, 93, 124, 125, 145
Parmenter, Wayne, 63
Parsons, Alexandra, 85
Passover As I Remember It, 61
Patent, Dorothy Hinshaw, 28, 30, **45**, 59, 65, 82, 137, 140, 141, 144
Paterson, Katherine, 21
Patrick, Diane, 48, 170
Paulsen, Gary, 41
Peace and Bread: The Story of Jane Addams, 181
Peace Three, 139

Pearce, Q. L., 28, **30**, 133
Peeples, H. I., **81**
People of the Breaking Day, **101**
People Who Make a Difference, **76**
Petey Moroni's Camp Runamok Diary, 35
Pettit, Jayne, 83
Picture Book of Abraham Lincoln, A, 75
Picture Book of Christopher Columbus, A, 130
Picture Book of Martin Luther King, Jr., 22, 55
Picture Book of Rosa Parks, 55, **171**
Picture Library: Pandas, 110
Pienkowski, Jan, 61
Pigeons, 44
Pilgrims of Plimoth, 101
Pilots: A Pop-Up Book, 52, 70
Pilots and Aviation, 69
Pinballs, The, 20
Pinkerton, Behave!, 36
Pinkney, Andrea Davis, 22, **89**, **172**
Pinkney, Jerry, 36, 122
Pippi Goes on Board, 167
Pippi in the South Seas, 167
Pippi Longstocking, 167
Pirates, 111
Pirates: Robbers of the High Seas, **110**
Pish, Posh, Said Hieronymus Bosch, 35
Pizer, Vernon, 170
Place My Words Are Looking For, The, **112**
Plane Song, 67
Planets, The, 127
Play-Off, 126
Playtime Treasury, The, 79
Polacco, Patricia, 61, 94
Polar Express, The, 37
Pond Life, **114**
Pop! Goes the Weasel and Yankee Doodle, 100
Porter, A. P., 89
Porter, Janice Lee, 89
Post Office Book: Mail and How It Moves, The, 115
Postcards from Pluto, 73, 107, **127**
Potter, A, 52
Potter, Beatrix, 69, 121
Potter, Tony, 73
Powzyk, Joyce, 28
Prairie Alphabet, A, 50
Prelutsky, Jack, 145
President Builds a House, The, 81
Prince, Amy, 36
Pringle, Laurence, 85, 135
Probosz, Kathilyn Solomon, 22, 172
Promise to the Sun, 43
Psyched!, 126
Public Defender: Lawyer for the People, 51

206 / AUTHOR/TITLE/ILLUSTRATOR INDEX

Pueblo Boy, **105**
Pueblo Stories and Storytellers, 106
Pueblo Storyteller, **104**, 105
Pumpkin Patch, The, 65
Punching the Clock, 27
Puzzle Maps U.S.A., 73

Quackenbush, Robert, 23, 67, 100, 138, 185
Quiri, Patricia Ryon, 138, 185, 189

Raccoons, 25
Race of the Golden Apples, The, 35
Rachel and Her Children, 78
Rachel Carson, **168**
Rachel Carson: Voice for the Earth, 168
Racing Indy Cars, **40**
Radin, Ruth Yaffe, 46
Rain Forest, 117
Rainbow Balloon, 42
Rainbows Are Made, 165
Rainforest Secrets, 117
Random House Book of How Things Work, The, 93
Random House Book of Poetry for Children, The, 145
Ray, Deborah Kogan, 94
Ray, Delia, 51
Real McCoy, The, 22
Rechenka's Eggs, 61
Recycle! A Handbook for Kids, **118**
Recycling, 118
Red Leaf, Yellow Leaf, 35
Reddix, Valerie, 88
Reed, Don, 59, 122
Relatives Came, The, 20, 167
Remarkable Children, 46
Reptile, 45, 54
Research Balloons, 42
Rhodes, Patricia, 88
Rhodes, Timothy, 61
Richards, Norman, 86, 175
Riley, Helen, 71
Ring Out, Wild Bells, 165
Ringgold, Faith, 164
Ritz, Karen, 155
Roaring Reptiles, 29
Roberts, Naurice, 95
Rochelle, Belinda, **55**
Rockwell, Anne, 45
Rodgers, Mary M., 117
Rogers, Barbara Radcliffe, 110
Rojany, Lisa, 93
Rolling Harvey Down the Hill, 145
Roocroft, Alan, 29
Roop, Connie, 92, 130, 155

Roop, Peter, 92, 130, 155
Rosa Bonheur, 161
Rosa Parks, 55, 171
Rosa Parks: My Story, 55, 171
Rosa Parks: The Movement Organizes, 171
Roth, Harold, 115
Roundtree, Katherine, 89
Royal Kingdoms of Ghana, Mali, and Songhay, The, 177
Royston, Angela, 29, 128
Rust, Graham, 116
Ruth Law Thrills a Nation, 23, **67**, 68
Ryden, Hope, **53**
Ryder, Joanne, 31, 49, 128, 139
Rylant, Cynthia, 20, 115, **167**

Sailboats, Flagpoles, Cranes, 93
Sam Ellis's Island, 63
Sam Johnson and the Blue Ribbon Quilt, 36
Samuel Goldwyn: Movie Mogul, 175
San Souci, Daniel, 121
San Souci, Robert D., 36, 121
Santoro, Christopher, 27, 71
Sarah, Plain and Tall, 21
Sattler, Helen Roney, 29, 136
Save the Earth, 113
Saving the Peregrine Falcons, 32, 33
Say, Allen, 88, **169**
Say Woof! The Day of a Country Veterinarian, 52, **135**
Scarebird, 121
Scarecrow!, **120**
Scarecrow Clock, The, 120
Schafer, Susan, 133
Schaub, Janine, 145
Schlein, Miriam, 29, 44, 110
Schotter, Roni, 76
Schwartz, Alvin, 35
Schwartz, Amy, 36
Schwartz, David M., **97**, 98
Schwinger, Larry, 144
Science Book of Machines, The, 93
Scieszka, Jon, 36, 37
Sea Around Us, The, 168
Seals, 140
Seals, Sea Lions and Walruses, 59, 140
Search for the Right Whale, The, **139**, 141
Second Street Gardens and Green Truck Almanac, The, 116
Secret Garden Notebook, The, 116
Seeing in Special Ways, 47
Seesaws, Nutcrackers, Brooms, 93
Seizas, Judith, S., 125
Selsam, Millicent E., 42

Author/Title/Illustrator Index / 207

Seminoles: A First Americans Book, The, 103, 106
Sense of Wonder, The, 169
Seven Candles for Kwanzaa, **89**
Sevengill: The Shark and Me, 122
Sewall, Marcia, **101**
Seymour, Peter, 52, 70
Shachtman, Tom, 81
Shaka: King of the Zulus, 178
Shark, 122
Sharks and Other Creatures of the Deep, 59, 140
Sharks: Challengers of the Deep, **122**
She'll Be Comin' 'Round the Mountain, 101
Shebar, Sharon Sigmond, 42
Shebar, Susan E., 42
Shh! We're Writing the Constitution, 56, 134
Shooting Stars, **94**
Shortcut, 133
Shorto, Russell, 52
Shot from Midfield, 126
Showers, Paul, 124, 125, 145
Shumate, Jane, 157
Sicilia, D. B., 87
Sid and Sol, 35
Side by Side, 165
Siebert, Diane, 67, 133
Siegel, Beatrice, 63, 171
Silent Spring, 168
Sill, Cathryn, 44
Silverstein, Alvin, 114, 118, 125
Silverstein, Robert, 118, 125
Silverstein, Shel, 98
Silverstein, Virginia, 114, 118, 125
Simon Says—Let's Play, 79
Simon, Seymour, 57, **121**, **143**
Simple Machines, **92**
Sioux: A First Americans Book, The, 103, 106
Sis, Peter, 121, 130
Six Bridges of Humphrey the Whale, The, 141
Skeleton, 124
Skirt, The, 97
Skurzynski, Gloria, **114**
Skyscraper Book, The, 143
Slither McCreep and His Brother, Joe, 35
Smell, the Subtle Sense, 125
Smith, Eileen L., 95
Smith, Elizabeth Simpson, 23
Smith, Lane, 36
Smith, Robert Kimmel, 21
Sneve, Virginia Driving Hawk, **103**, 106
Snowy Day: Stories and Poems, 122
Sobel, R., 87

Soccer: A Heads-Up Guide to Super Soccer, 126
Sojourner Truth: Ain't I a Woman?, **156**
Sojourner Truth and the Voice of Freedom, 157, 183
Solberg, S. E., 39
Something Special for Me, 21
Soon, Annala, 96
Sorcerer's Apprentice, The, 37
Soto, Gary, 87
Souza, D. M., 128
Souza, Dorothy M., 29
Spanenburg, Ray, 70
Spider, The, 85
Spiders, **128**
Spinelli, Eileen, 131
Spirit of St. Louis, The, 68
Spring Fleece: A Day of Sheepshearing, 65
Squirmy Wormy Composters, 145
St. George, Judith, **188**
Stanley, Diane, 178
Stargazing Sky, 94
Stars and Stripes, **134**
Stars Come Out Within, 47
Stateswoman to the World, 182
Steele, Philip, 59, 140
Stevenson, James, 61
Stewart, Edgar, 72
Still, John, 49, 128
Stinky Cheese Man and Other Fairly Stupid Tales, The, 37
Stolz, Mary, 35
Stone, Lynn M., 29
Stop, Sue, 126
Story Behind Great Inventions, The, 86
Story of Frederick Douglass, Voice of Freedom, The, 22
Story of Hanukkah, **75**
Story of Jean, A, 47
Stranger, The, 121
Stringbean's Trip to the Shining Sea, 73, 90, 91
Stwertka, Eve, 168
Sugaring Season, 64
Sullivan, George, **40**
Sullivan, S. Adams, 43
Sun: Our Nearest Star, The, 127
Sundiata: Lion King of Mali, **175**, 177
Sunken Treasure, 123
Superdupers: Really Funny Words!, 27
Surcouf, Elizabeth Gillen, 178
Surprising Myself, 185
Surrounded by Sea, **66**
Swan Lake, 37

208 / AUTHOR/TITLE/ILLUSTRATOR INDEX

Swimming with Sea Lions and Other Adventures in the Galápagos Islands, **72**, 73

Tainos: The People Who Welcomed Columbus, **129**
Taitz, Emily, 157, 183
Taking My Cat to the Vet, 135
Taking Sides, 87, 97
Tale of Benjamin Bunny, The, 121
Tale of Mandarin Ducks, The, 35
Tale of Peter Rabbit, The, 69, 121
Talking Eggs, The, 36
Talking with Artists, **34**
Tar Beach, 164
Tarantula, The, 128
Taylor, Barbara, 72, **114**, 117
Taylor, Dave, 29
Taylor, David, **27**
Taylor, Paul D., 71
Terban, Marvin, 26
Tester, Sylvia Root, 135
Thanksgiving at Our House, 131
Thanksgiving at the Tappletons', 131
The Amazing Potato, 82
The Writing Bug, **165**
There Is No Rhyme for Silver, 112
There'll Be a Hot Time in the Old Town Tonight, 101
This Is a House, **80**
Thomson, Bob, 81
Three Days on a River in a Red Canoe, 21
Three Little Pigs, The, 144
Through Grandpa's Eyes, 47
THUMP, THUMP, Rat-a-Tat-Tat, 36
Thurgood Marshall: A Life for Justice, 158, 183
Tibbitts, Alison, 29
Titanic: Lost ... and Found, The, 123
T. J. and the Pirate Who Wouldn't Go Home, 111
To the Rescue, 52
Tobias, Tobi, 170
Tokuda, Wendy, 141
Tolstoy, Aleksey Nikolaevich, 116
Tomes, Margot, 122, 130, 143
Tommy at the Grocery Store, 35
Tongues of Jade, 37
Too Hot to Hoot, 27
Too Many Tamales, 97
Total Soccer, 126
Towle, Wendy, 22
Train Song, 133
Trains, 133
Trains at Work, **132**
Tree of Cranes, 88

Tropical Rain Forests Around the World, 117
Trucker, 52
True Stories About Abraham Lincoln, 75
True Story of the Three Little Pigs by A. Wolf, The, 36
Truth About Santa Claus, The, 143
Tseng, Mou-Sien, 88
Tub People, The, 35
Tuesday, 37
Turner, Dee, 73
Turner, Robyn Montana, **160**, 161, **163**
Turtle Watch, 134
Turtles, 133
Twentieth-Century Inventors, 175
Two and Too Much, 35
Two Bad Ants, 84

Ugh, 35
Under the Sea-Wind, 168
Unhuggables, The, 145
Up Against the Law, 52
Urban Roosts, **44**

Van, Allsburg, Chris, 37, 84, 121
Van Rynbach, Iris, 131
Vare, Ethlie Ann, 181
Vennema, Peter, 178
Venus, 127
Very Hungry Caterpillar, The, 84
Very Young Gardener, A, 116
Victory Garden Alphabet Book, The, 81
Victory Goal, 126
Viorst, Judith, 98
Visit of Two Giant Pandas at the San Diego Zoo, **109**
Visit to the Zoo, A, 135
Visual Dictionary of the Human Body, The, 124
Vogel, Carole G., 141
Voyage of the Frog, The, 41
Voyages: Poems by Walt Whitman, 165

Wade, Mary Dodson, 67, 68
Wadsworth, Ginger, 168, 179
Waiting to Waltz: A Childhood, 20, 167
Waldron, Ann, **162**
Waldrop, Victor H., 32, 110
Wallner, Alexandra, 130
Wallner, John, 130
Walter, Mildred Pitts, 35, 89
Walter Carroll, 59, 114
Walter Warthog, **136**, 137, 159
Walter's Tail, 36
War with Grandpa, The, 21

Author/Title/Illustrator Index / 209

Washington, 138, 187
Wasps at Home, 31, 128
Watson, Wendy, 131
Watts, Barrie, 84
Way Things Work, The, 93
W. E. B. DuBois: Crusader for Peace, 157
Week in the Life of an Airline Pilot, A, 52
Weidt, Maryann N., **173**, 182
Weil, Lisl, 98
Weiner, Eric, 22
Weird and Wacky Inventions, 86
Westward with Columbus, 130
Wetterer, Margaret K., 92, 155
Wexler, Jerome, 71, **115**
Whale, 139, 141
Whale Song, 141
Whales and Other Creatures of the Sea, 59, 140, 141
Whaling Days, **140**
What Bit Me?, 128
What Is a Cat?, 54
What's Hatching Out of That Egg?, 54
What's Inside? Insects, 128
What's the Big Idea, Ben Franklin?, 56
What's Your Story?, **39**
Whelan, Gloria, 46
When I Was Young in the Mountains, 20, 167
Where Are My Bears?, 34
Where Are My Prairie Dogs and Black-Footed Ferrets?, 34
Where Are My Puffins, Whales and Seals?, 34, 59, 140
Where Are My Swans, Whooping Cranes, and Singing Loons?, 34
Where Butterflies Grow, 31, 49, 128
Where Did Your Family Come From?, 95
Where Do Cats Live?, 54
Where Do You Get Your Ideas?, 40
Where Do You Think You're Going, Christopher Columbus?, 130
Where Does This Come From? Ice Cream, **81**
Where in the World Are You?, 73
Where the Sidewalk Ends, 98
Where to Find Dinosaurs Today, **57**, 58, 99
Where Was Patrick Henry on the 29th of May, 56
White, Florence M., 95
Whitfield, Philip, 57
Who Comes to the Water Hole?, **28**
Who Is the Beast?, 117
Why Don't You Get a Horse, Sam Adams?, 56
Why Is a Frog Not a Toad?, 28, **30**, 133
Why Mosquitoes Buzz in People's Ears, 35
Wiesner, David, 37
Wild, Wild Wolves, 30, 144

Wildsmith, Brian, 26, 61
Wilkinson, Brenda, 183
Will You Sign Here, John Hancock?, 56
Willard, Nancy, 35
Williams, Jennifer, 73, 90
Williams, Linda, 120
Williams, Sylvia B., 22
Williams, Vera B., 21, 73, 90
Willie's Not the Hugging Kind, 35
Willow, Diane, 29
Wimmer, Mike, 133
Wind Warrior, **87**
Windows on Wildlife, 27, 34
Winning Ways in Soccer, **125**
Winter Across America, 121
Winter Whale, 139
Wisniewski, David, **175**, 177
Witnesses to Freedom, **55**
Wizard of Oz, The, 120
Wolf and the Seven Little Kids, The, 144
Wolkomir, Joyce Rogers, 60
Wolkomir, Richard, 60
Wolves, 30, **143**, 144
Wonderful Pussy Willows, **115**
Wonderful Worms, **144**
Wood, Linda C., 29
Wood Hoopoe Willie, 89
Workers' Detective, The, 181
World of Honeybees, The, 85
Worth, Valerie, 112
Wright, Nicola, 73
Wright, Rachel, 111
Wright, Joan Richards, 28
Wright Brothers: How They Invented the Airplane, The, 69
Write Your Own Story, 40
Writing for Kids, 40
Wurmfeld, Hope Herman, 52
Wynne, Patricia, 122

Year They Walked, The, 171
Yep, Laurence, 37
Yorinks, Arthur, 35
You Call That a Farm?, 65
Young, Jerry, 71, 144
Your Cat's Wild Cousins, **53**
Your Foot's On My Feet! And Other Tricky Nouns, 27
Your Skin and Mine, 125
Yukon, 50

Z was Zapped, The, 37
Zebra, 29
Zebras, 29
Zinnia and Dot, 36
Zoo Clues, 28

Subject Index

Aakioloa bird, 32
Abanaki (Native Americans), 101
Abolitionists, 156-57
Accuracy, 5
Activists, 171, 181
   union, 96
Actor, 38, 96
Adams, Samuel, 56
Addams, Jane, 161, 181
Adopt-a-Horse Program, 79
Adoption, 20-21
Adventure, 23
Africa, 33, 176
   southern, 28
African-American family, 122
African-American holidays, 89
African-American stories, 164
African-Americans, 21-22, 171, 172, 192
African Fund for Endangered Wildlife, 136, 137
African wildcat, 53
AIDS patients, 77
Ailey, Alvin, Jr., 22, 172
Ailey's inspiration, 172-73
Air force pilots, 51. *See also* Airline pilots; Pilots
Aircraft, 26
Airline pilots, 52. *See also* Air force pilots; Pilots
Airships, 22-23
Alabama, 58
Alaska, 106
Albatrosses, 72
Allergies, 125
Alligators, 29, 30, 31, 65
Almaraz, Hector, 94-95
Alphabet books, 32, 50-51, 60, 72, 81-82, 128
"Amazing Grace" (song), 100
Amazon rain forest, 117. *See also* Rain forests
American Bashkir Curly horse, 31
American Mammoth jackstock, 31
American Minor Breeds Conservancy, 31
American Revolution, 22, 119
Amish, 24
Amish stories, 24
Ammann, Jacob, 24
Amnesty, for illegal residents, 95

Amphibians, 45
Ancestors, 83
Ancona chicken, 31. *See also* Birds
Anderson, Marian, 22, 164
Andretti, Michael, 41
Animal researcher, 158-59
Animal rights, 155, 166
Animal shelters, 25
Animal words, 26-27
Animal world, mysteries of, 27-28
Animals, 28, 72
   in Africa, 25-26, 28-29, 136-37
   in Australia, xiii
   differences among, 29
   egg-hatching, 54
   endangered, 27, 31-32, 33, 34, 60, 65, 72, 110, 136, 139
   extinct, 28, 31, 32, 136
   farm, 31
   habitats of, 27-28, 32, 33, 34
   intelligence of, 28
   jungle, 29, 117
   luminous, 27
   protection of, 32
   in rain forests, 29
   of the Savannah, 29
   skeletons of, 27
   social behavior of, 25
   tools of, 33
Antelope, 26, 28, 30
Anthropologist, 155
Anthropomorphism, 6
Antiochus, 75
Ants, 26, 84, 117
Apatosaurus, 58
Apes, 26, 30, 31, 33
Appalachian Mountains, 20, 167-68
Apple orchards, 65
Aquarium, 122
Aquino, Benigno, 37
Aquino, Corazon, 37
Arachnids, 128
Archaeologists, 123-24
Archbishop, 96
Archipelago, 72
Architects, 38, 75, 80, 81, 137
Arizona, 103, 169
Army ants, 117. *See also* Ants
Art, Impressionist, 161
Artists, 22, 34, 160-61, 162, 163

212 / SUBJECT INDEX

Aruba, 78
Aruego, Jose, 37
Asia, 25, 33, 39
Asian Americans, 37, 39
Asiatic bear, 43. See also Bears
Aspirin, 86
Assassinations, presidential, 75
Assembly-line workers, 51
Asses, 31
Astronauts, 22, 52
Atlases, 73
Atocha (ship), 123
Attorneys, 96
Attucks, Crispus, 22
Australia, 25, 71
Authors, 37, 38, 165, 166, 167, 168
Authorship, 39-40
Auto mechanics, 52. See also Mechanics
Automobile racing, 40-41
Autumn, 121
Avery, John, 111
Aviators, 68. See also Air force pilots; Airline pilots; Pilots
  female, 67

Baboons, 28, 29
Bacon, Henry, 75
Badgers, 26
Bahamas, 129
Baking bread, 104, 105
Bald eagles, 60. See also Birds; Eagles
Ballerinas, 170
Balloon enthusiasts, 41-42
Ballooning, 42
Bandicoots, 60
Banking
  and finance, 52, 98
  and investing, 98
Banks, 96
Banneker, Benjamin, 137
Bartholdi, Frederic Auguste, 135
Baseball, 105
Basi Gou, 109
Basketball players, 170
Batik illustrations, 26
Bats, 27, 42-43, 135
  greater horseshoe, 124
Bearden, Romare, 22
Bears, 1, 34, 43-44
  black, 135
Beavers, 25
Bees, killer, 85
Beetles, 85, 114
Bell, Alexander Graham, 189
Bethune, Mary McLeod, 164
Big Dipper, 94
Bill of Rights, 56, 134

Biographies, 155-89
  collective, 21-22
Biography bookshelf, 156-189
Biologists, 117
Birds, 25, 26, 32-33, 34, 44-45, 72
  feathers of, 45
  land, 54
  tropical, 29
  water, 54
Bismark (ship), 123
Black Australorp chicken, 31. See also Birds
Black Bart, 111
Black-footed cat, 53. See also Cats
Black-footed ferrets, 34
Black Muslims, 22
Black rhino, 31, 137. See also Rhinoceroses
Blackbeard, 111
Blimps, 22-23
Blindness, 46-47, 188-89
BLM (Bureau of Land Management), 79, 80
Blood plasma, 21
Blood system, 145
Bobcat, 53. See also Cats
Body, human, 109, 145
Bonaparte, Joseph, 163
Bonaparte, Napoleon, 163
Bonheur, Rosa, 161
Bonnet, Stede, 111
Bonney, Anne, 111
Boobies, 72. See also Birds
Books, 8
  alphabet, 32, 50-51, 60, 72, 81-82, 128
  choosing, xv-xvi, 3, 19-20
Booth, John Wilkes, 74
Borges, Jorge Luis, 96
Borneo, 33
Boston Harbor, 91
Boston Light, 91
Boston Massacre, 22
Boston Post Road, 119-20
Box cars, 132
Bozeman Trail, 102
Braille, Louis, 46
Brain, 125
Bread baking, 104, 105
Bridgman, Laura, 189
British Colombia, 50
Broadcasters, television, 38. See also Journalists
Brontosaurus, 58
Brooks, Anne, 76-77
Brooks, Gwendolyn, 112
Brown, John, 157
Brown v. Board of Education of Topeka, Kansas, 55

Subject Index / 213

Bryceson, Derek, 159
Buffalo Bill, 102
Buffalo dance, 105
Bugs, 128
Bullfighters, 169-70
Bunche, Ralph, 22
Bureau of Land Management (BLM), 79, 80
Burgess, Abbie, 92, 155
Bus boycott, 55, 171
Business, 47-48
Business executive, 96
Business owners, 22. *See also* Entrepreneurs
Butcher, Susan, 11
Butterflies, 30, 31, 48-49, 84, 117, 128

Cactus finch, 72. *See also* Birds; Finches
Caddis fly, 114
Caddis-fly larva, 25
Caimans, 29. *See also* Crocodiles
Calico Jack, 111
California, 49, 58
Cambodia, 39
Cambodian people, 37
Camouflage, 4, 28
Canada, 49, 58
Canada lynx, 53
Captain Greavs, 111
Captain Hook, 111
Captain Kidd, 111
Captivity, 34
Capuchin monkeys, 77
Caracal, 53
Careers, 51, 52-53, 98
Caribbean, 111, 129
Caribou, 50
Carrot seed, 116
Carson, Rachel, 168
Carter, Jimmy, 81
Carter, Roslyn, 81
Cartier, Jacques, 119
Cash, Johnny, 100
Cassatt, Mary, 160-61, 162
Caterpillar, 84
Caterpillar equipment, 86
Catfish, 65
Catkins, 115
Cats, 26, 28, 53-54, 124
Cayley, Sir George, 69
Cebus monkeys, 117
Challenger (space shuttle), 38
Challenges, 170
Chameleons, 27
Chang, Michael, 38
Charles, Prince, 178
Chau, Hoang Anh, 83, 96

Chavez, Cesar, 95, 96
Checking accounts, 96
Cheetahs, 28, 29, 53, 124
Cherokee (Native Americans), 106
Chess, Victoria, 34, 35
Cheyenne (Native Americans), 102
Chickens, 31, 54
Chief Joseph, 102
Chief Seattle, 113-14
Children, handicapped, 47
Children's Crusade, 55
Chimney sweeps, 142
Chimpanzees, 33, 124, 158-59
ChimpanZoo, 159
Chimps, 159
China, 39, 78, 109
Chinese, 20, 37, 38
Chinese American, 169
Chipmunk, 25
Chisholm, Shirley, 22
Chopsticks, 143
Christmas, 63, 64, 88
Chrysler, 47
Chung, Connie, 37, 38
Chung, Myung-Whun, 38
Circulatory system, 145
Cisneros, Henry, 96
Civil rights, 21, 55, 155, 171
    activists, 171
    movement, 183
Civil War, 74
Class trips, 108-9
"Climbing Jacob's Ladder" (song), 100
Clinton, Bill, 155
Clinton, Hillary Rodham, 155
Cobra, king, 124
Coca-Cola, 86
Cochiti drums, 105
Cochiti Pueblo, 105
Cochran, Jacqueline, 23
Coelacanth, fish, 32
Coelurosauravus (gliding reptile), 32
Cole, William, 112
Collages, 120
Collective biographies, 34-39, 48, 51, 76-77, 85-86, 96, 112, 170
Colonies, 56
Colonists, 119
Columbus, Christopher, 5, 129-30
Comanches, 102
Commodity Futures Trading Commission, 38
Computer programmers, 51, 105
Computers, 52, 105
Conductors, 38
Congressman, 96
Congresswomen, 22

214 / SUBJECT INDEX

Constables, 26
Constitution, the, 56, 134
Constitutional convention, 56
Construction, 80, 81
Continental Congress, 134
Cookies, 85-86
Corn, 81
Corn farming, 65
Costa Rica, 117
Cousteau Society, 133
Cowper, William, 100
Cows, 31, 63, 81
Coyotes, 30
Crafts, three-dimensional, 43, 71
Cranberries, 2, 11, 65
Cranes, 34
Crayfish, 114
Cree (Native Americans), 144
Crews, Donald, 132-33
Crocodiles, 26, 28, 29, 30, 31
Crocodilians, 29
Cronkite, Walter, 136
Crows, 26, 44
Crum, George, 85
Cummings, Pat, 34, 35
Cuts, 145
Cynthia Rylant, 167-68

Dairy farming, 63-64
Dampier, William, 111
Dancers, 172
Dandridge, Dorothy, 164
de Champlain, Samuel, 119
de Rozier, Jean Francois Piltre, 69
Deafness, 188-89
Decorated eggs, 61
Deer, 30
Degas, Edward, 161
Delaware, 49
Detectives, 51
Diademed squid, 27
Dialogue, in writing, 39-40
Dillon, Diane, 34, 35
Dillon, Leo, 34, 35
Dineh, Navajo, 103
Dinosaurs, xiii, 57-58, 71, 99, 118, 125
Diplomats, 22
Directors, film, 96
Dirigibles, 23
Diving beetles, 114
Doctors, 181
Dodo bird, 32-33. *See also* Birds
Dogs, 135
Dogsled race, 11
Dolls, 105
Dolphins, 26, 59, 114, 140
Douglass, Frederick, 22, 157

Dow Chemical, 47
Dr. Susan Picotte Memorial Hospital, 181
Dragonfishes, 27
Dragonflies, 83-84, 114
Drake, Sir Francis, 111
Dreidels, 76
Drew, Charles, 21
Drums, 105
DuBois, W. E. B., 157
Ducks, 30, 114
Dunham, Katherine, 22, 172-73
DuPont, 47
Dutch Belted cows, 31

Eagles, 26, 59-60, 124
Earhart, Amelia, 23, 67, 68
Earth (planet), 73, 109, 127
Easter, 60-61
  baskets, 61
  dinner, 61
  parades, 61
Eastman, George, 175
Eastman Kodak, 86
Economists, 38
Ecuador, 72
Edison, Thomas A., 22, 86, 175
Educators, 38
Eels, 26, 27, 114
Egg hunts, 61
Egg-rolling contests, 61
Eggs, 26, 54
  painting, 61
Egielski, Richard, 34, 35
Egypt, 91
Ehlert, Lois, 34, 35-36
El Chino, 169
Electric eels, 27
Electric motors, 175. *See also* Engines; Motors
Elephants, 26, 28, 31
  African, 124, 137
  Asian, 137
Elevators, Otis, 86
Ellis Island, 61-63
Endangered animals, 27, 60, 72, 110, 136, 139. *See also* Animals; Extinct animals
Endangered planet, 117
Endings, in writing, 39-40
Endpapers, 119
Engines, 132. *See also* Electric motors; Motors
Entrepreneurs, 173-75. *See also* Business owners
Envelopes, 11, 115
Environment, 118
Environmental projects, 113-14

Environmentalists, 168, 169
Eponyms, 26
Equal rights, 21, 157-58
Equality, 183
Equipment, manufacture of, 52
Equipment, sports, 52
Ernst, Lois Campbell, 34, 36
Everett, Edward, 74
Executives, business, 96
Explorations, in space, 127
Explorers, 22, 119
Extinct animals, 28, 136. *See also* Animals; Endangered animals

Failures, 47-48
Faith Ringgold's work, 164
Falcons, peregrine, 32, 33, 44
Fall. *See* Autumn
Families, 20-21
 African-American, 122
Farm animals, 31. *See also* Animals
Farmers, cotton, 51
Farming, 64-65
 dairy, 63-64
 pumpkin, 65
 trees, 64-65
Farms, 108
 types of, 64-65
Fashion retailing, 52
Feathers, 45. *See also* Birds
Feelings, Tom, 34, 36
Ferrets, 26, 34
Fetterman, Captain William J., 102
Fiction, 39-40
Field trips, 108, 127
Figure skaters, 170
Film directors, 96
Finches, 72. *See also* Birds
Fire prevention, 66
Firefighters, 52, 65, 66
Fireflies, 129
Fires, forest, 66
Fish, 32, 45, 65, 114
Fishermen, 50
Fishing, 66
Fishing cat, 53
Fishing village, 66
Flags, 134
Flamingos, 26
Fleischman, Paul, 112
Flies, 26
Flight, 23, 67
 adventurous, 23
 aviators, 67-68
 historic, 67
 history, 68-70
Flores, Patrick, 96

Florida, 104, 132-33
Flowers, 116
Flying gecko, 117
Folk songs, American, 100
Folk stories, Hmong, 83
Food products, 81-82
Football coaches, 22
Football players, 170
Forest fires, 66
Forks, 143
Fossil bones, 57
Fossils, 32, 70-71
Foster homes, 20-21
Franklin, Benjamin, 56
French and Indian War, 119
French, Daniel Chester, 75
French Open (tennis), 38
Frigate birds, 72. *See also* Birds
Fringed flowers, 114
Frogs, 10, 25, 28, 30, 31, 71, 114, 117, 133

Galápagos Islands, 72-73, 133
Gamble, David, 86
Gamble, James, 86
Games, 79
Garbage, 118
Gardening, 11, 116
Gardens, 81, 116
Gavials, 29
Geese, 26, 30. *See also* Birds
Geography, 73
Georgia Department of Natural Resources, 139
Gettysburg Address, 74
Ghana, 177
Gharials, 34
Giant kelp, 34
Giant Pandas, 109
Gibbons, 33
Giblin, James Cross, 142-43
Gibson, Althea, 170
Gifts, 88
Gillette razors, 86
Giraffes, 28, 33
 reticulated, 124
 Rothschild, 29, 31, 136, 137, 159
Gladiator tree frog, 25
Glass, 142
Gloucester Old Spots pig, 31. *See also* Pigs
Gnats, 26
Goats, 135
Goddard, Robert, 175
Gold, 129
Gold rush, Canadian, 51
Goldfinches, 26. *See also* Birds; Finches
Goldwyn, Samuel, 175

216 / SUBJECT INDEX

Golfers, 96, 170
Gondola, 23
Goodall, Jane, 33, 155, 158-59, 169
Goodyear, Charles, 175
Gorillas, 33
  mountain, 27
Gould, Gordon, 175
Goya, Francisco, 162
Gramm, Wendy Lee, 38
Grandparents, 20-21, 94, 104, 105, 107, 167
Graphics, 6
Great Lakes, 119
Great Lakes Lighthouse Keepers Association, 92
Greece, 70
Green Corn Dance, 131
Green sea turtle, 133. *See also* Turtles
Greenpeace USA, 139
Griots, storytellers, 177
Ground finch, 72. *See also* Birds; Finches
Groundhogs, 116, 135
Guide dogs, 46
Guinea hog, 31
Gulls, swallow-tailed, 72. *See also* Birds
Gutenberg, Johann, 187-88
Gutenberg, and printing, 188

Habitat for Humanity, 81
Habitat, of animals, 27-28, 30, 32, 33, 34. *See also* Animals
Habitats, 29, 53, 133
Hallmark, 47
Hamer, Fannie Lou, 21, 164
Hamilton, Alice, 181
Hancock, John, 56
Handicapped children, 47
Hannotte, Dean, 58
Hanukkah, 75-76
  symbols of, 76
  traditions in fiction, 76
Hares, 26, 30
Harrison, Ted, 50
Harvest, 2
Harvest Feast, 131
Harvest mice, 25
Hearing, 125
Hearn, Michael Paul, 112
Hedgehogs, 26
Heinz, 47
Helping others, 76-77
Henry, Marguerite, 80
Henry, Patrick, 56
Henson, Matthew, 22
Hillert, Margaret, 112
Hippopotami, 28, 26, 29
Hispanic Americans, 95
  in fiction, 96-97

Historical sites, 10
Historical topics, 5
Hmong, 83
Hoban, Russell, 112
Hogan, Ben, 170
Holidays, African-American, 89
Homelessness, 77-78
Homographs, 26
Homonyms, 26
Honeybees, 27, 30. *See also* Bees
Hopi Pueblo, 105
Hopkins, Lee Bennett, 165
Hopper cars, 132
Hopscotch, 78-79
Horsemen, 26
Horses, 26, 31, 79-78, 135
Hospice program, 77
Hot air balloons, 23, 41, 50
Hounds, 26
Houses, 80-81
  building, 80, 81
Huerta, Dolores, 96
Human body, 109, 145
Humanitarianism, 81
Humanitarians, 181-82
Hummingbirds, 27
Hunkpapas (Native Americans), 102
Hurston, Zora Neale, 164, 181
Hyenas, 28

Ice cream, 81
Idaho, 104
Ideas, 40
Idioms, 26-27
Iditarod, 11
Iguanas, marine, 72
Illustrations, 4, 14
Immigrant Wall of Honor, 62
Immigrants, 62-63, 82, 94-96
  experiences of, 95-96
  in fiction, 83
  and immigration, 134
Impressionist art, 161
Incandescent lamp, 175
Inclined planes, 92, 93
Income tax, 96
India, 43, 78
Indianapolis 500, 40-41
Information, seeking, 19
Information books, using, 8-14
Information literature, 15
Injuries, 145
Inner-city schools, 77
Inouye, Daniel K., 38
Insects, 27, 34, 83-84, 114, 128
Intelligence, of animals, 28. *See also* Animals

Subject Index / 217

Interest, monetary, 96
International Whaling Commission, 140
Inuit, 50
Inukshuk, 50
Inupiat (Native Americans), 106
Inventions, 22
 accidental, 85
 and inventors, 86-87
Inventors, 22, 69, 86, 87, 175
 African American, 175
Iowa, 49, 58
Irish immigrants, 62. See also Immigrants
Isis (ship), 123
Isshinryu (Okinawan karate), 87
Ivory soap, 86, 87

Jackals, 135-36
Jackson Elementary School project, 113
Jackson, Jesse, 157, 182-83
Jackstock, 31
Jaguars, 30, 117
Jaguarundi, 53
Japan, 39
Japanese, 37, 38
Jeans, 86, 173-75
Jefferson, Thomas, 56, 183
Jenkins, Carol Heiss, 170
Jewish symbols, 76
Jewish traditions, 61
Jews, 75
Job opportunities, 51-52
Johns, Barbara, 55
Jokes, 26
Jordan, Barbara, 22
Journalists, 37, 38
 television, 41
Judah, 75
Judges, 51
Jungles, 34
Jungle animals, 29, 109, 117. See also Animals
Justininano, Erik, 77

Kalona Historical Society, 24
Kalona Historical Village, 24
Kangaroos, 26
 great gray, 124
Kansas, 144
Karate, 87
Karate instructors, 77
Karenga, Maulana, 89
Katz, Bobbie, 112
Keita, Sundiata, 175-76

Keller, Helen, 188-89
Kellogg, Steven, 34, 36
Kelly, Grace, 178
Kelp, 34
Kennedy, John F., 156
Kennedy, X. J., 112
Kenya, 136
Keresan language, 105
Keresan pueblo, 105
Khan, Chingis, 178
Khmer Rouge, 38
Killer bees, 85. See also Bees
King, Coretta Scott, 157, 183
King, Martin Luther, 22, 55, 171, 182
Kings, 175, 177-78
Kingston, Maxine Hong, 38
Kiskadees, 117
Kites, 88
Kittens, 135. See also Cats
Klondike, 51
Knives, 143
Korea, 39
Korean, 37, 38
Koto, 38
Kramer, Jerry, 170
Kroll, Steven, 112
Kumin, Maxine, 112
Kuramoto, June, 38
Kuskin, Karla, 112
Kwanzaa, 89

L'Enfant, Pierre, 137
Labrador, 50
Ladybugs, 84, 129
Lakota (Native Americans), 103
Lamps, incandescent, 175
Landfills, 118
Larks, 26
Larva, 25
Latimer, Lewis Howard, 175
Lava lizards, 72
Law enforcement, 51-52
Law, Ruth, 23, 67, 68
Lawick, Hugo Van, 159
Laws, changing, 80
Leakey, Louis, 158
Leeches, 65
Legal rights, 52
Legends, 105
Leopards, 26, 28, 30, 31, 53. See also Cats
Leslie-Melville, Betty, 169
Letter writing, 90, 107
 in fiction, 90-91
Letters, 11
Levers, machine, 92, 93
Levi jeans, 86

218 / SUBJECT INDEX

Life
  of Lincoln, 74-75
  in medieval Africa, 176-77
  in Spain, 163
Lighthouse organizations, 92
Lighthouses, 91
Lilienthal, Otto, 69
Lincoln, Abraham, 74, 131
Lindbergh, Charles, 23, 67-68, 70
Lindgren, Astrid, 155, 166
Lions, 26, 28, 29, 53. See also Cats
Liquid paper, 87
Lithographs, 162
  stone, 74-75
Little Brewster Island, 91
Little, Jean, 47
Little Rock Nine, 55
Livingston, Myra Cohn, 112
Lizards, 72
Loans, 96
Loons, singing, 34
Lopez, Nancy, 96
Louis XIV of France, 177
Lynx, 53

Macaws, 117
Maccabee, 75
Machines, 92-93
Madison, Dolley, 138, 184-85
Madison, James, 138, 163, 183-85
Magicians, animal, 27
Mail, 11, 114-15
Maine, 48, 91
Malaysia, 33
Malcolm X, 22, 157
Mali, 176, 177
Malinke, 177
Mallee fowl, 25
Mandela, Nelson, 100, 157-58
Manitoba, 50
Manufacturing, 52
Maple sugar farm, 64
Maple syrup, 10
Maps, 39, 73-74, 79
Marbled cat, 53
Marches, 55
Marine biology, 168
Marine iguanas, 72
Marshall, Thurgood, 158, 183
Martial arts, 87-88
Martinez, Maria, 106
Martinez, Vilma, 96
Mary Rose (ship), 123
Massachusetts, 91
Massachusetts Institute of Technology, 181
Massasoit, 131

Matador, 169
Matinicus Rock Lighthouse, 92
Matzeliger, Jan, 175
Mayflower (ship), 131
Mayors, 96
McNair, Ronald, 22
Mechanics, 52
Medicines, 65
Meerkats, 28
Mema, 176
Mendes, Chico, 117
Mennonite Historical Society of Iowa, 24
Mennonite Museum, 24
Mennonites, 24
Mercury (planet), 127
Merriam, Eve, 112
Metamorphosis, 85
Meteorite, 94
Meteors, 94
Mexican Americans, 87, 94-95
  achievers, 96-97
Mexico, 49, 95
Mice, 25
Microscope, 114
Middle ages, 177-78
Migration, 84
  of birds, 60
  of butterflies, 49
  of whales, 139
Milk, 81, 143
Milking, 64, 81
Millionaires, 22
Mimicry, 4
Missouri, 49
Mistakes, 85
Monarch butterflies, 48-49, 54
Money, 96, 98
Mongooses, 28
Monkeys, 26, 28, 30, 77, 117
  spider, 124
Montana, 104
Montgolfier, Etienne, 41, 68
Montgolfier, Joseph, 41, 68
Montgomery, Alabama, 171
Morgan, Sir Henry, 111
Moths, 27, 30, 49, 128
Motorcycles, manufacture of, 52
Motors, 175. See also Electric motors; Engines
Muir, John, 169, 178-79
Muir Glacier, 179
Muir Lake, 179
Muir Park, 179
Muir Woods National Monument, 179
Museums, 98-99
Music, origin of hymns, 99-100
Musical origins, 100-101

Musicians, 38
Muskrats, 114
Mustangs, 79-80
Mysid shrimp, 65
Mysteries, 27-28

Nacona, Peta, 102
Names, 62, 63
Narragansett (Native Americans), 101
National Inventors Center, 86
National Inventors Day, 86
National Museum of Natural History, Nairobi, 158
Native Americans, 5-6, 59, 85, 101, 102, 103, 119, 131, 140, 144
   Abanaki, 101
   Cherokee, 106
   Cheyenne, 102
   Cree, 144
   history of, 102
   Hunkpapas, 102
   Inupiat, 106
   Lakota, 103
   Narragansett, 101
   Navajos, 103, 106
   Nez Perce, 102, 104
   Oglala Sioux, 102
   Omaha, 180-81
   Pawnee, 144
   Pawtoxet, 131
   and Pilgrims, 101-2
   Pueblos, 103, 104
   Seminoles, 103, 104, 106
   Shoshoni, 102
   Sioux, 102, 103, 106, 181
   Teton Sioux, 102
   Wampanoag, 101, 131
Natural history museums, 71, 98
Naturalists, 178-79
Nature museums, 71
Navajo-Churro sheep, 31
Navajo Curriculum Center, 103
Navajos (Native Americans), 103, 106
Nebraska, 144
Nepal, 43
Neptune (planet), 127
Nervous system, 125
Nests, 25, 44
New Brunswick, 50
New England, 66
New England Aquarium, 139
New Mexico, 79, 103, 105
New Mexico State Penitentiary, 79
New York City, 107
News journalists, 37, 38
Newton, John, 99, 100
Newts, 114

Nez Perce (Native Americans), 102, 104
Ngor, Haing, 38
Nguyen, Dustin, 38
Nigeria, 78
Nobel Peace Prize, 22
Nobel Prize, physics, 38
Nogales, Luis, 96
Norman, Jessye, 100
North Pole, 22
North Star, 94
Northern neighbor, 50
Northwest Territories, 50
Nouns, 26-27
   about animals, 26
Nova Scotia, 50
Nurse, 51
Nutrition, 82
Nye, Naomi Shihab, 112

"O Canada" (song), 50
O'Keeffe, Georgia, 161
Ocean, 108
Ocean life, 108
Ocelot, 53. *See also* Cats
Oglala Sioux (Native Americans), 102
Oil paintings, 186
Oklahoma, 104
Old Glory, 134
Olmos, Edward James, 96
Olympic Mountains, 121
Omaha (Native Americans), 180-81
Ontario, 50
Opera, 38
Opera singer, 22
Orangutans, 33
Orchestra conductor, 38
Orchids, 117
Oregon, 104
Organization, 6, 14
Original Lighthouse Collection, 92
Ortega, Katherine Davalos, 96
Ostrich, Masai, 124
Ostriches, 28, 29, 54
Otters, 26, 65
Owls, 26, 44
   barn, 44
   snowy, 44
Oxen, 26
Oysters, 27

Pacific Islanders, 39
Paleontologists, 57
Palindromes, 27
Pallas's cat, 53
Pandas, 27, 109, 110
Paper towels, 86

Paper wasps, 25
Parakeets, 135
Parker, Cynthia Ann, 102
Parker, Quanah, 102
Parks, Rosa, 55, 164, 171
Parrots, 26, 65
Partridges, 26
Passover, 61
Pasteurization, 143
Patent and Trademark Office, 86
Paulsen, Gary, 41-42
Pawnee (Native Americans), 144
Pawtuxet (Native Americans), 131
Peacocks, 26
Pearls, 27
Pelicans, 72
Penguins, 26, 34
Pepperidge Farm bread, 86
Peregrine falcons, 32, 33, 44
Permits, work, 95
Persian Gulf War, 100
Personification, 6
Pheasant chick, 54
Pheasants, 26
Philippines, 37
Photo-essays, 65, 80, 94-95, 128
Photography equipment, 86
Physician, 180-81
Picotte, Susan LaFlesche, 180-81
Pigeon Creek, 113
Pigeons, 44
Piglets, 26
Pigs, 31, 135
Pilgrims, 130-31
Pilgrims, and Native Americans, 101-2
Pilots, 51, 52, 69, 70
Pinkney, Jerry, 34, 36
Pioneers, 175
Pippi Longstocking, 166, 167
Pirates, 110-11
  in fiction, 111
  in poetry, 112
Pisanky (decorated eggshell), 61
Planets, 118, 127
  endangered, 117
Plants, growing, 116
Plasma, 21
Pledge of Allegiance, 134
Plot, Robert, 57
Plots, in writing, 39-40
Plover, 26
Pluto (planet), 127
Plymouth, Massachusetts, 101, 142
Poems, 165, 168
Poetry, 165
Poetry writing, 40
Poets, 112
Point of view, in writing, 39-40

Poison dart frog, 117
Political leaders, 22. *See also* Politicians
Politicians, 37, 182. *See also* Political leaders
Pollution, 113
Pond snail, 114
Ponds, 114
Pop-ups, 71-72, 85, 93
Popsicles, 86
Porcupines, 117
Porpoises, 59
Portuguese man-of-war, 25
Post-it notes, 86
Postal service, 114-15
Postcards, 73, 90-91, 107, 127
Postman, 115
Potato chips, 85
Potatoes, 82
Potters, 52
Pottery, 104, 105
Pourquoi stories, 43
Powell, Colin, 22
Prairie dogs, 34
Praying mantis, 27, 128
Predator, 60
Prelutsky, Jack, 112
President of the United States, 183-84, 185-87
Presidential Medal of Freedom, 171
Presidents, 138
Price, Leontyne, 22
Prince Edward Island, 50
Princess Diana, 178
Printers, 187-88
Programmers, computer, 51, 105
Protection, of animals, 32. *See also* Animals
Public defenders, 51
Pueblo, 104
Pueblos (Native Americans), 103, 104
Puffins, 34, 59, 140
Pulleys, 93
Puma, 53. *See also* Cats
Pumpkin farming, 65
Pumpkins, 2
Puppies, 10
Pussy willows, 115-16
Python, 54

Qionglai Mountains, 109
Quadriplegics, 77
Quagga, 32
Quebec, 50
Quilts, 163-64

Subject Index

Rabbits, 30
Raccoons, 25
Race cars, 40-41
Rackham, Captain Jack, 111
Railroad disasters, 92
Rain forests, 25, 109, 117
  African, 29, 34
Ramirez, Blandina Cardenas, 96
Rays, 27
Read, Mary, 111
Readers of nonfiction, 2-3
Reading, 4
  collaborative, 10-12
  for information, 8-14
  motivational, 9-10
  oral, xv, 14-15
Reading aloud, 8-9, 14-15
Rebuses, 132
Recycling, 118
Red Cloud, 102
Reptiles, 26, 27, 28, 29, 30, 31, 32, 45, 54
Research, 9-10
Research balloons, 42
Researchers, animal, 158-59
Response activities, 15-17
Restaurateurs, 51
Retail, 52
Reuse, 118
Revere, Paul, 56
Revision, in writing, 39-40
Rhinoceroses, 31, 137
  black, 31, 137
  white, 28
Richards, Ellen, 181
Riddles, 26
Right whales, 139
Ringgold, Faith, 161-62, 163-64
Rivero, Juan, 117
Rivers, 114
Roberts, Bartholomew (Black Bart), 111
Robinson, Eddie, 22
Rock and Roll Hall of Fame, 38
Rolls-Royce automobile, 86
Roosevelt, Eleanor, 155, 181-82
Roosevelt, Franklin D., 155
Roosevelt, Theodore, 1, 43-44
Rothschild giraffes, 29, 31, 136, 137, 159
Royal Canadian Mounted Police, 50
Royalty, 177-78
Roybal, Edward R., 96
Roybal, Timmy, 105
Russian Jews, 62
Ryder, Joanne, 112
Rylant, Cynthia, 112, 167

Sailors, 26
Saint Lawrence River, 119

Saint Lawrence Seaway, 51, 119
Salamanders, 114. *See also* Lizards;
  Reptiles
Salmon, 26, 113
Salmon, Chinook, 124
San Diego Zoo, 109
San Francisco, 122
San Ildefonso Pueblo, 105
Santa Claus, 142, 143
Saskatchewan, 50
Satin bowerbird, 25. *See also* Birds
Savage, Augusta, 164
Savannah, the, 29
Savannas, 136
Save the Whales, 139
Scarecrows, 120-21
  history of, 120-21
Schwartz, Amy, 34, 36
Scientists, 123
Scorpions, 27
Scotchgard, 86
Scrapes, 145
Scratch board (illustrations), 89
Scratches, 145
Screws, machine, 92, 93
Sculptor, 75, 135
Sea creatures, 109
Sea lions, 59, 72, 140
Seals, 34, 59, 140
Seasons, 121
Seeds, 11, 116
Selachiphobic, 122
Seminoles (Native Americans), 103, 104, 106
Senators, U.S., 38
Sending mail, 115
Senses, 125
Serval, 53
Settler's family, 66
Seven principles of Kwanzaa, 89
Sharks, 59, 114, 122
  great white, 27
Sheep, 26, 31
Sheep farming, 65
Shelley, Kate, 92, 155
Shelters, animal, 25-26
Ships, 26
Shipwrecks, 123
Shoe-lasting machine, 175
Shooting stars, 94
Shorinji kempo (Japanese martial arts), 87, 97
Shoshoni (Native Americans), 102
Shrimp, 65
Silly Putty, 86
Sioux (Native Americans), 102, 103, 106, 181
Sitting Bull, 102

222 / SUBJECT INDEX

Skeletal system, 124-25
Skeletons, 27, 124
Skin, 125
Skunks, 145
Skyscrapers, 143
Slave trader, 99-100
Slaves, 22, 156-57
Sled dogs, 11
Slugs, 145
Smell, sense of, 125
Smith, Bessie, 164
Smith, Lane, 34, 36-37
Snakes, 124, 145
Snipe, 26
Snohomish County Adopt-A-Stream Foundation, 113
Snow, 121
Snow leopard, 53. *See also* Cats; Leopards
Snowshoe hares, 53
Soccer, 125-26
 in fiction, 126
Social activists, 182, 188-89. *See also* Activists; Civil rights
Social behavior, of animals, 25
Social workers, 51, 181
Solar system, 73, 107, 109, 127
Songhay, 177
Songs, 131
Soninke, 177
Sosa, Dan, 96
Soto, Gary, 112
Sound barrier, 70
South Carolina, 98
Southern Africa, 28
Southwest Voter Registration Education Project, 96
Soviet Union, 78
Space, 70
Space explorations, 127
Spain, 129, 162
Sparrows, 44
Speech, 125
Spiders, 11, 25, 128, 145
Spirit of St. Louis (plane), 68
Spirituals, 100
Spoons, 143
Sports figures, 37
Spring, 122
Squanto, 131
Squid, 27
Squirrels, 25, 26
Sri Lanka, 43
Starlings, 44
Stars, 26
Statue of Liberty, 92, 134-35
Stewart, Maria W., 164
Stickleback fish, 25, 114
Stone, Lucy, 181

Stories
 African-American, 164
 Amish, 24
 of Columbus, 130
 Thanksgiving, 131
Storks, 28
Story quilts, 163-64
Storytellers, 104-5, 106
Storytelling, 104, 105
Strauss, Levi, 173-75
Streams, 114
Style, 14
Sumanguru, 176
Sumatra, 33
Sun, 127
Sundiata, Keita, 175-76
Sunflowers, 50
Sunken ships, 123
Swallow-tailed gulls, 72. *See also* Birds
Swallows, 25, 44. *See also* Birds
Swans, 26, 34. *See also* Birds
Swine, 26. *See also* Pigs
Swiss Mennonites, 24

Tailorbird, 25
Tainos, 5, 129, 130
Taiwan, 33
Tallchief, Maria, 170
Tanzania, 158
Tarantulas, 128
 curly-haired, 117
Tash, 118
Teach, Edward (Blackbeard), 111
Teachers, 51
Teenagers, 46
Teleological explanations, 6
Television broadcasters, 38. *See also* Journalists
Television journalists, 41. *See also* Journalists
Tennis players, 170
Termites, 25
Tet celebration, 83
Teton Sioux (Native Americans), 102
Tewa (language), 105
Tewa pueblo, 105
Thailand, 33
Thanksgiving, 101, 130-32
Thanksgiving stories, 131
Themes, 1
3M, 47
Three-spined stickleback, 25
Thuy, Dan, 82
Tidal pool, 114
Tigers, 25, 53, 117
Ting, Samuel C. C., 38
Titanic (ship), 123

Toads, 10, 26, 28, 30, 31, 71-72, 133
Tollhouse Inn, 85
Tools of animals, 33. *See also* Animals
Toronto Blue Jays, 50
Tortoises, 30, 54, 72, 133
   giant, 27
Toucans, 117. *See also* Birds; Tropical birds
Traditions, 105, 131-32
   of Easter, 61
   from history, 134
   of Passover, 61
Trains, 132-33
Transportation, history of, 119
Treasure, buried, 123
Tree finch, 72. *See also* Birds; Finches
Trees, 26, 64
Trejo, Frank, 77
Trevino, Lee, 96
Tropical birds, 29. *See also* Birds; Toucans
Tropical rain forests, 29. *See also* Rain forests
Truckers, 52
Truth, Sojourner, 155, 156-57, 164, 183
Tubman, Harriet, 164, 183
Tupperware, 86
Turnips, 116
Turtle frog, 114
Turtles, 30, 31, 54, 133, 134
   land, 133
   painted, 124

Ukrainian art, 61
Underground railroad, 164
Union activists, 96
United States, history, 134
University of Iowa, 58
Urban roosts, 44
U.S. Commission on Civil Rights, 96
U.S. Lighthouse Society, 92
Utah, 103
Utensils, eating, 143

Valdez, Luis, 96
Van Allsburg, Chris, 34, 37
Velasquez, William, 96
Venezuela, 78, 117
Venus (planet), 127
Veterinarians, 52, 135
Vietnam, 83
Vietnamese, 37, 38, 82, 83
Virginia, 49, 167
Volunteers, 81
Voting rights, 55

Wagener, Isabella Van (Sojourner Truth), 156-57
Wakefield, Ruth, 85
Walker, Madame C. J., 22, 48, 164
Walruses, 26, 59, 140
Wampanoag (Native Americans), 101, 131
Wang, An, 37, 38
Wang Laboratories, 37
Warthogs, 28, 136, 159
Washakie, 102
Washington, George, 56, 131, 138, 185-87
Washington, Martha, 186
Washington (D.C.), 104, 137
Washington (state), 113
Wasp nests, 10
Wasps, 25, 30, 128
Water beetles, 114
Water boatmen, 114
Water buffalo, 26
Water department, 108
Watercolors, 93, 131
Watering holes, 28-29
Waterman, Clara, 49
Waterworks, 108
Wedges, machine, 92, 93
Weeds, 65
West Africa, 176
West Indies, 129
West Virginia, 20, 167
Whale poems, 141
Whale watch, 141
Whales, 26, 34, 59, 114, 140
   blue, 27, 124
   endangered, 139
   in fiction, 139
   history of, 140
   humpback, 139
Whaling, 140, 141
   history of, 139
Wheels, machine, 92, 93
White rhino, 28. *See also* Rhinoceroses
Whooping cranes, 34
Wiesner, David, 34, 37
Wild Free-Roaming Horse and Burro Act (1971), 79
Wild Horse Annie, 79
Wild pigs, 28. *See also* Pigs
Wildcat, African, 53
Wildebeests, 28
Wildflowers, 116
Wildlife Research Education and Conservation, 159
Willard, Mary Jane, 77
Willard, Nancy, 112
Wilson, Woodrow, 67
Windows, 142
Winter, 107, 121, 122

Wisconsin, 178-79
Witches, 26
Wolf trail, 50
Wolves, 26, 30, 143
   history of, 143
   portrayal in folk literature, 143-44
Women
   of achievement, 161
   who inspire, 181-82
Women's rights, 181
Wong, Bong Way (El Chino), 169-70
Woodpecker finch, 72. *See also* Birds; Finches
Woods, Granville T., 175
Woolly-necked storks, 28
Woolworth, Frank W., 48
Woolworth's, 47
Word play, 26-27
Work permits, 95
Workers, assembly line, 51
World War II, 23
World Wildlife Federation, 139

World Wildlife Fund, 60
Worms, 144, 145
Worth, Valerie, 112
Wounds, 145
Wright Brothers, 69, 175
Writers, 96, 181
Writing, 39-40, 72-73, 90, 165
Writing letters, 115

Yellow-billed storks, 28. *See also* Birds
Yellow jackets, 30
Yellowstone National Park, 121
Yosemite Falls, 179
Yukon Territory, 50

Zambonis, 86
Zebras, 28, 29, 32
Zeppelins, 23
Zoos, 28, 34, 53, 65, 135
Zucchini, 116

About the Author

The author was just a young girl when reading for pleasure and information became fixed for life. She enjoyed reading the stories of Hans Christian Andersen, but also read nonfiction stories about him, making connections between Andersen's life and the stories he wrote. Her favorite books included folklore and books about real people and real things. Now she enjoys reading hundreds of books each year—books that she shares with elementary school students. For several years her book critiques were aired over a local public radio affiliate. Her book reviews have appeared in national and local periodicals and newspapers. Through *Great New Nonfiction Reads* she is able to share information about some of the best information books published in the last five years.

Sharron L. McElmeel is a full-time educator, consultant, and author who lives in the Iowa countryside, where horses graze beside her house, tractors hum in nearby fields, and the bookshelves in her house are filled with wonderful literature to read and share.